About the Author

Glen Humphries has been writing and publishing books since 2017. *Lull City* is his 11th book and he's still not sure how he's cranked out that many, given that he likes snoozing on the lounge so much. Along the way he's managed to win a few awards, one for a book about beer and another for a true crime book he wrote about a serial crim who was the source of many urban legends in the suburb Glen grew up in. He has played tambourine onstage for several bands – usually only for one song – but has never actually been in a band himself. When some friends at uni formed a band, he wanted to be part of it so badly he put his hand up to be a roadie. He even fibbed and told them he'd played drums in a high school thrash band in the hope it would boost his credentials. That led to the unfortunate situation where they recommended he jam with some other musos who needed a drummer. So he sat behind the kit, with pretty much no idea what to do. What a schmuck. He has played tambourine on one recorded song – *Glen's Wish* – which features on The Adam Buckland Ensemble's *Soundtrack From a Noisy Mind*. He's still available for tambourine recording, if anyone needs it. He wrote the book *Lull City* because he wanted to read a history of the Wollongong music scene but got sick of waiting for someone else to do it, so he decided to write the damn thing himself. He finds he drinks a lot more coffee when writing than is really good for him. He has great ideas for book subjects when he's drunk, only to realise the next morning that they're actually pretty stupid. He's of the age where an afternoon nap is the best thing ever. But if he's drunk too much coffee that morning, then the afternoon nap window is well and truly closed. He thinks people should spend their money buying albums from local artists rather than listening to them for free online. Cheapskates. He would be surprised if anyone is still reading this far down. If anyone is, send him the phrase "Scooter Party" via email or any of his social media accounts. It'll be a little in-joke between you and him. The older he gets the more he comes to the conclusion that afternoon gigs are far more civilised that night-time shows. But mainly because he has trouble staying up past 9.30pm.

Also by Glen Humphries and published by Last Day of School (www.lastdayofschool.net)
The Slab: 24 Stories of Beer in Australia
James Squire: The Biography
The Six-Pack: Stories from the World of Beer
Friday Night at the Oxford
Beer Is Fun
Sounds Like an Ending: Midnight Oil, 10-1 and Red Sails in the Sunset
Night Terrors: The True Story of the Kingsgrove Slasher
Healer: The Rise, Fall and Return of Tumbleweed
Alright!: Queen at Live Aid

Lull City

The Wollongong Music Scene 1955-2020

Glen Humphries

ISBN: 978-0-6489911-3-7
Lull City: The Wollongong Music Scene 1955-2020 is copyright Glen Humphries 2021

For more information email dragstermag@hotmail.com. If you loved this book so much that you want to buy some more copies then head over to my micropublishing site Last Day of School (find it at www.lastdayofschool.net). And maybe buy some copies of my other books. They're good, I promise you. And all so reasonably priced.

This book is copyright. All rights reserved. Except for private study, research, criticism or reviews, as permitted under the Copyright Act, no part of this book may be reproduced, stored in a retrieval system, or transmitted in any form or by any means without prior written permission. Look, I spent two years researching and writing this book. I even put a lot of the original pieces I dug up in the bibliography to make it easier for future researchers. So it's surely not too much to ask for you not to steal my stuff, is it?

To Warren Wheeler, who did a lot of the heavy lifting to show both myself and others that the story of the Wollongong music scene is important.

Listen up

I'm the first to admit that reading about music is not the same as listening to it. That's why I've created a Spotify playlist to accompany this book. Just search for "Lull City soundtrack" (or my profile page) to listen to a lot of bands mentioned in this book – as well as many who aren't. The publication of this book doesn't mean the end of updating the playlist, I see that as an ongoing project.

If you're a Wollongong band and you're on Spotify but not on the playlist, get in touch with me at lastdayofschool.net and I'll add a song or two.

Also, if you listen to the playlist and find some tunes you like, do the right thing and buy the bands' vinyl or CD, go to one of their shows. If they made some music you liked, then they deserve to be paid for that. A play on Spotify doesn't earn them any cash, selling you an album or a ticket to a show does.

Introduction
The Sounds of the City

Captain James Cook would have been the first white man to overlook Wollongong in favour of Sydney. In April 1770 Cook was in the Endeavour, cruising up the coast looking for a place to make land so he could "discover" Australia. On the afternoon of April 28 the Endeavour anchored off the Wollongong coast near a place now known as Woonona.

A small boat was dispatched to the shore to suss things out. But the surf was too rough, so Cook thought "bugger this, let's go up the coast for a bit". And the very next day he lands in Sydney's Botany Bay. And so began the habit of people overlooking Wollongong for the big smoke around 80 kilometres up the road.

Over time that would be accompanied by negative images of the city of Wollongong. If you're not from here, for a long time it was likely the only thing you heard about Wollongong was something bad. For years it wore the tag of an industrial steel town, a place where out-of-towners envisaged you could wipe your fingers on any building in the city and they'd come away coated in grime. Then, when the steelworks slashed the workforce in the early 1980s, it became the depressed steel town, where the dominant source of income was the dole.

Or maybe it's the story of the corrupt council, where a town planner slept with developers and approved their buildings, where self-important types sat outside a kebab shop on plastic seating they dubbed the Table of Knowledge and felt like kings of the city, where two conmen pretended to be corruption investigators and got councillors to fork over cash.

Perhaps it's the darker tales of murders – and even more horrible acts – that would spring to people's minds when they thought of Wollongong.

But it's an attitude that is slowly shifting as Sydney becomes more crowded and people look to find a house to buy that won't leave their grandchildren still paying off their mortgage. And so they look to Wollongong. So the far northern suburbs became dormitory areas as Sydneysiders bought what were cheap homes, planning to get up really early and catch the train into Sydney every morning.

Soon enough that saw real estate prices go up in the far north, prompting others look slightly further south. What followed was those price rises slowly crept further south, at least as far as Woonona, just 14 minutes from the Wollongong CBD (and that place Cook overlooked back in 1788), where the median sale price for a house doubled in the last decade to over $1 million.

Before, out-of-towners tended to look down their noses at Wollongong – but now they pay millions to live here. The reason the prices are so high up north is geographical. In part because those suburbs are close to Sydney but there's also hardly any space to build any more homes. Hemmed in by the escarpment to the west, homes in some northern suburbs cling to the coastal fringes. It's really not until you reach the areas south of Wollongong that there is any space for the urban sprawl to occur – which is partly why houses are usually cheaper down there than up north.

The Illawarra's northern suburbs has long been a draw for the artistic type. Dancing was a big part of life in the northern suburbs just after World War I. A beachside facility dubiously dubbed the Thirroul Pleasure Grounds included what was tagged as an open-air dancing arena. The grand opening of the venue saw a range of activities that causes one to consider people back then had a curious idea of pleasure. Among the attractions that night was a performing baboon ("the only one of its kind in Australia"), an "educated donkey", a talking parrot and a dog that could do tricks.

Even after the baboon left, the dancing arena was very popular with the locals through to the mid-1920s. From there attendances tapered off until in 1926 it was destroyed by fire. New owners had recently taken over and, with the newspapers suggesting business wasn't good, the fire reeked of an insurance job.

In May 1922 English author DH Lawrence, just before he made his name with *Sons and Lovers*, and wife Frieda stepped off the Sydney train at Thirroul station. There's no word of them being tempted to get off a stop early at Austinmer, which had by then decided to call itself "the Riviera of NSW".

While others may have come to the Illawarra for a holiday, Lawrence was at work. In six weeks at a Craig Street house overlooking the ocean he cranked out the novel *Kangaroo*, in which Thirroul features, albeit under the guise of a town called Mullumbimby.

Painters too have found inspiration up north, including Brett Whiteley. The artist, who used the northern suburbs coastline in his paintings – though rarely indicated in the works' names – would stay at the local motel in Thirroul to both work and detox from heroin. On Monday, June 15, 1992, the motel owner entered Room 4 and found Whiteley's body in bed under the covers. On the bedside table was a bottle of whiskey, orange juice and a jar of pills. The coroner found he had died of a coronary embolism, likely brought on by the detox cocktail of methadone, whisky and juice.

More recently the north has been home to musicians like Rob Younger from Radio Birdman, Jodi Phillis of The Clouds and Midnight Oil songwriter Jim Moginie, who can be sometimes seen strolling through the Thirroul CBD.

While Wollongong's southern suburbs lack such celebrity residents, the area does have its own notable musical past.

Lake Illawarra has contributed a few footnotes to the musical history of the Illawarra. In the 1920s and 1930s, dressed-up locals and people from the northern suburbs boarded boats and sail to Gooseberry Island, just over 400 metres offshore, where someone had constructed a dance hall. They don't seem to have been sedate affairs, attendee Sonny Massey said a keg of beer always made its way over to the island. "The dances started before sunset," he said, "and when you'd come home, the sun would be rising."

The lingering effects of the Great Depression saw the end of the dances, and residents started to pull apart the hall to put the materials to better use making humpies on the mainland.

More recently, starting in 1987, the lake was home to the "floating restaurant" (ie: boat) known as the Merinda. It plied its trade along Lake Illawarra, booking musicians for the night-time dinner cruises.

The owners had tussles with council over car parking and with the unions over claims non-union labour was used to repair and repaint the boat after it had been lifted out the water. "At this stage the bans are still on but we need to get the Merinda back into the water because we have 300 people booked for cruises at the weekend," operator Graham Bath said at the time. Luckily for him the bans were lifted in time for the weekend.

By 1992, Bath – who had been taking a bath financially speaking for years – decided to move the vessel to Sydney. He said the Merinda had been losing around $100,000 a year on Lake Illawarra. "You cannot afford to keep operating a business with those types of losses," he said. "The business has been on the market now for six months and there has been no local interest shown to purchase or lease it so we are relocating the tourist asset."

***

This is a story of the Wollongong music scene, focusing

on four golden ages. The most recent of those – which we're still enjoying – was sparked by a combination of people from the northern and southern ends of Wollongong. It's also a story of the changing face of the city, which undeniably played its own part in this golden period. It's a period where bands went from hiding their Wollongong roots and claiming they were from Sydney to proudly staying put and letting the world know where they were.

The first golden age kicked off at the tail end of the 1950s, when teens were inspired by this glorious sound known as rock and roll to start their own bands. The second era took hold in Wollongong as the calendars turned to 1980 and some sections of the city embraced the DIY attitude of punk – and not just the music. It sparked art, movies and a well-organised protest movement designed to help the young unemployed in a city that sometimes felt hollowed out.

The third is of course the Oxford era, the period in the city's musical history that has received the most attention. Its heyday was from 1989 to the turn of the century and saw the biggest explosion the local music scene had ever witnessed. The Oxford – along with the opening of the city's first independent music store in Redback Records – sparked a growth in bands and led to others being inspired to create all-ages venues and street press.

By the 2000s, the Oxford had begun to slide, as did the music scene. Other venues that had been there in the 1990s – The North Gong, Sunami, the University of Wollongong bar – either closed or ditched the idea of local bands. A city council crackdown on gig posters wrapped around light poles or plastered on walls didn't help matters.

As music historian Warren Wheeler put it, that just left the Oxford. "This concentration of the scene would ultimately have a direct impact on the quality of music coming from the area, with bands no longer needing to compete for crowds as the Oxford provided a captured audience."

To be sure, there were still good bands playing around town early in the 21st century but even they would admit the scene wasn't in the healthiest state.

As an arbitrary starting point for this latest golden age, well, 2014 works. That was the year Jeb Taylor from Music Farmers and Yours and Owls' Ben Tillman – both from the far north – joined forces to create the Farmer and the Owl label, releasing Hockey Dad's first recording, the *Dreamin'* EP. Of course, all three had been around for a while – Taylor had been working in the music industry since at least 1999 (he had even been the Oxford Tavern booker at one stage), Tillman was one-third of Yours and Owls, which started as a café in 2010 – but he had been booking shows for a year or two before that.

As for Hockey Dad – who proudly called the far southern suburb of Windang home – well they'd been around for a whole year by that point but Zach Stephenson and Billy Fleming had spent a few years in the band Abstract Classic, which had caused a few ears in the Illawarra to prick up.

That label would sign up a number of Wollongong artists, including Bec Sandridge, Totally Unicorn and The Pinheads, as well as re-releasing old albums from the likes of local acts Tumbleweed and Mother and Son. In time it branched out to sign bands from out of Wollongong – both within Australia and internationally.

It's worth pointing out that this book was never intended to be a complete and detailed history of the Wollongong music scene. No doubt readers will wonder why a band they loved doesn't make an appearance, others may wonder why, say community radio station Vox FM, 1990s music venue Sunami or the Musicoz Awards – which started in Wollongong as a work for the dole program before going national – barely get a mention. Telling a story is like mixing a song; some things get pushed to the front while others end up buried in the mix somewhere. It's just not possible to include everyone and everything that happened in the Wollongong music scene since the mid-1950s.

Still, I hope the reader comes away from *Lull City* with a stronger understanding of the history of the Wollongong scene and an appreciation of just how good it is now.

1

At first the Illawarra wasn't too keen on this strange new beast known as rock and roll. In October 1956, the city's first "rock and roll" dance – held at the Corrimal Community Centre – made the front page of the *Illawarra Mercury*. It wasn't to mark the first event of its kind, but to note the heavy presence of police outside the venue.

Four cops in uniform were stationed outside, with more plainclothes police inside, fooling no-one. They were there to stop the kids from going crazy after being whipped into a frenzy. But no rioting occurred – there weren't enough people inside for that. As many as 20 people milled outside along with those uniformed police, but none dared go inside.

"The dance was scheduled to start at 8pm, but by 9.30pm only four couples were on the lonely floor," the paper reported. "And only one couple was 'hepping' it up. The rest of the dancers were dancing in a conventional manner." None of the dancers were undercover cops, by the way.

The police had a theory for the low attendance; the mums wouldn't let their kids go after hearing of the wild behaviour in London a month earlier at screenings of the Bill Haley movie *Rock Around the Clock*.

Almost a year later, the city seemed to have made its peace with this music the young folk loved. Little Richard was on a tour of Australia. It was one of the first rock tours of this country, and the first to reach Wollongong.

Bringing along the likes of Johnny O'Keefe and Eddie Cochrane, Little Richard kicked off the tour with a gig at the Crown Theatre, then on Keira Street. The local paper again gave the concert the front-page treatment, but this time there was no mention of the cops. O'Keefe and his band the Dee Jays started the show "with a twang of electric guitars and a clash of cymbals".

"The Australian group, with its wailing saxophones, provided the 'shocker' of the night, sung by Johnny O'Keefe," the reporter wrote. "O'Keefe swaying in all directions, sung a number, *Flip, Flop and Fly*, which is a current hit in America. He finished on his knees wrestling with the microphone. The audience screamed and stamped their feet while O'Keefe sang." O'Keefe biographer Jeff Apter paints a different story of the Wild One's Wollongong show. Apter writes that the crowd was booing O'Keefe, calling for the American headliner instead. No shrinking violet, O'Keefe called on his band to stop, and then gave the rowdy crowd a response that has gone down in history. "You may boo me and you may throw things at me. But you all pay your money to see me – because you love me!".

According to the *Mercury*, Cochran's performance "put the

audience into full swing", followed by "the female Elvis Presley" in one-hit wonder Alis Lesley. "She squealed instead of grunting, as Presley does, after each line," the *Mercury* noted.

As would be the case for every rock and roll show from here on, the headliner got the most attention. "His version of *Tutti Frutti* and *Lucille* were met with tremendous applause and he could be barely heard above the screaming and stomping of feet," the front page of the *Mercury* read. "Besides being an expert showman, Little Richard also appeared to be an expert gymnast."

The *Mercury* interviewed Little Richard in his hotel room after the show, where he revealed his desire to turn to God. The performer – who had thrown religious booklets into the teenaged crowd – told the reporter this music caper was only temporary. "Rock 'n' roll to me is a living. Everyone has to have a living," he said. "But my real ambition is to become a minister." That came sooner than expected – when the tour reached Newcastle, Little Richard famously chose to forsake rock and roll for the Lord, throwing his jewels into the Hunter River.

The show had an effect on Wollongong teens, and local bands started to form. According to music historian Warren Wheeler, the first may have been Johnny Johnson and the Rebels. Forming in late 1957, the band played venues like the Patch, The Rex at Thirroul and Fairy Meadow's Charles Hotel. They even travelled to Victoria to record an album's worth of tunes, though apparently no copies have survived.

To the likely befuddlement of parents, rock and roll was still around when the 1960s arrived. In 1960 American singer

Crash Craddock toured Australia. He hadn't set the charts on fire in his own country, but Australians went crazy for him. On February 2, he played two shows at the Crown Theatre and drew in around 4000 fan across both shows. The *Mercury*'s coverage of the show paints a wild scene, with fans waiting outside rushing every taxi that pulled up in case a rock star was about to climb out.

Things were also frenetic inside. "Teenage girls swarmed around the foot of the stage," the *Mercury* reported, "when the star of the performance, Crash Craddock, began to sing the final number at the end of the second session. As Craddock came off, a burly bodyguard and offsider threw themselves around the star and tucked his head under their arms to get him through the throng of screaming girls milling around the stage."

By this time, the city was experiencing what would be the first of four eras where the music scene was strong. It was also around the time of The Beatles, who were creating hysteria wherever they went; and not a little inspiration too. The band never played in Wollongong on their 1964 tour, though four imposters in suits and moptops caused a minor disturbance when they appeared in Keira Street in March that year.

A northern suburbs musician found himself as the support act to the real Beatles. Johnny Devlin had been a rock star in his native New Zealand in the 1950s, dubbed that country's answer to Elvis Presley. By the time the '60s rolled around Devlin's heyday had been and gone but he moved from New Zealand to Corrimal and kept writing and releasing tunes. He also wrote songs for others and dabbled in booking bands.

He was actually looking for someone else to take up the support slot when the organisers asked why he wouldn't do it himself. "I had a very serious think about it because I knew it would be very difficult singing with The Beatles – they were the hottest act in the world at the time," Devlin said.

"I told them I'd do it on two conditions. Number one, that I went on first because I wanted to get on and off as quick as possible and, number two, they double the money they offered me, which was peanuts."

He got to witness Beatlemania up close; seeing the intense media coverage of the band's every move and the girls trying to sneak into the Fab Four's hotel rooms. "I was approached by numbers of girls saying they'd make it worth my while if I could get them up to see The Beatles," Devlin said.

There was also a bit of songwriting interplay backstage. "I remember they called me backstage at one stage and they were all grouped around Ringo, who had a little Korg drum pad," Devlin said. "They played a song and asked me, 'what do you think of this one?'. They played *A Hard Day's Night* to me before it was even released.

Paul McCartney also had a hand in Devlin's last top 40 single *Won't You be My Baby?*. Devlin was tinkering with it backstage and McCartney didn't like what he was hearing. "He just sort of took the guitar and fiddled around with it a bit," Devlin said. "He said 'why don't you do this?'. He put a couple of chords in here, there and everywhere, and it sounded better."

It went to No29 when released, though McCartney didn't get a songwriting credit. If he had, there's every chance it would have climbed even further up the charts.

In the early 1960s, the first golden age of the Wollongong music scene saw the formation of The Tornadoes, who were still going five decades later. Doing what Tumbleweed would do years later, The Tornadoes were made up largely of brothers. Four of them in fact – John, David, Peter and 12-year-old Robert. The band, from Windang, rehearsed in a shed at the back yard of the Goodger home. The only ring-in was Fred March, who was a classmate of David's at Berkeley High School.

That school and surrounding suburb was a fertile ground for bands in the early 1960s. The suburb was the location of a migrant hostel, which meant plenty of teenagers living in close quarters and discovering rock and roll was the easiest way to fit in with others in this new country. One such band was The Coffin Cheaters, and guitarist Arnie Olbrich later sung the praises of the suburb. "If you take the working class suburb of Berkeley, one small area of Wollongong, it has a greater concentration of musos than anywhere, and that's no shit," he said in 1984. "Heaps and heaps of players and bands, all from Berkeley."

The first Wollongong band to make a mark outside the city also came from Berkeley High – The Marksmen. They started out in 1961 as a surf instrumental band called The Tremors before changing their name to The Marksmen in 1964. Their lasting claim to fame is the self-financed single *But Why* backed with *Moonshine*. Released in 1966, it was recorded in Sydney with Ossie Byrnes producing. The band had known Byrnes from his days in the early 1960s when he had a recording studio in Brooker Street, Tarrawanna –

before he made his name as the producer of The Bee Gees early hits.

The Marksmen's single has become the rarest of the Australian garage 45s, with copies selling for more than $1000 on the few times the single turns up in the marketplace.

The band members themselves can't recall how successful the single was at the time. Singer Bob Kerr told the Garage Hangover site he reckoned they sold around 10,000 copies. That's a figure bassplayer Neil Porter disputed.

"If we had sold 10,000 copies of *But Why/Moonshine* in the mid-'60s we would have, because of the very small population of Australia, quite a huge national hit," he said. "This certainly did not happen."

In fact, he said they only pressed 500 copies, many of which were sent to radio stations. "As far as I know they did sell as many as we put into stores but in spite of our local popularity, we didn't even chart in our own home town."

In the last months of The Marksmen's existence in 1968 they made the front page of the *Mercury* over fears of violence at a Wollongong Town Hall gig. The show – the Pink Pussy Cat Ball – was organised by Miss Australia entrant Margaret Brodie as a fundraiser for disabled children.

The Marksmen and another local band called The Minutes had both been booked, for the princely sum of $60 each. But Brodie ditched The Minutes in favour of The Checkmates, who offered to play for $40. In protest, The Marksmen refused to play the Pink Pussy Cat Ball.

"Organisers are playing one band off against another," The Marksmen's manager Doug Joyce said. "They book one band then contact another and offer it the booking if it will play for less money. "It is time someone made a stand."

With the gig on August 30, 1968, the *Mercury* carried the front page story reporting that Brodie had requested a police presence at the ball because she feared "groups of local pop musicians will try and cause disturbances". No such disturbance occurred, though there was no report of what the 350 people who turned up felt about The Checkmates' performance.

In 1969, The Marksmen disappeared; to cash in on the hippie vibe of the time, they changed their name to The Imagination and moved to Sydney with a new lead singer named Alex Stefanovic (the dad of TV celeb Karl). The move was prompted by the same issue that plagued Wollongong bands for decades afterwards. Unless you were from Sydney, venues and labels really didn't want to know about you – it's why a Wollongong band with just one member living in Sydney would call themselves a "Sydney band". The Imagination released two singles on the Parlophone label (home of The Beatles) and proceeded to not set the world on fire at all.

Ossie Byrnes also had a hand in another Wollongong act, the Del-Fi's. He was managing them from 1961, drilling into them the need to perfect their sound before pushing for their big break on TV shows like *Bandstand* and *Six O'Clock Rock*.

"The band has already had TV offers but I advised the boys not to consider it yet," Byrnes told the *Mercury* in 1961. "You see, with my experience in recording, I am in a position to pick out their little faults. I know the boys are keen to appear on television but they agree with me that it would be better to wait until their arrangements are perfected."

They had to wait three years, until 1964, when they became the first Wollongong band to appear on a national TV show. They played three tunes on Johnny O'Keefe's *Sing, Sing Sing*, two of which the instrumental band were joined by vocalist Derek Lee.

The Tarrawanna-based Lee had his own success on that show several months earlier, winning the Star Quest talent show and landing a record deal with Festival Records and a trip to the UK (the female winner was a singer by the name of Olivia Newton-John). He recorded two singles, one with the Del-Fi's before heading to the UK and signing a trial contract with EMI in 1965. Returning there in 1966, his EMI deal fell through and Lee effectively disappeared from the scene. His old band never heard a word from him, his name appeared nowhere in Australian rock encyclopaedias and songs he'd written were credited to other writers.

Researcher Bill Casey solved the mystery years in 2003, finding him in southern Italy, where he was running a charter boat service. He had continued to sing in the UK and Europe but rarely recorded anything. "I was too busy with the singing," he told Casey, "I hardly found time to get married. In fact, only four times."

Another 1960s band that achieved some success were The Executives, founded in the far northern Illawarra suburb of Helensburgh. Back in the day when the music charts were state-based, the band had a string of hits in 1967 and toured the US but by 1970 the Executives had had their day in the sun. The band reformed briefly in the 1970s to not much success, though they did record the theme tune to popular

TV soapie *The Young Doctors*.

A few members of The Executives had success outside the band. Guitarist Ray Burton co-wrote the Helen Reddy hit *I Am Woman*, while drummer Rhys Clark played with Billy Joel for the piano man's first few albums.

The mid-1960s saw a Wollongong singer record a seven-inch single that became a collector's item. England-born Elizabeth Reed arrived in the city with her family in 1964. Going by the stage name of Wee Liz, she performed at various venues around the city before hooking up with Ossie Byrnes, who had moved to the Sydney suburb of Hurstville by this time, setting up another recording studio. The mainstays there were The Bee Gees, whom Byrnes had faith in and so gave them almost unlimited studio time to hone their sound.

Byrnes also had a small label, Downunder, which released singles by forgotten entities like Derek's Accent, Rick and the Bad Boys and Soul Agents during the five months it existed in 1966. Wee Liz recorded a single for Downunder, *Tiny Little Pebble* backed with *Lonesome 409* (there are rumours the Bee Gees' Robin Gibb played triangle on the B-side). Of the 13 singles released by Downunder, Wee Liz's is by far the rarest, with copies reported to have sold for as much as $240.

With Wollongong being just over an hour south of Sydney, it was common for bigger performers to play shows in the city. One of the more notable was Normie Rowe's 1965 show at the Wollongong Town Hall. The sorts of fears people had about the rock and roll crowd at that first dance at Corrimal in 1957 came to life at this Rowe show.

A council report after that town hall gig listed the

destruction made by frenzied Rowe fans – all of which sounds remarkably tame to modern-day music fans. Before the doors opened the hundreds of fans waiting outside trampled the grass and gardens. During the show some fans had the audacity to stand on the seats for a better view and council staff were so concerned about the behaviour that the police had to be called. The men in blue prowled the aisles of the town hall and even dragged a few unlucky punters to a waiting police wagon outside. The devices that held the exit doors open had been ripped off and toilet paper was thrown around the hall like confetti.

When Rowe wanted to return to Wollongong in 1967, it was a case of once bitten, twice shy for the council. In a saga that made the front page of both local papers – the *Mercury* and *The South Coast Times* – the council refused Rowe's request to play the town hall again. Even with the promise of a $2000 security deposit.

So the promoters went and booked the Corrimal Community Hall instead (or maybe they had already booked it as a Plan B, while asking for the town hall – media reports were conflicting). *The South Coast Times* predicted unruly teenage behaviour at the concert. "Police and Wollongong City Council officials are ready for a riot at the Normie Rowe show in Corrimal on Sunday night," it stated on the front page.

Unsurprisingly, the paper had gilded the lily just a bit. No riot took place at the Princes Highway venue. Teenage girls lined up outside the venue from 8.30am, waiting for Rowe – who didn't take the stage until 11pm. Rather that rioting, the papers that day were more concerned about these girls missing breakfast and going hungry. Around 450 fans watched the show, which led some critics to suggest it had been a flop and the promoter conceding that Rowe's 11pm start time may have kept some of his younger fans at home.

In August 1969, local music fans got very excited with the news that Russell Morris – who had released his iconic hit *The Real Thing* a few months earlier – was playing a show at an Albion Park dance. They were soon disappointed when they turned up and realised it was all a hoax. In her weekly Gong Beat music column, *Mercury* journo Sharyn Kennedy implied the hoax was perpetrated by the other band on the bill. "The dance had been planned with the Solomon Wright Crusade playing and Russell Morris' name was advertised to attract a larger crowd. The organisers of the dance were upset at discovering the hoax. They were under the impression Russell Morris would be appearing." Or maybe it was the organisers' doing – after all they would have benefited the most from the increased door take.

Morris actually did turn up in Wollongong later that year for Outset – dubbed the city's first pop music festival. Held at Wollongong Showground on December 28, 1969, Morris was the headliner, with Jeff St John and Copperwine, Tamad Shud and local act Tin Pan Alley on the bill. Morris got the crowd revved up, the front page of the *Mercury* saying reporter Christine Blanche was "scratched and kicked" as she fought through the crowd to interview Morris. "As Morris left the stage, girls raced after him," the paper's front page stated. "They tried to kiss him and souvenir his clothes and hair but he managed to escape into his car. As Miss Blanche climbed into Morris' car, the frenzied girls grabbed at her hair and thrust their arms and bodies in front of her."

The front-page story, obviously not written by Blanche, reflected the era by making note of what the women in the crowd were wearing (accompanied by a relevant photo). "Several girls watched the show in bikinis, others wore 'in' gear of today and others still in jeans and t-shirts," the story read. "There was no evidence of drugs or alcohol in the audience. All were there to listen to the 'groovy' music."

The mid-1960s also saw the rise of music venues more receptive to younger fans. Before then, it was halls like Corrimal, the Wollongong Town Hall and Pioneer Hall that put on bands. The Pioneer Hall in particular was restrictive, with its strict dress regulations and staff ensuring dancers left sufficient space between their bodies lest they be corrupted.

One of the first was the Mocambo upstairs in Crown Street, roughly opposite the Church on the Mall. Leased and operated by 16-year-old Toni Knipe – who had never been to a nightclub – the Mocambo opened in December 1963 (with the help of a £300 loan from mum and dad). The plan was to hold stomp sessions, and serve nothing stronger than soft drink and coffee. The stomp sessions didn't go so well with downstairs tenants, who found ceiling flakes all over the floor when they turned up for work the next day. After the landlord had enough of their complaints, the Mocambo was closed in March 1964.

One of the better-known venues was Zondrae's. Located in Keira Street (in a building that backed onto MacCabe Park, years later the home of the Farmer and the Owl festival), it was set up in 1965 by ambitious teen Zondrae King, with the help of her mother and a wealthy aunt who stumped up the finances. Due in part to the rise in quality local bands in the late 1960s, Zondrae's quickly became a popular place for teens and those in their early 20s to hang out, feeling like a home away from home. That in turn led to Sydney acts deciding that was the place to play when visiting Wollongong. By 1967, after a falling out between mother and daughter, Zondrae's was no more.

King soon ended up managing the beautifully named Wonderland Ballroom, a venue in what is now Northern Bowl at Bellambi.

Another entrepreneur who set up a venue in the 1960s was Brian Neville – and he was nothing if not persistent. He had been running the so-called "Apple Candy" dance at Warrawong, when he decided to launch a nightclub in Crown Street called Oliver's. The doors opened on March 14, 1969, with a performance from Doug Parkinson in Focus. Two months later he booked Johnny Farnham for a gig. Still riding high on the success of *Sadie the Cleaning Lady*, Farnham was mobbed at an appearance at David Jones on the afternoon of the gig.

Four months later, the doors were closed, due to "safety regulations" according to the officials. For a few months Oliver resurrected the Apple Candy dances, moving them to Corrimal, before giving Oliver's another crack in September at a new location in Flinders Street. Things weren't any better this time around, with Neville having to defend his venue against complaints about noise and drunken patrons (the more things change, the more they stay the same) just a month after opening.

The *Mercury*'s Gong Beat music columnist took Oliver's

side against the complainants in a strident piece published in October 1969. "The older generation never let up on us, do they? Most of them forget they were once our age too," Sharyn Kennedy wrote. "They think that the music we like is nothing but rubbish, but times change and our duty is to see that trends do change. After all, the older generation hasn't made a smashing success of the world, has it?

"The kids that are in the disco are not harming anyone. They are simply sitting down listening to the music; most of them don't even dance."

The support didn't really help. In March 1970, council forced the closure of Oliver's II because of a curious reason – it lacked a car park. Neville had made a deal with a service station across the road to use its driveway for parking after hours. He then made an agreement with council that, if that deal fell through (as it did), he would either find alternative parking or close.

"There's no parking in the area, so I have no choice but to close," Neville told the *Mercury*. "The station cancelled its arrangements when a car radio was stolen from a customer's car and our patrons were blamed."

As a farewell of sorts for Oliver's, in March, Neville organised a rock festival at Wollongong Showground featuring Taman Shud and a bunch of lesser known acts – Leo de Castor and Friends, The Cleves, The Turkish Green Electric and Freshwater. He'd been banking on as many as 5000 teens showing up, an ambitious target given the Capitol Hall (which was previously Wonderland before a sponsorship from Capitol Motors led to a name change) was holding its own festival that same night – with a stronger line-up. Johnny Farnham was headlining, with Masters Apprentices, Jeff St John and Copperwine and Flying Circus also on the bill.

It didn't help Neville that he'd arranged an outdoor concert at night in autumn. The temperature dropped to at least 15 degrees, which was likely why 3000 fewer teens turned up than he expected. "Many were wrapped in blankets and fur coats as they listened to the ear-splitting cacophony," a snobbish *Mercury* journalist wrote.

By the middle of the year, the failed venues continued to haunt Neville. In July, he appeared in Wollongong court charged over the fact he'd been organising shows at Oliver's new Flinders Street location without a licence. During the hearing, his lawyer J Geddes said Neville owed about $3000 to creditors following the March closure of Oliver's. "Mr Geddes said Neville had done his best to 'make a go' of the discotheque in Flinders Street, Wollongong, as there was nothing of this sort for the young people of Wollongong," the *Mercury* reported.

But Neville had a change of heart; in 1971 he opened the Boogaloo at the Royal Hotel on the corner of Crown and Keira streets (at what is now the top end of the mall). It's unclear how successful the venue was; after its opening in August – ominously enough on Friday the 13th – there are no further mentions of it in the local papers.

2

Wollongong was part of a national event that straddled two decades. From 1966 to 1972 confectionary maker Hoadley's (responsible for the Violet Crumble) sponsored the Battle of the Sounds. It was a high-profile event that attracted big bands like Sherbet, Fraternity (featuring a pre-AC/DC Bon Scott), The Masters Apprentices and The Twilights (with Little River Band's Glenn Shorrock). Bands from across the country entered, with local radio stations sponsoring the show in their own areas – in Wollongong that was 2WL.

Wollongong bands The Wanderers (1967), The Marksmen (1968) and Tin Pan Alley (1969) made it from the NSW Country final all the way to the grand final. None of them ended up winning, or making the top three. Things weren't as good for Wollongong bands after that – in the last three years of the competition no local band made it past the NSW Country Final. That was perhaps a reflection of the quality of the local scene at the time.

Wollongong in the 1970s was still a pretty conservative place especially where the arts were concerned. This can be seen in two incidents; one at the start of the decade and one at the end. In March 1970 there were concerns about the touring stage play *Pyjama Tops*, featuring four female actors. The problem for some was that each actor appeared nude at least once during the production. Not surprisingly, ticket sales for the five-night Wollongong run were strong. But just to make sure the show was "appropriate" two Wollongong police detectives watched the first night's performance.

The following day the *Mercury* reported thusly on the show: "Ten displays of bare bosoms and bottoms raised not a whimper of protest at Wollongong Town Hall last night. Even Sergeant K Prosser of the 21 Division said he found nothing offensive in the nudity." That the issue warranted any coverage at all suggests there was still a conservative streak in Wollongong in 1970.

It was a streak still present in 1979, when staff pulled the plug on a gig at Collegians due to offensive language. In May 1979 six people were arrested by police after a brawl broke out at a Dave Warner gig. The crowd got rowdy when a Collegians employees tried to remove Warner from the stage for swearing. During the song *Half-Time at the Football*, an employee warned Warner about using rude words.

He made light of that, which prompted the staff to cut the power and then charge at Warner with a view to getting him out of the auditorium. The road crew warned there would be a riot if the power wasn't restored.

The club had an over-the-top response to the situation –

banning all future Tuesday night rock concerts. "It was a sad night indeed for Wollongong rock and roll," said Collegians' John Preston, who booked the bands, "because this incident – the first one for four and a half years – looks like destroying so much good groundwork.

"The future looks grim. For instance the club had contracted to book Jimmy and the Boys, The Sports, Dragon and Mother Goose … now these bands have been axed because of the Tuesday night ruling."

The decision didn't really affect local bands, who already had almost nowhere to play – if they wanted to play their own songs. If Wollongong acts wanted a gig, they were forced to into the beer barns where they played cover versions. That cover band blight lasted well into the 1980s and provided something for younger bands in that decade to kick against.

But the decade of tie-dye and bell bottoms wasn't a complete waste. Wollongong was by now well and truly on the map for touring bands. In 1970, The Beach Boys – minus Brian Wilson – played at Capitol Hall. They played two shows – 7.30pm and 10.30pm – to mark the Captain Cook holiday, which was April 28, 1970. It marked the 200th anniversary of Cook's failed attempt to land the Endeavour at Woonona. Only in Australia would you get a public holiday to commemorate a failure.

The Wollongong stop was one show on a 20-date tour, half of which was a 10-night residency at the Silver Spade Room in Sydney's Chevron Hotel. The band cost Capitol Hall manager George Russell almost $7000, and he aimed to recoup that by charging $2 a ticket. Russell would have made his money back – Capitol Hall was packed, with more than 4000 people turning up to see The Beach Boys.

For some touring acts, Wollongong wasn't a happy place to visit in the 1970s. UK act Manfred Mann's Earth Band turned up in May 1972, playing to just 400 people at Wollongong Showground on a cold, windy day. The promoter responded in the way future promoters would – by criticising the city rather than accepting their act was past it. "Similar results for future concerts could lead to groups bypassing the South Coast," they said. "Wollongong youth has been crying out for decent groups in recent years. Now the groups are coming to the district, the crowds are staying away."

In April 1976, Billy Thorpe had a crowd of just 170 for a Wollongong Town Hall show, while in July 1978 former rock legend Johnny O'Keefe found himself reduced to playing Westfield Figtree.

But the punters would come out for the good bands. The first Wollongong show for Skyhooks in December 1975 – which was the heyday for the band – pulled in more than 5000 to the showground. "We are Skyhooks and they say we are filthy," Shirley Strachan said from the stage, "and we don't deny it." It was clear the police were expecting something filthy from the band; there were more than 100 officers on duty at the show. Some who were unhappy their leave had been cancelled so they could police the show would have been even more unhappy with the crowd's good behaviour showing they didn't need to be there at all.

Sherbet brought their chest hair and satin jackets to town a few times. In 1976, over a photo of screaming girls, the headline read "Sherbet lays 2200 in aisles". Just two years later the band's fortunes had diminished; while the *Mercury* headline stated they rocked Wollongong, just 900 fans turned up to see them. The year 1979 saw Little River Band, Rose Tattoo and the Kevin Borich Express play the Dapto Showground before a crowd of more than 5000.

One gig from the 1970s has gained a bit of notoriety – a July 1974 AC/DC show at the Corrimal Community Hall (now the home of the Arcadians theatre group). AC/DC weren't the headliners for the July 7 gig – their name appeared in small print underneath that of the headliner, former Easybeats frontman Stevie Wright, hot on the back of his newly released *Evie* single. Despite the fact Wright had a charting single, tickets were really cheap – just $1.

Years later organiser Rob McKie spoke to the *Mercury* about that gig. "The promoter approached me asking if I wanted to bring down the Stevie Wright Band and as part of that act, a young band called AC/DC," McKie said. "My first response was 'how much?'. I paid $250 for Stevie Wright and $50 for AC/DC and I thought I got robbed at the time." He needn't have worried; AC/DC wowed the crowd and he ended up booking them for another 10 shows.

Another regular visitor to the Illawarra was punk act Radio Birdman, thanks in part to band leader Deniz Tek finding a receptive crowd in an earlier group. Tek played the Charles Hotel at Fairy Meadow in the 1970s with a band known as Cunning Stunt and Screaming White Hot Razor Blades, before eventually settling on TV Jones. On vocals and guitar was Tek (another member, Chris Jones, was briefly a part of the Birdman line). Their drummer was a leftie who chose to play a right-handed kit, which Tek said gave him a really weird sound. TV Jones played in Wollongong regularly, as Tek told Vivien Johnson in Birdman's biography.

"The Charles Hotel in Wollongong was the biggest gig and later there was a bar called Caesars [located in Kenny Street]. This was late 1972, 1973 and it was a fantastic scene down there. The Charles was amazing – always packed, we'd usually get about 600 people in there… We would wear clear plastic raincoats – a lot of really bizarre things, hacking things up onstage, did a lot of things with food. Fruit and peanut butter, making big explosions on stage and food goes all over everybody. We were covering a lot of Alice Cooper. I was emulating Alice on stage, copied a lot of his moves. I used to explore his ideas about insanity being a theme."

TV Jones' explosive show rocked Wollongong – Tek said the audience connected to his over-the-top stage persona – and so the band decided to make the move to Sydney, where they weren't able to replicate that vibe. Tek was kicked out while the band was recording an album, taking with him songs like *Monday Morning Gunk*, *Man with Golden Helmet* and what was to become *I-94* to the new outfit he formed – Radio Birdman.

On November 12, 1976, Birdman also played at the Corrimal Community Hall, on their *Blitzkrieg* tour. That show didn't start out looking like anything special. As bassplayer Warwick Gilbert said in the Birdman documentary *Descent into the Maelstrom*, there were just four people in the hall and the mood in the dressing room was quite sombre. It was then that Tek revved up his bandmates with a General Patton-like speech.

"It was this electrifying call to arms and everyone got all wired up," Gilbert said. "We went out there completely wired up. We went out there and thought 'bugger it, let's just take the brakes off and go for it, do anything'.

"We went out there, took our hands off the instruments and everything started feedbacking, then Rob (Younger) goes, 'Arrrggghhh!'. In the end we had a pretty good crowd going nuts – it was great. But really inspirational, for me it was one of the best gigs, converting that situation."

The 1970s also saw the creation of the region's first record labels – if you count cassette-only releases as a "record". Based out of a house in Tarrawanna Street, Corrimal, 2-Tapes was created by Tim Vandenberg, also a member of the N-Lets. That act was a few degrees apart from the increasingly cover-band dominated music scene, as this description from a 1979 issue of *Roadrunner* street press illustrates.

"Only [Christopher] Croot uses his instrument in anything approaching a conventional manner, but what can a person do with an old-fashioned acoustic drumkit besides hit it? [Paul] Groch, when he hasn't left it unattended on someone's speaker cabinet, slings his bass at an almost unpluckable knee height, rarely playing it as such, rather using it as a noise-making device.

"Vandenberg – the extrovert, public image and suspect character of the group – also frequently prefers to rest his guitar on the floor, laying baking trays across its mangled frets, throwing tinkling pieces of metal at the pick-ups and even rummaging around in an accompanying amplified suitcase."

2-Tapes released the N-Lets' *Organised Noise* cassette, as well as recordings from Carmel E-Klastic, The Slugfuckers and Sydney's Voight/465.

The Butterfly label of local promoter Peter Evans also started up in the 1970s, releasing a handful of singles – including one by Tarquin, a popular local band of the decade. Evans' label name lives on today in his band booking business Butterfly Promotions.

3

At this point, it's worth stepping out of the chronology of the music scene to cover off the history of radio in the Illawarra, which is the main way people heard new tunes in the time before streaming services.

As strange as it may seem today, the region was serviced by just one commercial radio station for ages. That was 2WL, which started broadcasting from the front room of a Smith's Hill house back in 1931. It soon moved to premises in Edward Street, Wollongong, and would have the city's airwaves to itself for almost half a century. For most of that time, the station only broadcast in the evenings; a 1956 program guide shows the schedule taken up by serials with surprisingly few music shows. It wouldn't start broadcasting 24 hours a day until 1972.

It would seem not everyone was a fan of what 2WL was playing. In August 1966, a firebug ran riot through the building, emptying filing cabinets and using the papers to start fires in the accounts section, manager's office and reception area. There were only two fatalities in the fire – a pair of goldfish owned by an employee died in the overheated water of their bowl. Amazingly despite a $25,000 damage bill, the transmission and broadcasting sections were untouched and the station was able to go to air that morning.

In May 1970, the station would take part in a little-known piece of Australian music history – the radio ban. In what was a real act of stupidity, the major record companies had tired of giving singles to radio stations and wanted them to pay. The radio stations rightly pointed out they were a major source of promotion for these singles and so commercial stations nationwide banned major label songs from their airwaves from May until September, when the record companies acknowledged their stupidity.

The ban saw Australian acts record covers of the banned songs and release them on independent labels, which then became hits due to radio stations desperate for local artists to fill their playing quota. However, there is no indication that any Wollongong bands were able to take advantage of the ban to secure airplay on 2WL.

The radio landscape in the city changed on New Year's Eve 1978, when 2 Double O announced its arrival with a concert in MacCabe Park to announce its arrival. Jon English and Doug Parkinson were the top of the bill and, at midnight, the crowd sang *Auld Lang Syne* – which was broadcast live by 2 Double O.

The station had gotten its broadcasting licence a year earlier, despite rival bidders concerned it could become a mouthpiece for the trade union movement. That was due to the NSW Trades and Labour Council holding 14 per cent of shares in parent company Wollongong City Radio and six unions each holding 2 per cent.

In good news for the city's youth, 2 Double O announced it intended to aim its programming at the younger market. "We hope to have young people running the station and they will decide what is played," Wollongong City Radio chairman Ralph Hopkins said. It was a smart move to target younger listeners; given 2WL was at the time operating under the uninspiring slogan of 'Gently Rockin'', it would seem that market was largely untapped.

The new station was operating out of the Grand Hotel in Keira Street after buying it from Tooheys for $250,000 and then leasing out the pub. The unusual arrangement caused it a few headaches with the licencing police. The station had tried to get the licence removed from the upper floor of the hotel so it could broadcast but a district court judge refused the bid.

The station won an appeal, but then found itself fined $300 for breaching the Liquor Act after having already started on alterations to the upper floor before getting court approval. It was back in court again in October of its first year because work it had promised to undertake as a condition of the appeal – construction of a unisex toilet and a better communications system for the use of after-hours hotel guests – had not been done.

Later in September, 2 Double O notched up a musical first for the region when it set up a simulcast of a live show at the Wollongong Workers Club. Two local bands – Scamm and Mirage – were on the bill, with the former having its set broadcast live on 2 Double O.

That same month, the station created headlines and controversy by signing up none other than John Laws after he had just left Sydney's 2UW. It was a move designed to improve the station's poor ratings; in the first year it had captured just 18.8 per cent of the market compared to 2WL's 57.1 per cent. The signing didn't sit well with the city's labour council, who promised a black-ban on the station if it allowed Laws to go to air due to his "union-bashing" record.

"If the station thinks it is going to increase its listening audience by employing Mr Laws, it could be in for a shock," South Coast Labour Council secretary Merv Nixon said. "There are 93,000 wage and salary workers in the city of Wollongong. If the initial response to his appointment is any indication, none of those 93,000 people will be tuning into 2 Double O."

Laws' appointment was curious, given the station's large shareholdings held by the state labour council and union movement. Mr Nixon said locals were unhappy with the NSW Trades and Labour Council for allowing it to happen. Council vice-president Barrie Unsworth offered the interesting explanation that its representative wasn't at the board meeting when the decision was made. "We weren't pleased when we found out what was going on," Unsworth said. "We will be making enquiries about the matter."

Laws, who thought the union response to his appointment was "childish crap", met with Nixon twice – the second time the union boss scrapped the ban. It is unclear what, if any, broadcasting Laws did for 2 Double O, as he signed with Sydney station 2UE just a month later.

Over the years, 2 Double O struggled to overcome the dominance of its older rival. In 1983, four years after arriving on the scene, 2 Double O's audience share was still less than half that of 2WL – 15 per cent compared to 49.4 per cent. Despite that, WIN TV owner Bruce Gordon chose to buy the station in 1987, moving it to the TV network facilities in Mt St Thomas.

The younger station wouldn't seriously challenge 2WL until both switched to the FM band in 1992. The former station became i98FM while 2WL turned into Wave FM. It was a good change for i98FM, which had previously been dogged by poor reception in the northern suburbs. It meant both stations were competing on an equal footing, which was borne out in the first ratings survey since the FM change. Wave had 23.4 per cent of listeners, with i98FM not far behind with 21.4 per cent (newcomer Power FM broadcasting from Nowra managed to take almost 20 per cent of the market). In early 1993, i98FM found itself in front for the first time since its birth in 1979 – even it if was just by 0.2 per cent. By 1995, Wave's 50-year dominance was well and truly over; from that point on it would be i98FM who finished on top in almost every ratings survey.

In terms of the local music scene, the biggest boost radio-wise came on Australia Day 1995 when Triple J arrived. Before then the JJJ signal was sent from Sydney, which only reached the far northern suburbs of the Illawarra. In 1995, the Illawarra got its own frequency for the station – 98.9. "At least a bit of justice is now being done," said station manager Stuart Matchett. "No longer will people have to listen to a poor reception. It's not going to knock over every other radio station in the first few months, nor should it. It will just be an extra choice for people in the Illawarra to listen to."

It wasn't the first time Triple J had moved to broadcast in Wollongong. Back in 1982, the station had planned to relay its early morning programming through local ABC affiliate 2WN. The idea was sparked by a local ABC announcer mentioning the city had a large population of shift workers.

So Triple J started the ball rolling, printing up promotion programs and sending DJs to Wollongong for public appearances with a targeted July 1 start date after approval from the ABC bosses. "All that was needed for JJJ broadcasts to reach Wollongong was for a guy in central control Sydney to flick a switch," Triple J co-ordinator Marius Webb said.

But nothing happened. Twelve days later, Triple J got an answer – federal Liberal Communications Minister Neil Brown had decided the relays would not go ahead. He just apparently didn't bother telling anyone at Triple J or the ABC.

Back to the 1995 arrival, as was the case with the network's regional rollout, Triple J held an Unearthed competition in Wollongong, which was won by Evol. But the biggest advantage was the easier access for listeners in the Illawarra to hear independent music – and the chance for local bands to get national airtime for their CDs. In the era before music streaming, where almost any song can be listened to at any time you wanted, the arrival of Triple J was a big deal.

The city's community radio station Vox FM, was a very, very long time in coming. It started out as 2WCB in 1981, in the bathroom of the Wollongong Migrant Resource Centre, before moving to a somewhat more suitable premises upstairs on Keira Street a year later. By June 1986, it became 2 Vox-FM and moved to a home backing onto MacCabe Park in Ellen Street – but they still hadn't really started broadcasting.

At that time they were promising to start in August of that year, but that would be one of a number of promised deadlines the troubled station missed. There were several test transmissions since 1981 and the broadcasting licence had been granted in March 1986, but by 1989 still nothing had happened. A large part of the impasse was infighting and indecision, with some Vox members more interested in being DJs than filling the charter of helping groups that didn't have access to the media.

"I think Wollongong needs a radio station that is accessible, equitable and responsible," former Vox FM secretary Wayne Davis told the *Mercury*.

"We are not there to replicate existing services. Several community stations have simply turned themselves into clones of Triple M."

Vox president David Brown resigned in 1989 over what he said was the wrong direction the station was being pushed towards, rather than providing access for ethnic, women's and student groups.

"Our licence obliges us to provide a certain amount of space for these groups," Brown said. "But I think the directors are tending to move away from that."

A key stakeholder in the community station was the University of Wollongong Students' Representative Council. By 1989, the impasse had become so great SRC President

Daniel Morrissey was considering getting the university to take over the licence. "I will be initiating discussions with the vice-chancellor in the near future over the possibility of a student/university radio station," he told the *Mercury*. "One of our strongest arguments for the establishment of a student/university radio station is the new post-graduate school of journalism which will be running courses in 1989."

The university never did get their radio station; Vox FM soon sorted itself out and was broadcasting in the early 1990s. It also satisfied its community remit, with shows devoted to a wide range of migrant groups as well as the LGBTQI community. Music featured heavily as well, including a focus on home-grown talent via shows like *Doing It Locally* and *The Australian Independent Music Show*.

4

The early 1980s period saw another upswing for the Wollongong music scene, which was ironic given that same period coincided with a low point for the city. The Illawarra at the time was heavily dependent on coal and steel. Around half of the workforce was employed by those two industries. The Port Kembla steelworks was such a big employer that the suburbs surrounding it were full of steelworkers, many of them migrants.

When the recession of the early 1980s hit, Wollongong took a battering. The steelworks had stopped hiring in 1981 and brought in a voluntary redundancy scheme to reduce numbers. But it wasn't enough; a few years later more than 10,000 workers had been shed. Apprentices faced the horrible reality that they had to stay to finish their apprenticeship, all the while knowing there was not a job at the end of it.

In her book *Steel City Blues*, Julianne Schultz paints a grim picture of the city's economy in the early 1980s. "By the middle of 1983, 30,000 people and their families were dependent on government support to survive, 19,001 people were registered as unemployed and the three local Commonwealth Employment Offices listed only 108 vacancies. Businesses were closing each week. The number of people living in poverty increased five-fold, the crime rate escalated, the number of marriage breakdowns soared and the number of alcoholics seeking help more than doubled."

The 1984 state election, the first after the massive job cuts, showed just how angry people in the Illawarra were. Having little faith in the newly elected federal Labor government of Bob Hawke, voters in the Wollongong electorate (which included the steelworks) lodged a huge protest vote and ousted the sitting Labor MP Eric Ramsay – who had held the seat since 1971 – in favour of independent and then Wollongong Lord Mayor Frank Arkell. In the 117-year history of the seat, Arkell remains the only independent to hold it.

A sense of punk-flavoured activism rose up in the city in the early 1980s with the formation of the Wollongong Out of Workers Union. Controlled by unemployed people, WOW produced its own newspaper and established a food co-op, drop-in centre and a welfare rights centre for those out of work.

Much of their operations were run out of a house in Market Street (where the entrance to the Wollongong Central car park now is) seized during a 1983 winter campaign outside the Social Security office across the road.

"When some of the WOW members taking part were

hospitalised," Nick Southall wrote in the journal *Illawarra Unity*, "as a consequence of exposure [to the winter weather], it was decided to break into and occupy one of the empty houses across the road.

"With community support, including that of the South Coast Labour Council, who put pressure on the police and the owner, this house became WOW's office for the next six years."

Around 20 WOW members moved into the house, sharing a few of the rooms to sleep in. During the 1980s, the group occupied the Social Security office across the road, the ATO office and the national headquarters of the Labor Party in Canberra.

The organisation and its actions were very much influenced by the punk ethos of the late 1970s. "The freedom and creativity in music and art at that time," WOW member Gillian Pope told Southall, "was really a big release and broke down barriers for people who were out there in the suburbs. They weren't going to get a mainstream job and all those things. So there were a lot of avenues for their creativity to come out through punk."

Another member, Craig Donarski, cited the DIY aspect of punk as crucial for WOW. "Punk said it didn't matter how well you did things," he said. "It just mattered that you did … WOW had that punk thing that said if you're in a position to say something and if you don't say something you are morally bankrupt."

Other protest groups sprung up in the city in the early '80s, including the graffiti group Young and Pissed Off, who spray-painted slogans like "It's unemployment not leisure" on the Novotel Northbeach, in response to a campaign that branded the region "the Leisure Coast", or "Make BHP pay" on the walls of the city's Social Security office.

Redback Graphix, which worked closely with WOW, was started up by Michael Callaghan and Gregor Cullen in the 1980s. Working out of a disused kiosk in Stuart Park (later the home of the Yours and Owls festival), Redback produced brightly-coloured posters for WOW and other activist groups – which were plastered around the city – as well as on T-shirts and banners.

Callaghan told the *Mercury* in 1982 that he saw Redback as an alternative advertising agency. "Look at the capital available to big companies for advertising," he said. "The labour movement and community groups haven't got that sort of money to get their messages across, which is where we come in. We also act as general consultants for community-based campaigns."

Some of these included posters for various WOW fundraisers held at the Ironworkers at the top end of town near Wollongong train station. One of Redback's most recognisable posters posed the question "if the unemployed are dole bludgers, what the fuck are the idle rich?". The answer was given in pictorial form – a monkey reclining under a beach umbrella sipping a drink through a straw.

That poster was one of several created by Callaghan to help raise funds for his sister Mary's film company Steel City Pictures. The most well-known of the company's productions was *Greetings From Wollongong*, a 43-minute film partly funded by multi-band bill in Wollongong and Sydney.

Featuring a cast of unemployed young people, it's an

often-depressing film that shows the boredom and alienation of the city's youth who can't find a job and need other ways to fill up their day. It screened at the Sydney and Melbourne film festivals, but wasn't favourably received in some areas of Wollongong. Retailers in the CBD were unimpressed, claiming some scenes were shot in their stores without permission, and Wollongong council led a group of community leaders looking to prevent its distribution because of its negative portrayal of the city.

Musically speaking, two of the most pivotal 1980s Wollongong bands were The Sunday Painters and Proton Energy Pills. The former actually formed at the fag end of the '70s but began recording and playing in earnest in the 1980s. The band was formed by school friends Peter Raengal and Peter MacKinnon (who met in Year 5 at Wollongong Public and went to Wollongong High together). They picked up guitars and $30 amps and played in Raengal's bedroom. "I don't really consider myself a musician as such," MacKinnon explained years later. "I don't think I'm good enough. We used to joke that the reason we played our own material was that we weren't good enough to be a covers band."

While other members would come and go, bassist Dennis "Resident" Kennedy would join the two Peters in what was the longest consistent line-up of the band. Very much into the punk DIY aesthetic, the band released a handful of EPs and albums – all in small runs – on their own label, Terminal Records. The releases were works of art – one EP came with three different covers, another featured an individually made and coloured cover for each of the 250 vinyl EPs while a cassette release featured Raengal's bloodstains on each of the 100 copies. And every release was hand-numbered.

All of this contributed to the band's output being highly sought-after to this day; it's not unusual to see one of them being offered online for a few hundred bucks.

The other reason for their collectability is that their sound was so different to whatever else was going on around them. That sound – a mix of full-on electronic noise, rock, discordant pop, classical, punk, jazz and whatever else they wanted to play – was both ahead of its time and perversely timeless. But MacKinnon said the band wasn't to everyone's tastes – but not only when playing a hometown show.

"We would find the same when we played in Sydney or Melbourne. I remember one gig we did and at the end of the set, we tended to do a fairly full-on number that would go completely off. At the end of it there was just stunned silence from the audience. We were the support for what was essentially a pop band. The audience was there to see this pop band and we came out and just played this completely off the wall, almost wall of noise music and they just didn't know how to respond to it."

Being a university town, gigs at house parties in the 1980s weren't uncommon. The Sunday Painters played at uni students' homes in Corrimal Street, Gipps Road and West Street. Their home base was a former bakery nicknamed The Coke Ovens located in Findlay Place in the Wollongong CBD, a pokey little street few would even notice these days. The ovens served as a rehearsal space for a few bands, and a venue for gigs as well. The band also gigged regularly at a restaurant known as The Plant Room on Crown Street, near the Denison Street intersection. "That was our central hub as a community," Kennedy said. "Everyone knew of it, frequented it and enjoyed it. It must have been made in the late 1940 and was gorgeous, it was truly a wonderful place – we played there a number of times."

A number of other venues opened their doors to bands – in some cases to tap into a new market after the steelworks retrenchments led to fewer drinkers coming through the door. Among these were the Coniston Hotel, where 1960s music fans The Unheard played regularly, The Balkan Club at the top end of Atchison Street and the Ukrainian Club in Auburn Street.

Another band playing at all those venues was the Proton Energy Pills. These days that band is often thought of as a footnote to a bigger act – Tumbleweed formed after some members decided to end the Proton Energy Pills. But that doesn't do the band justice; what they did was send a vital message that you could come from Wollongong and make something of yourself.

The seminal line-up of the Proton Energy Pills were the Curley brothers Dave, Jay and Lenny (on vocals, bass and guitar, respectively), guitarist Stewart Cunningham and drummer Richie Lewis. Formed in the Curleys' home suburb of Tarrawanna, the band mucked about with local gigs until Dave joined in 1988 and forced the band to get serious. They started gigging in Sydney, and Lewis' regular visits to the Waterfront Records shopfront led to the band signing to that label.

The Protons cranked out two singles, *Survival* and *Less Than I Spend*, in 1989 and 1990. That year, they also featured on *Steel Town Sounds*, a documentary of the local scene that also featured the likes of Mutated Noddies, Man Bites Dog, The Unheard and Svegie's Vegies (whose members all worked at the local TV station WIN).

The year of 1990 also saw the demise of the Proton Energy Pills, during the recording of their self-titled EP (though some also call it *The Sun It Shines*). In liner notes to a later Protons' retrospective Cunningham explained the reasons for the band's end. "In hindsight it was clear (to me anyway) that Lenny wanted to go in his own direction and maybe there was some brotherly tension between him and Dave and myself because of this. Throw in some misunderstood words, a bit of stress, the pressure of recording and the next thing the Proton Energy Pills were breaking up."

That self-titled EP was a posthumous release and featured a sticker than read "Proton Energy Pills have changed their name to Tumbleweed". Which wasn't really true – they were two separate bands. That sticker came as a surprise to Cunningham, who didn't see it until the EP was in the record store racks.

Outside of local shows, one of the biggest gigs was when Midnight Oil came to town in 1986. The band had been regular visitors to the Illawarra and South Coast for years, as far back as the 1970s when they gigged under the name of Farm. On Saturday, February 1, the popular band headed a concert at Brandon Park at Fairy Meadow (now the site of the University of Wollongong's Innovation Campus) – their first appearance in the Illawarra since an October 1984 show at Port Kembla. Also on the bill for the concert, organised by the Steelers Club as a fundraiser, were Spy Vs Spy and Strange Tenants, as well as local acts Mistaken Identity and Happy Accident.

There was a booze ban at the '86 show, justified by Steelers manager Bob Millward because of a 1984 concert at Brandon Park where inventive individuals had gone into the ground a week earlier and buried booze, while others took in oranges injected with vodka on the day of the gig. He warned "smugglers" not to try and sneak anything into Brandon Park this time around. "It doesn't matter how many times we say it – people still think they'll get a dozen cans or a bottle of bourbon through the gates," he said before the show.

The move resulted in anger from fans at what they claimed was the "heavy-handed" behaviour of security searching people. "Security guards at the entrance gates confiscated all food from fans despite the fact that the well-publicised 'don't take' list included only alcohol, soft drink, glass and plastic containers," the *Mercury* reported the day after the concert.

Millward apologised for the issue, stating they only found out about the food ban at the last minute. Kerry Smith, who had travelled from Jervis Bay for the show, started a petition about the conditions at the show. "I'm a veteran of at least 50 outdoor rock concerts and I can honestly say that was the worst I have ever been to," she said. Smith claimed a security guard tipped out the contents of her handbag. "I was then forced to grovel on the ground amongst the crowd to pick up my personal belongings," she claimed.

The furore saw Millward swear it would be the last Brandon Park show for the Steelers. It caused further problems for the club with the Wollongong Licencing Squad recommending never granting the Steelers another liquor licence for an outdoor show unless improvements were made.

Things had gotten so bad that, at one stage during the concert, police had to close down the alcohol sales for two hours. Another issue that caught police attention was the lack of differentiation between tickets for purchasing soft drink, food and alcohol, meaning under-age fans could buy tickets for food and then use them to get beer.

Millward was not impressed with the suggestion that youngsters were buying booze. "I am adamant that underage patrons were not served with alcohol," he insisted. "Our information is that a great many of the underage drinkers arrived at the concert already drunk."

The coming decade of the 1990s brought with it what was the high point to date for the Wollongong music scene. The focal point was a pub on the corner of Crown and Corrimal streets, a few blocks from the beach. During the 1980s, the Oxford Tavern had acquired the nickname of "the bloodhouse", due to the rough nature of the clientele. It was rumoured that drugs smuggled in off the ships docking at Port Kembla quickly found their way to the Oxford. It was an unlikely place to become the home of the Wollongong music scene, especially given that most people were too scared to venture through its doors.

But through hard work, one man set the Oxford Tavern up as a place that would become legendary in the local music scene.

5

There's been a lot going on at the Oxford Tavern site at the bottom end of town. In the 1870s, when the temperance movement (which took a very dim view of alcohol) was in full swing, a temperance hall was part of the site. So the people of Wollongong had a place to go and not have fun.

Residents didn't seem to warm to the whole not drinking thing and the hall was sold in 1888. A year later the site became, of all things, a skating rink. When you think of what went on in the Wollongong of the 1880s who the hell comes up with skating? But right there, on April 3, 1889, the Elite Skating Rink opened its doors. "A scene from cloud land! An orgy with the fairies!", an ad in the *Mercury* proclaimed, suggesting the word "orgy" had a very different meaning back then.

The fun didn't last too long at the skating rink. Just four months later, on the night of August 30, the rink burned down, due to negligence by persons unknown, a coronial inquiry found. Basically, someone left a lit candle inside all night, never a good idea in a building made almost entirely of wood.

The Oxford rose up in late 1916, "furnished in a most modern and up-to-date style", according to a newspaper ad of the time. In words the Oxford's music fans would later find true, the ad also promised "the visitor will find the Oxford a home from home".

The venue made make headlines in 1951 when licencee Lucy Burrows was found dead upstairs, lying in a pool of blood. Using the vernacular of the time, three "new Australians" were charged with her murder; one of them, 22-year-old George Gach, was in possession of her stolen jewellery. Gach said he and Istran Gal waited outside, while Laszlo Kerekes carried out the foul deed. Kerekes insisted it was he who waited outside while the other two committed murder.

In the end, not even Gach suffering a heart attack in the dock could save him and his accomplices – they were all found guilty and sentenced to death.

In the late 1960s, there was talk that a $60,000 renovation to the Oxford could serve as one of the catalysts to rejuvenate the eastern end of Crown Street. In 1968, a group of developers pointed to the Oxford, the city council building (which is now the art gallery) and a new ice-skating rink at the showground as signs "the most valuable area in Wollongong" was on the rise.

The developers wanted to cash in on that, with construction plans for a "luxury motel" in the area. That ended up being the Downtown Motel, which suggests the word "luxury" meant something different in the 1960s than it does today. As for that skating rink – or "glaciarium" as people were wont to call it – that opened in 1967, the owners offloading it two years later. In 1970, those new owners announced the rink would shut down due to the high electricity bills – $250 a week. The rink had been popular in the first months when it was still a novelty but attendance wound down to the point the new owner was losing $200 a week.

In the 1970s, the Oxford played a part in the criminal underworld of Wollongong. Not that there was a wealth of dirty deeds going on in the city, but enough to raise a few eyebrows. Along Keira Street, where Amigo's Mexican restaurant now sits was once the home of the Tiki Coffee Lounge. It wasn't just coffee that was for sale either; if you liked the look of one of the waitresses, you could pay a bit extra for some private time upstairs. Charles Berry was the manager, until Sydney muscle Michael 'Big John' McHannigan was offered the job by the boss – as long as he could get rid of Charlie. He was fine with that and so on January 5, 1971, he went upstairs, whacked a sleeping Berry in the jaw with a hammer to wake him and then shot him twice.

With the help of an accomplice Big John stuffed the body in the ceiling. And there Charlie lay for several days in the heat of the summer, perfume and Brut 33 having to be sprayed to mask the odour. Finally, they removed the body and had it buried in Bendalong on the South Coast. McHannigan faced trial and was sent to jail. In later years, owners of the Mexican restaurant would insist Berry was still there, in spirit form.

Also in the 1970s, an illegal casino was around the corner from the Oxford, in Kembla Street. In 1977, that casino was named by a witness to a NSW Parliamentary Committee on drugs. That witness, former addict Gordon Lance Gately, also claimed the proceeds from the casino found their way to various city clothing boutiques. Those boutiques were also involved in the importation of heroin, he claimed. "I have come across certain clothing articles that have come out of the boutiques that have totally irrelevant tailoring features in them," Gately told the committee.

"They have come from Thailand. They have been cut and opened and there is enough room in them to bring in a kilo at a time." He added the boutiques were also selling sandals with false bottoms.

The Kembla Street casino was run by Sydney crime figure Barry McCann, who was also reportedly getting into drug dealing in the city. McCann is widely believed to have bumped off standover man Charles 'Chicka' Reeves, who was trying to take over his business. Reeves was found slumped in his car on the southern edge of Wollongong golf course in 1979, having been hit in the face with a shotgun blast.

That same year, Richard Vereker bought the Oxford Tavern. In his book, he paints an interesting picture of the pub; saying it was home to sportsmen, politicians, bookies, unionists and even staff from McCann's place around the corner.

"The Oxford was always busy and in the early 1980s was probably the biggest SP bookie pub outside of Sydney," he wrote. "We supplied all the booze for the cops' Christmas barbecue, and the senior guys from the unions and the ALP were looked after when they drank there. When the general strikes were called the Oxford would be exempted."

On New Year's Eve 1981, the Oxford Tavern was the scene of a riot of sorts, with around 30 people arrested for assaulting police, malicious injury and resisting arrest. The trouble occurred on the road outside the tavern, as punters leaving other nearby venues created a throng of around 1500 people. Tavern owner Lois Considine was quick to point out to the *Mercury* there had been no fights inside the venue that night – just outside. "The Oxford used to have a bad image but [husband] Kevin and I have worked hard to clean it up," she said. "Our plumbers and electricians have had their work halved because of the decrease in vandalism."

Nick Southall was among the punters who spilled out onto the street. "Soon any cars attempting to drive along the main street were being slowed, rocked to-and-fro and occasionally kicked or hit," he wrote in a blog post. Things got hairy when a car hit a person sitting on the road and drove off. An ambulance was called but, confronted by the crowd, they weren't going any further until the police turned up.

"By now the crowd numbered in the hundreds and the sight of the approaching police was met with jeers, taunts and a couple of beer cans thrown in their direction," Southall wrote. "Rapidly there were more cop cars and paddy wagons on the scene. Determined to advance, the cops inched forward, as the crowd grew and consolidated."

One of the officers pulled their gun and pointed it at the

crowd, prowling along the police line. "While his gun held the crowd at bay, the snatch squads began lunging into the throng," Southall wrote. "Under direction from their boss, small groups of cops targeted the biggest, angriest and most defiant. Known local toughs and trouble makers were amongst those snatched." They were thrown into waiting paddy wagons, with cops jumping in behind them – to lay into them with fists, Southall reckoned.

***

But for many, the memories of the Oxford Tavern are far more positive. For more than a generation of bands and music lovers from the late 1980s through to the mid-2000s, the Oxford was the place to be if you were into music. It wasn't because the acoustics were great – because they weren't. It was a rectangular-shaped room, with a shin-high stage wedged into one corner and the bar in the opposite corner. If you wanted a good sound you stood at the corner of the bar, with the stage facing you. Anywhere else and the bands sounded a bit ordinary.

What the real appeal of the Oxford was a sense of belonging. It took all comers; from the goths, the metalheads, the punks, the Steelers fans sporting footy jerseys who ducked in after a game at the showground down the road. No matter who you were, you were welcome. Also, in a city where the various slices of musical subculture were small, it made sense to band together – safety in numbers.

"The Oxford ultimately was a pub for the social groups that would have been harassed at 'normal' pubs," hotel sound engineer and musician Pete Conran told Ben Gallan for his University of Wollongong honours thesis. "Punks, mods, bohemians, skinheads, you name it. And at the Oxford they all got along. There was no rivalry, and any fights that ever broke out were never because of them. When 'normal' people would come into the pub, they'd be the ones who would be 'offended' by the other groups and would be the ones to start the fight."

In Gallen's thesis, photographer Ian Laidlaw explained there was no need to find out where your friends were going on a Friday or Saturday night, "… by nine or 10 o'clock you'd walk in the back door or the front door of the pub and you'd know 95 per cent of the people in there and it'd be packed."

All of those good vibes and memories people hold of the Oxford can be traced to one man – Steven Robinson. In the late 1980s, Robinson was the singer and songwriter of A Comedy of Errors (who, in 1991, became the first Wollongong band to release a CD).

"In Wollongong at that time, you couldn't play a gig anywhere as a local band and play original songs," Robinson told the *Mercury* in 2010. "You had to be either a covers band or be a touring band.

"We were really lucky, we got this gig at the Oxford and a lot of musos came down to see why this original band was getting a gig. 'I said give me your number and I'll try to get you in'."

In the end, Robinson was sending so many bands in the direction of the Oxford's manager that they asked him to start booking the bands for the venue. He made it a point to book 100 per cent local acts and even introduced a cabaret night called the Flying Fish Café, where people could get onstage and perform whatever their little hearts fancied.

Robinson admitted to Gallan that "locals only" policy did mean the bands weren't always up to scratch – at first. "Man, I had some crap onstage … but after a few gigs they got it and all you had to do was give them a couple of gigs. A few of them, after they heard recordings or heard themselves back, they think 'God, What!?' and so they really worked on it. Then you only needed a few gigs and they'd come up really well."

In later years, others took over from Robinson, including Zambian Goat Herders drummer Dillon Hicks and Jeb Taylor (who went on to play a big part in the Wollongong music scene's fourth golden age).

One of the significant things about the Oxford was that almost all the shows were free. For Taylor, himself a musician, that made it easier for young bands to grow. "You can't expect people to pay for a band when it's their first gig," he told Gallan. "Maybe their first gig is easy 'cause all their friends will come but, you know, their third or fourth gig … There are so many bands in Wollongong that wouldn't have got anywhere if they hadn't been able to play free gigs at the Oxford."

That also led to an expectation in the Wollongong music scene that *all* gigs should be free. Other venues tried to replicate the Oxford scene by putting on bands once or twice a week but the cover charge they placed on shows saw people shy away. Those venues overlooked that the Oxford's success was due more to the scene it had created rather than just booking bands. Even at the Oxford, when a touring band played with a cover charge at the door, a different crowd showed up. The regulars just didn't want to reach into their pockets to pay to get into their local.

Having a place to play was part of the reason the local scene was strong in the 1990s. Also in the mix was Redback Music, the only record store in the city that sold independent music. The store was also the only place that stocked releases by local artists. Owner John Jenkins also started the Redback Music label releasing CDs by Wollongong bands like Zambian Goat Herders, Mudlungs, Pounderhound, Dettol and FUgG.

In 1993, the scene got its first music press – the *Independent Music Monthly*. Put together by Kim Waters in the northern suburb of Austinmer, the free magazine featured stories on local bands and included a monthly gig guide showing where those bands were playing – as well as noting local music shows on community radio station Vox FM as well as other events in the scene. The *Independent Music Monthly* wound up in 1996, with music mags *Pulse* and then *Bulb* stepping into the breach, the latter finishing up in 1999 due to what publishers claimed was a lack of local support.

In the 1990s Waters also started up an all-ages venue Sunami in the same upper Crown Street location that once housed the Ironworkers Club. One of the more notable acts that played there was Blink-182, just before they became superstars.

The Oxford saw the birth of a number of iconic Wollongong bands in the 1990s. Among those was The Culprits, fronted by singer-songwriter David Beniuk, who had honed his craft as a solo performer at the Illawarra Hotel on the corner of Keira and Market streets in the Wollongong

CBD. The Culprits lasted from 1990 to 1991, coming runners-up in the state final of the national campus battle of the bands.

A few years later, the Merry Widows formed out of a few pieces of The Culprits. That band went all the way to the national band comp finals, finishing in second spot and releasing the CD EP *Waltz*. The Widows broke up after finding the grind of driving up and down the east coast for gigs while holding down full-time jobs too much to hack. Beniuk continued on as a solo performer, releasing albums well into the 2010s.

Another band big in the 1990s was FUgG. A pop-punk act featuring songs written by guitarist-singer Adam Buckland and bassist-singer Ronny van Dyk, they created a lasting image by dressing up onstage in women's clothes, pyjamas, as priests, Elvis or whatever else took their fancy. The band pushed out a few releases on cassette before their 1997 CD EP *Drucked* scored Triple J airplay with van Dyk's song *Distortion Saved My Teenage Arse*.

In retrospect, that would be the band's high point. The follow-up EP *Altar Ego* scored Triple J airplay via the song *Pale Edwards* (again written by van Dyk). Soon after the release, Buckland left the band – going on to release a wealth of albums under the names of Dodgy World, Sweet Sweet Bulbs and The Adam Buckland Ensemble.

With a new line-up, FUgG released two full-length albums in the early 2000s, *Art Brut* and *No Left Turn Unstoned*. The first of those was released by Taylor's label High Beam Music (which also put out releases by local acts Thumlock, the Monstrous Blues, Shifter and Hee Haw). The latter was also slated for release on High Beam but that never happened due to the label's financial difficulties. While both albums were strong, they didn't achieve the same success as earlier EPs, which suggested the band's time in the sun was over.

While Wollongong of the 1980s and 1990s was focused on guitar rock and punk, some acts chose to push against the tide. One of them was Erika's Jive, an acoustic-electric duo made up of guitarist and singer Denise Thomas and bassplayer Mary-Anne Cornford. With songs about love, desire, gun control and conservative politics, the duo had a hard time finding appropriate places to play. "We played the Oxford for about four years," she told Warren Wheeler for UOW newspaper *Tertangala*, "and we just can't do it any more due to the late times and the drunkenness."

Their music was more suited to the intimate venues like The Plant Room in the CBD and the Fireworks Cafe in the north; places where volume wasn't required to reach anyone at the opposite end of the room. Musically, they saw themselves as offering strong female role models that served as an alternative to the standard manufactured girl pop star. "We want to make women aware that you don't have to do that sort of thing," Thomas said. "You can actually be whoever you are and be who you want to be within the entertainment industry." They left behind the self-produced album *Who's Erika*, released in 1997 and which still stands up decades later.

Without doubt, the biggest Wollongong band in the 1990s was Tumbleweed. Rising out of the break-up of the Proton Energy Pills, Tumbleweed showed the local scene that a band from Wollongong could make a name for themselves outside the city. Following a few EP releases in 1991 and 1992, late that year they released their first, self-titled, album – still regarded by fans as their best. Having signed to Atlantic Records in the US, the band had figured they were set for stardom.

But Atlantic wasn't able to hear the quality in the follow-up *Galactaphonic* and lost interest, even though that album became a success in Australia. Guitarist Paul Hausmeister felt they were one of loads of bands Atlantic signed up in the wake of Nirvana's breakthrough with the view that one of them might become successful. "We would have been one out of 20 bands they signed with the same objective," Hausmeister said. "And one of those 20 was a band called Stone Temple Pilots. All [the label] needed was one of those bands to start charting well and the others mean nothing."

The band didn't make it easy on themselves either. After *Galactaphonic*, guitarist Lenny Curley and singer Richie Lewis sacked Hausmeister, which saw his friend and drummer Steve O'Brien quit in sympathy. That was the beginning of the end for the band. They trundled along for another five years, releasing the albums *Return to Earth* and the oft-forgotten *Mumbo Jumbo*.

That last release saw interminable delays due to record company takeovers, which was the final nail in the coffin for Tumbleweed. A decade of animosity between the original members followed, before managing to patch up their differences in 2009 and reform. They soon found their hardcore fanbase had never left them and their second coming ended up lasting longer than their first go-round.

For local bands in general, promotion was much harder in

the era before the internet took hold and music streaming meant bands could get send their sounds around the world at the push of a button. In the 1990s, one popular way for a band to get some exposure for their music was via album and single compilations.

One of those was sparked by Protons singer David Curley in his role as a youth worker at Wollongong Youth Centre. Curley did much for young bands in this decade, being heavily involved in allowing bands to rehearse in the centre and setting up all-ages shows.

One of his earliest efforts ended up getting state-wide recognition. Tied in with state and federal initiative, The Drug Offensive – which tried to talk to kids in their own language about drugs and alcohol – Curley organised a split seven-inch called *The Good Trash*. The single featured two local bands, Eat My Chainsaw and Social Outcasts. Both were anti-drug songs, but Eat My Chainsaw's *Choose* was a lot more subtle. The Social Outcasts' *Wasted Youth* featured the opening lines "I'm sick and tired of drugs that wreck my brain/My memory will never be the same".

The Good Trash won recognition in the 1990 *Sydney Morning Herald* Youth Awards. "It gave young people the chance to express themselves on an issue which is important to them," Curley told the *Herald*. "I had always wanted to find a way to integrate music with my work with kids because music is a good way for kids to channel their energies."

In 1994, Wollongong City Skillshare released the classic local compilation *Socketwood*, named for a rainforest tree found only in the Illawarra region. The disc featured 19 Wollongong bands, none of who went onto fame and fortune, but it still provides a snapshot of the local scene. While the majority of the songs come from heavy guitar bands like Mudlungs, Shifter and Dinky Crash (featuring future Museum of Contemporary Art curator and noted ceramic sculptor Glenn Barkley on vocals) that dominated the Wollongong scene at the time, it also made space for other styles. That included the folk sound of The Hunt Brothers, a solo acoustic performance from Greg Gluyas, blues-rock from Alloy Forces (who were tipped to be going places at one stage) and early dance music from Cosmic Z.

A few years later in 1997, another Dave Curley initiative saw the light in the form of the compilation CD *No Dress Regulations*. Recorded by Zambian Goat Herders' Brent Williams, it was a collection of tunes from bands that had played at the Wollongong Youth Centre and was arguably better than *Socketwood*. It was certainly more comprehensive, boasting 26 tracks compared to *Socketwood*'s 19. It also showed a growing local music scene, with only five of the 26 bands having also appeared on *Socketwood*. The *No Dress Regulations* disc featured a variety of styles – punk, metal, hip-hop, singer-songwriters and indie – and included an early recording of Thumlock, who went on to have international success.

The youth centre was also perhaps the only venue in town putting on all-ages shows. Opened with a show by Tumbleweed, the venue was a haven for kids looking to see bands or even perform. It was also noted for staging shows by the likes of international acts like Fugazi, NOFX and All.

6

The Oxford's demise was long and it was slow. The ball started rolling in late 2005, when the Belmorgan property development group announced its $350 million plan for both the Oxford Tavern block and what was the Dwyer's Holden site just across the road in Corrimal Street. Called Gravity, it would include a seven-storey shopping centre on the Dwyers site, as well as two residential towers more than 90 metres high, with a pedestrian bridge over Corrimal Street. It was to be bigger than any other building around it at the time.

Seventeen storeys of apartments would go up on the Oxford site, with a three-storey tavern located at the corner of Corrimal and Burelli streets (though anyone with a brain could see the tavern would be doomed after residents in the expensive apartments above started complaining).

City councillors weren't fans of what was tagged "a Gold Coast-style development" – an apt description given the architect had worked on heaps of buildings along that tourist strip. "I don't believe this is what our residents want," Cr Anne Wood told the *Mercury*. Council knocked back the part of the development featuring the towers, and state planning minister Frank Sartor was not impressed either.

A development application for the Oxford site was lodged in April 2006 and the debate was brought back to council after some councillors objected to the proposal being rejected in the first place. One of those councillors was embroiled in the corruption scandal two years later that saw the council sacked.

It got the nod from council by a vote of 7-4 when it went back in mid-2006 – despite some councillors still finding the project on the nose. With the green light, the Oxford part of the development was meant to be finished in 2009. But it never actually began – at least not by Belmorgan's hands. The Oxford Tavern site was up for sale in mid-2008 and the arm of the Belmorgan group that owned the land went into receivership by the end of that year. But boss John Kosseris was still upbeat, "it's all good ... it's all pluses, not doom and gloom," he said.

He was wrong. The company holding the land went into receivership through lender Suncorp in April 2009, with three more businesses in the Belmorgan stable being liquidated in July. A year later creditors were still owed more than $200 million.

While all this uncertainty was buzzing around in the mid-2000s, worrying both bar staff and bands, the Oxford had stayed open. That uncertainty had an effect on the health of the scene, which had lost some of the lustre of the golden age of the 1990s. Other venues like the North Gong, which had been a hotel known for bringing down independent bands from Sydney to play on its stage wedged into the back of the band room, had been fighting a losing battle with residents behind the pub complaining about the noise. It led to earlier finishing times for gigs to appease the neighbours, before opting to forget about bands altogether on the path to turning the band room into an upmarket dining and drinking area.

While places to play might have been disappearing, there were still some notable bands in first decade of the 21st century. A game-changer on the scene was the often-confronting theatrical rock and roll of Bracode.

Fronted by the operatic stylings of singer Zec Zecher, the band often took the stage in costume and facepaint. But it wasn't all style, there was real substance there – shown in the fact they took out the 1999 band comp at Wollongong Uni, beating out the likes of Porcelain. "We are not into 'beating the boys' or anything like that," guitarist Rebecca Mayhew said. "We are just there to play from a female point of view about issues that concern us, have fun and do the best we can."

The foursome put out two albums in their time, *Over The Shoulder Boulder Holder* and *Greatest Tits*. For years, Bracode also strongly championed the participation of women in rock and roll. In 1998 they worked with the Women's Music Collective, where they found their work cut out for them.

"We all sat around in a circle of women," Bracode's Erica Lewis told the *Mercury*. "Everyone talked about what they played and what they were into. The first thing out of anyone's mouth was 'I play guitar but I'm not very good' or

'I play this, but I'm pretty crap'."

The band took part in the Wollongong Youth Centre Utterbox project, aimed at highlighting violence against women, contributing the song *Side Saddle* to a CD compilation. "It's about being a second-class citizen," Zecher said, "how man has designed things, like the side saddle, for women." The centre also ran Girls Get Loud music workshops, in which Lewis and Mayhew held classes, and were major players in the Scooter Rock Chix movement. In addition to Bracode, Mayhew and bassist Jacqui Besgrove formed the long-running Babymachine.

That band saw the members take up the Ramones-like idea of adopting the same surname – Machine. Like Bracode, Babymachine had a message to send out. "We do have a political agenda, a feminist agenda, but we don't believe in getting all preachy," Bec Machine said. "We take a more tongue-in-cheek attitude, we get our message across by taking the piss."

Babymachine released three albums in the 2000s – *Birth is Imminent* (2004), *Appetite for Reproduction* (2011) and 2019's *Abort! Abort! Abort!*. With the help of the internet (which wasn't the instant music delivery device it is today), the band ended up with fans around the world, due in part to some of their albums being picked up by overseas labels.

"I get emails from people I've never met saying 'your record's really important' and telling me how the songs are inspirational or how it speaks to them," Kristy Machine said. "That's really encouraging. When you get that kind of feedback from someone you haven't met or who is not part of your crowd, it feels like what you're doing is a little more legitimate."

Unlike many other Wollongong bands, who splintered apart after a few years, Babymachine stuck around and are still a going concern in the 2020s. "The key to why we have stayed together for so long is because we're really good friends," Kristy Machine said at the time *Abort! Abort! Abort!* was released. "We keep it easy, we keep it so that it fits into our lives. We practice most weeks but if one of us has got a crazy hectic week and practice is going to be a horrible thing, we just don't do it. We want to keep it fun and keep it as something that's enjoyable for us."

Another 2000s-era band worthy of attention is Dropping Honey. While formed in 1997, the fuzzed-up shoegazer band hit their straps at the turn of the century, releasing their debut album *Snakes & Ladders* in 2001. The band was fronted by singer-songwriter Damien Lane (who had also played in other '90s Wollongong bands like Pounderhound and The Gilded Kiln). The sound of Lane's songs bore the signs of bands like The Cure and My Bloody Valentine, especially the latter's penchant for difficult-to-hear vocals. "I really, really like that," Lane explained. "It's the whole thing of leaving it open to your own interpretation. Also it's a way of masking it if it's autobiographical, so you can't tell what it's about."

The band broke up in 2004, when Lane and guitarist Jolyon Pagett moved to the UK, leaving the recorded album *Dreams of Broken Teeth* unreleased (though some of the tracks later appeared on the group's Bandcamp page). After the pair's return, the band reunited for a short while, before taking another hiatus and then playing some more shows – 2021 saw them in the studio recording a new album.

During this time, Lane was making a living as a film score composer – albeit one who would sometimes argue for less music onscreen. "I don't like the music to be too manipulative or spoon-feeding people," Lane said. "Music can do a really wonderful thing in terms of being subtext. I just prefer to work that way rather than going 'well, this is a sad scene, so here's the strings'."

When his band Proton Energy Pills split up in 1990, guitarist Stewart Cunningham didn't let the grass grow under his feet. Instead throughout the 1990s he played in a number of respected indie bands like The Yes-Men, Asteroid B-612, Challenger-7 and Brother Brick. His longest-running band was Leadfinger, named for his own nickname garnered from an incident in his teens where his brother shot him in the finger with an air rifle (though there's also a bit of an homage to Leadbelly going on as well).

With a musical style resembling the underground guitar rock of the '70s and '80s Cunningham's first release under the Leadfinger name was 2007's *The Floating Life* (recorded in Cunningham's home studio in Helensburgh through 2005-06). Four more albums followed between 2009 and 2016, not to mention a few EPs and several compilations – some of which were released by Taylor through the Impedance Records label.

***

In the 2000s, the Musicoz Awards for unsigned artists started in Wollongong as a work for the dole program. In time, acts like Bluejuice, The Fumes, Felicity Urquhart and Bliss n Eso would be among the award winners. As would

Wollongong band Porcelain, who won in 2001. Driven by songwriters Lo Roberts and Ben Richards, the band moved to the United States in 2005 and signed with Universal.

Basing themselves in Los Angeles, the band played shows in the US for several years and worked with the likes of Linda Perry and Blondie's producer Mike Chapman. During that time Porcelain was also working on their debut album *Freedom and Release*. An album that would never be released and what could have been one of city's musical success stories appeared to peter out as Roberts and Richards went their own ways.

One act had to get out of Wollongong to become successful – electronica trio Infusion. Formed by high school friends Jamie Stevens and Manual Sharrad in the 1990s, with fellow local Frank Xavier joining later, they realised Wollongong didn't offer a receptive audience for their style of music. "Because we're an electronic band," Xavier said, "and there are a lot of primarily rock kids in Wollongong, we used to have bad shows. People would go 'what the hell is this?'." So they left town, first heading to Sydney and then Melbourne. And then the world, playing some of the big dance festivals. In 2004, they won an ARIA award for best dance release with the song *Girls Can Be Cruel*, repeating the feat a year later with their album *Six Feet Above Yesterday* while signed with Sony BMG. Infusion called it a day in 2013 after a show at Sydney's Enmore Theatre.

A combined effort from the website WollongongMusic Scene.com and advocacy group Wollongong Music Round Table captured some of the sounds of the early 21st century in a pair of compilation discs released in 2004 and 2005.

Volume 2004 featured 17 tracks and the 2005 volume 18, with only three bands doubling up. One of those was a band that went against the prevailing guitar rock sounds of Wollongong. The Dawn Collective was a five-piece that included a cello and played atmospheric orchestral tunes that at times sounded like they had been composed for a movie soundtrack. The year the compilation was released, The Dawn Collective finished second in the NSW final of the campus band competition.

Also on that first disc was The Monstrous Blues, which included former Tumbleweed members Paul Hausmeister and Steve O'Brien, a spin-off from long-running metal act Segression known as Side Effect X and punk act Hy-Test, which had yet another member of the Curley family in guitarist Michael. The 2005 edition showcased the likes of dance band The Fists, who performed with a mix of electronics and live drums, indie metal act Ohana, former Pounderhound frontman Tim Ireland with a more acoustic sound, and Dlivr's funk/afro Cuban/jazz hybrid.

***

Back at the Oxford, the end had arrived. The 2009 Christmas Party band showcase was axed in favour of pole dancing, which gave an indication of what the owners thought of the local music scene. Six months later, in July 2010, the white gates on the beer garden closed after the receivers terminated the tavern operator's lease. The *Mercury* ran the news the same day as its gig guide, which carried the disclaimer "Patrons are advised to check with the Oxford Tavern to see whether any gigs scheduled at that venue will still go ahead". They didn't – and the hundred-odd bands who had been booked to play in the coming months lost their gigs too.

The Oxford Tavern sat derelict at the bottom end of town for more than two years, until a Sydney developer plonked down around $7 million for the block in April, 2013. Eleven months later, a PSR Investments plan for a $38 million 14-storey apartment complex on the site was approved. The pub car park, long loved by tavern goers and those looking for a free CBD park, was still in use up until the sale. So the sudden loss of cheap CBD parking was another stinger.

Then the cyclone fencing went up and, in July, the wrecking ball was brought in. A month later it was gone (though someone managed to save the "Oxford Tavern" neon sign, which later turned up outside the Wollongong Art Gallery for the *Steel City Sound* exhibition).

It was small consolation, but the iconic venue's name would live on. In July 2016, the apartment and retail complex was officially opened – and it was called Oxford on Crown.

Ironically, while the local music scene justifiably bemoaned the loss of the Oxford back in 2010, two of the three pieces that would join up to make a new golden age for the city were already in place.

7

The first piece of that puzzle was a guy up north by the name of Jeb Taylor, who was inspired to dip his toes into the music scene after hearing a few songs from Tumbleweed. Discovering they came from a few suburbs down the road, he formed a band with friends from Bulli High School in 1996.

Taylor was the drummer, joining with schoolmates guitarist-singer Justin Roberts and guitarist Chris Rojas, roping in bassplayer Simon Dalla Pozza from a neighbouring school. Calling themselves Anomie they played their first show at the Wollongong Youth Centre, scoring a support slot with a band called Stumbling Jesus Mosquito (who was Tumbleweed road-testing songs for a new album under an assumed name).

A year later they changed their name to Ventolin, releasing their debut EP (somewhat confusingly titled *Anomie*) which boasted a heavy rock sound drawing comparisons to Shihad.

A second EP was recorded in 1998 but the band splintered before it could be released.

From there, Taylor started working behind the scenes, managing local stoner rock act Thumlock while still in his teens. He set up the High Beam Music label (which sprung out of his online music blog of the same name) to release their second record *Lunar Mountain Sunrise* in 1999. "There was no real intention to start [the label]," Taylor said. "It was just something I decided to do on the spur of the moment."

Taylor suddenly had his hands full – the album scored rave reviews here and overseas and the band followed it up with albums *Emerald Liquid Odyssey* (2000) and *Sojourn's Lucid Magic* (2002). The albums were released internationally, which was a much harder task in the era before social media channels and YouTube. It meant emails and cold calls to labels, trying to interest them in this Wollongong band they'd never met or seen play live.

Thumlock petered out in 2003 – the band insist they never broke up and a reunion is talked about from time to time. Taylor meanwhile kept developing his High Beam Music label from the front room of his home in the far northern Wollongong suburb of Wombarra. He put out releases from local bands like FUgG, Monstrous Blues (which featured his old bandmate Dalla Pozza), El Sanchez, Hee Haw and Shifter (which counted future Tumbleweed bassist Jamie Cleaves among its members). By forging connections in the music scene around the world, he also acted as the Australian distributor for several overseas labels.

In 2003 Taylor, Dalla Pozza and Roberts met up again and had a few jams for old time's sake. That led to the creation of a new band – How Machines Work. They dug out that unreleased Ventolin EP and sent one of the tunes – *Pilot Error* – to Triple J's Robbie Buck without an accompanying bio or information. Buck liked what he heard and started playing it on his *Home and Hosed* show.

From there it became a minor indie hit and meant Taylor's band was enjoying more success than most of the local bands on his label. "You've got so many bands who push so much and put so much work into stuff and to have it happen for us with absolutely no effort is kind of weird," Taylor said at the time. "I suppose it's the luck of the draw. We didn't have a full set when that started getting played. So we started getting offered shows without having a full set."

The popularity of the song saw the band release it as a three-track EP and later have to distance themselves from suggestions the song was about the September 11 terrorist attacks (it was written several years earlier).

Pilot Error was released by the band because Taylor shied away from signing them to his own label. For their 2004 follow-up *Address in White*, he and Dalla Pozza created the Trans Electric Records label for it – despite having bigger labels interested in signing them.

"We had a few but it ended up going around in circles a lot of the time," Taylor said. "We could have kept going at it and kept giving them demos, but it was getting close to a year since the *Pilot Error* stuff got some interest."

In order to move the label out of his house, Taylor teamed up with Dalla Pozza in 2004 to open the Music Farmers store. While in time it would become a focus for the local music scene, it was initially intended to be an office and storage space upstairs in the Crown Street mall, accessed by a door on the ground floor many wouldn't notice if they weren't looking for it.

In a short space of time, the label faded away and that office space became a music store, but focusing on CDs more than the vinyl records that later set the store apart. Starting a music store in the CBD didn't seem like a smart business move; at the time there were almost half a dozen CD stores in the mall, including the independent-music friendly Redback Music. But somehow the little guy would end up being the last man standing, Music Farmers continuing to exist, while those other stores disappeared. "I guess they were all competing with each other at the time and we were stocking a lot more obscure stuff, like local stuff," he said on the store's 15th anniversary in 2019. "That was our point of difference then and it just evolved over the years as the market changed."

Taylor opted for a bigger space in 2007, moving into large premises in Crown Lane opposite the western end of the mall. It was so large that the store – which was called 5 Crown Lane – could host shows by local and visiting acts, as well as holding art exhibitions from Radio Birdman' Deniz Tek and others. The venue was opened in May with a party and a free mix CD boasting the likes of Nick Oliveri and Taylor's own How Machines Work.

"We just wanted to be able to run shows and run in-stores," Taylor said of the bigger store. "And there were a few other people around at the time that were looking for the space to do different projects. It just gave us heaps of space – maybe too much space sometimes. We'd think 'what are we going to do with all this space?'."

Once the local council got word of what was happening there wasn't much Taylor could do there. While council could turn a blind eye to in-stores and the like during business hours, there was the problem of the after-hours gigs. In late 2008, council told Taylor he needed to apply for an entertainment licence if he was going to continue to have bands play at 5 Crown Lane. He felt the costs were too prohibitive and decided to close the space to the public, using it as a place to hold the stock for an online retail store.

Taylor picked up a new business partner for 5 Crown Lane in the form of Nick Irwin, a local metal bassist. Together they also launched the Impedance Records label, putting out releases by former Queens of the Stone Age bassist Nick Oliveri, New Christs and Hard-Ons. Also in the catalogue was a bunch of local bands, including BugGirl, HyTest, Mother and Son (who would soon inspire Hockey Dad), Leadfinger and Irwin's own band Immolate.

A massive shopping centre development across the road ended up being the venue's saviour. With construction crews smashing their way through bedrock to build the three-storey Wollongong Central development and making a real racket in the process, council realised it could hardly take issue with noise from a band playing across the road. So 5 Crown Lane reopened after being closed for about two years.

After putting up with the noise of construction for several years, once the centre was finished, Taylor got some bad news from the landlord. The cost of a new lease would be four or five times what they had been paying. "It was too far apart to even try and negotiate so we just thought 'let's look for something else'."

So in 2014, they moved a few hundred metres south to a smaller shop in Keira Street where there wasn't the space to do what they'd offered at 5 Crown Lane but, by moving a few things around, they'd be able to have bands turn up and play. Also, the Music Farmers name returned to the shopfront.

As well as running his own label, Taylor also did stints as a band booker through the 2000s, including at the Oxford, the Harp Hotel a few doors up the road, and The Patch in Fairy Meadow just north of the city. Shows at that last venue were killed off in 2013 in the same way as many other venues – complaints from neighbours who moved in near a pub and then didn't like the noise. "That section of the law," Taylor said at the time, "is very heavily weighted in favour of one person rather than the employment the place brings, the amount of people that turn up to watch bands."

He took things a step further in 2012, opting to start a music venue above the Grand Hotel in Keira Street. Called Barcode, it was aimed at a niche not well catered for in the Illawarra. "There's a level of bands that always come through Wollongong," Taylor said, "that get 80 or a hundred people that are probably too big for Yours and Owls or whatever, but when you put them out to the UniBar or The Patch, they're not big enough, so we're trying to look at that.

"There's a lot of shows maybe not coming through Wollongong because the right space isn't around."

8

Something else was going on in the first decade of the 2000s, something which centred around a non-descript plastic table and set of chairs outside a kebab shop in North Wollongong. The regulars took to referring to it as the Table of Knowledge, perhaps in a self-deprecating way, but perhaps not. The regular who sat at that table in the early mornings saw themselves as Wollongong's players – developers, lawyers and council officials including general manager Rod Oxley.

What some of the regulars got up to would strip the city of democratic representation for more than three years, put Wollongong on the front page of newspapers and the top of TV news bulletins for all the wrong reasons and turn the area into the source of sniggers. In time it even saw the end of one of the city's most-loved music venues.

In early 2008 the Independent Commission Against

Corruption began investigating the goings-on of council staff and several developers. At the centre of the growing storm was town planner Beth Morgan, who was having affairs with two developers – Frank Vellar and Glen Tabak. In the ICAC hearings she claimed she also had sex with a third developer – Michael Kollaras – though he denied any such thing ever happened.

While sleeping with Tabak and Vellar (and being presented with gifts, cash payments and even a holiday to China) Morgan also appointed herself the assessment officer for their developments. At times she used other workmates' log-ins to approve contentious aspects of these developments and cover her tracks. In the commission, Morgan justified the use of a workmate's computer thusly; "I believe he gave me the right to use the computer because when you leave your computer you're supposed to shut it down."

If the saga of sex and dodgy DA approvals wasn't enough of a drawcard, the scandal also threw up a few conmen. Ray Younan and Gerald Carroll told a number of participants they had links with ICAC or were even investigators and, for a cash payment, could affect the outcome. Plenty of money changed hands, according to the ICAC findings. Vellar coughed up a whopping $120,000 and Morgan paid $50,000. City councillors Val Zanotto and Frank Gigliotti were also caught up in it – the former paid $120,000 while the latter handed over a case of whiskey.

ICAC Jerrold Cripps handed down his findings in 2008. He took a very dim view of Morgan, Tabak and Vellar, saying they were "unconvincing and uncooperative witnesses who were prepared to disregard the truth and would say whatever they thought would best serve their own interests". Findings of corruption were delivered against all three of them. Morgan escaped punishment due to insufficient evidence and that the time to lay charges had lapsed.

Tabak was hit with a $2500 fine and a two-year-good behaviour bond, while Vellar served a 10-month sentence via an intensive corrections order (which meat he avoided seeing the inside of a cell) and a $3000 fine). The only person to go to jail was councillor Gigliotti, who served four months for giving false or misleading evidence.

Corrupt conduct findings were also made against councillors Zanotto, councillors Kiril Jonovski and Zeki Esen. Former council general manager Oxley was also found to have engaged in conduct "that was liable to allow, encourage or cause the occurrence of corrupt conduct". However, no charges were recommended against him. Oxley said the findings were shattering and that he didn't feel he had done anything wrong. "It has a connotation of being corrupt," he said, "you're taking backhanders, you're on the take, you're deceitful, dishonest and I don't believe I was any of those things." He later wrote a book called *Named and Shamed*, which outlined his view of events.

The saga gave the state government no alternative but to sack the elected council – regardless of the fact there were no findings against the bulk of councillors. From 2008 to 2011 the council was run by three administrators, which put the city into a holding pattern, with the administrators focusing on the day-to-day running of the council, rather than developing any far-reaching strategies.

Residents had to wait until September 2011 to get the chance to vote for their representatives. In a sign he was perhaps unable to read the room, Oxley announced he was having a tilt at the position of Lord Mayor. "This isn't out of self-interest," he said when he announced his candidacy. "I'm doing it because I think Rod Oxley has something to add to the city. I have the drive, the single-mindedness, the passion and I've got the interests of the city at heart."

If the vote counts were anything to go by, many of the city's residents preferred to put that time behind them. Oxley only managed to net a few thousand votes.

The scandal also left Michael Yaglinpinar with a bad taste in his mouth. He was the owner of that North Beach kebab shop, and the man who put out the white chairs and table every morning. The man who just made their coffee but didn't eavesdrop on their conversations.

"I'm really upset with it all," he said. "All the publicity that we've been getting is negative … it's just a table, it's nothing." The attention the Table of Knowledge gained drove the regulars away, and also perhaps played a part in Yaglinpinar selling up just a few months after the commission handed down its findings.

It took several more years for the effect to be felt in the music scene, but the Wollongong council corruption scandal also inflicted damage there.

9

While the council scandal wound its way through ICAC, some "demolition parties" were going on up north. University of Wollongong psychology student Ben Tillman moved out of home when he was 18, taking up residence in a waterfront sharehouse in the northern suburb of Sandon Point. The place was dirt cheap, with housemates paying around $30 each a week in rent. As uni students are prone to doing, Tillman and his housemates threw a few wild parties – tagged "barn parties" because the sharehouse resembled a barn. But things soon got out of control.

"Rumours got around they were called demolition parties," Tillman told *Coal Coast* magazine. "People would literally walk around and punch holes in the wall. We didn't get our bond back. The parties were pretty big – at one of the last ones we had about 600 to 700 people at our house."

Not surprisingly, the police started taking an interest in

what was going on in the beachside sharehouse. They gave the party throwers some advice – which the students unwisely followed.

"They told us if we wanted to have the parties we'd have to register them," he said. "So I was like 'sweet, we will register them', which was the dumbest thing we ever did, because we were giving police the heads-up! It got to the point where there'd be hundreds of people out the front and our friends were being arrested."

The police also handed out fines to Tillman who, as a uni student, wasn't flush with cash to pay them. So he had the bright idea to throw another party, sell tickets and use the proceeds to square up with the cops. But the party wasn't as his house, this time it was hosted at Castro's, a gay-friendly nightclub in the Wollongong CBD. To make it look professional, he created the promotion business Liberteen Ranch. "There is just a lack of live music down here and we sort of thought we should do something," Tillman told the *Mercury*. "We wanted to get a bit more of a live music scene and try and get more people interested in live music."

The parties went off well and Tillman paid off his fines – then things got serious when he was offered the chance to book cult US band Ratatat. "I remember the agent saying it would cost 15 for them to play – and I didn't know if that meant $1500 or $15,000, but either way I didn't care."

With other bands like The Vines and Tame Impala also on the band list, what got tagged A Night with the Phantom needed a bigger venue. So in May 2009, the show kicked off at the beer barn Waves in the suburb of Towradgi.

Among the partygoers in the Sandon Point days were

Tillman's friends Adam Smith and Balunn Jones (also uni students, studying psychology and economics respectively). While Tillman was doing his thing with Liberteen Ranch, they were travelling around South America. When they came back to Wollongong, they told Tillman of their plans to open a coffee shop. Burnt out from booking bands, Tillman threw in his lot with them. In the back end of 2010, they took out a lease on a hole in the wall on Kembla Street, at the eastern end of the mall. While in early coverage of the venue it was called Owls Café, it soon came to be known as Yours and Owls (a twisting of the phrase "Yours and Ours").

"In a way we set up the café in an effort to create the type of place we would like to go to that just wasn't on offer in Wollongong," Jones said.

In February of the following year, the place became more than a café, opening up at nights as a small bar. It wasn't the first small bar in the city – that honour went to trailblazer Otis Bar, up a narrow set of stairs on Crown Street opposite the western entrance to the mall. The venue – sitting on top of streetside shopfronts – opened in 2009 despite headaches in acquiring a small bar licence. "It's such a difficult process and it's so expensive that it puts a lot of people off," said co-owner Louise Keyte. "We have full-time jobs to cover the cost because we really want to do it but if you don't have a full-time job I think it would be difficult."

In mid-2011, Otis Bar was closed and the team moved to a nearby location in Globe Lane to open up The Little Prince which soon became a popular venue, due in part to the fact it was at ground level and visible to passersby.

Also an issue for small bars was a difficulty in councils

understanding they were distinct from a larger venue, therefore the old licencing rules shouldn't apply. In time, the recently elected Wollongong council got their heads around the change and more small bars would pop up, forever changing the nightlife in the Wollongong CBD.

Yours and Owls experienced this sense of confusion. They ended up with an on-premises licence rather than a bar licence, which put them in a similar class to a restaurant that could serve a patron wine. "Melbourne has had a small bar culture for 30 years or something and Sydney is still behind but they're slowly catching on," Tillman said. "I guess council didn't really know what to expect when we applied. They don't get that you can have a place that serves alcohol that's not necessarily dangerous."

It did turn out to be dangerous for the three owners still in their early 20s. "After we got the liquor licence things went a bit downhill," Tillman said several years later. "We were 23 and we were like 'Yes, we can have our own bar, we can drink whatever whenever we like. We got progressively worse at getting up early to do morning shifts."

At first glance, the tiny shoebox of Yours and Owls didn't seem like it was destined to become an iconic music venue just two years after opening. Fitting in around 80 people, there was no stage – bands played on the ground level on the same floor the punters stood on. It made for a tight squeeze for a local band like Tommy M and the Mastersounds, who had eight members. The venue was so compact that, sometimes, a band's singer looked like a member of the audience. A set of stairs led to a small area, which were also full on busy nights – with the occasional crowd surfer taking a leap from the stairs onto hopefully raised arms. Like the Oxford in its day, Yours and Owls engendered a feeling of ownership and belonging. Who cared if it wasn't the biggest venue ever, it was *their* venue, it was *their* place. A place that, like the Oxford, came to occupy a prime piece of real estate in the memories of the regulars.

Looking back after a few years, Tillman admitted the excitement of opening Yours and Owls meant they did things and then asked for official permission later. "We just opened and we got a letter in the mail that said if we didn't get a DA [development application] or close in two weeks we would be fined $1 million," he told the *Mercury*. "We pushed a few boundaries with council and brought a few issues to attention, but partly because we've naturally gotten into a bit of trouble."

By 2012 Yours and Owls had established itself as *the* music venue in town. And they got themselves into a bit of trouble too, with two of the owners finding themselves facing police charges following a decision to have an unauthorised mural painted on the wall facing the street outside the venue. Painted by local artist Simon Grant in December 2011, the landlord wasn't impressed by the mural and ordered it to be painted over. There was a delay in that happening because the owners were waiting to hear back about their plans to place three panels over the mural that could regularly be repainted by artists. Until then, Jones said, they had been under the impression the mural's removal was on hold.

In early February Tillman and Jones spent $50 on paint and brushes and covered over the mural. "It's drawn attention to how boring the CBD is without it," Tillman said.

A month later, the same wall was hit by vandals, who daubed phrases like "no teams born here council gay" and "have some fun you boring saps". Smith felt the removal of the mural had created a blank canvas for that sort of thing.

"What we had before was graffiti," Smith said. "As soon as that becomes taken over there's always the risk it's going to be bombed. It's just a target now. I have no idea what happened but it looks pretty bad."

The police had an idea what happened – two months after the March 2012 vandalism they used CCTV footage to charge Jones and Tillman with malicious damage. Those charges were later withdrawn and dismissed, with the help of a solicitor who was a regular customer and offered his services pro bono. When news of the charges being dropped was reported in the *Mercury* in late November, Jones said they were selling the business – but wouldn't elaborate on why.

One of those reasons stemmed from events on the night of October 26, 2012. That night Yours and Owls held a big show to mark their second birthday, in the town hall across the road. Tillman was at the show and caught a taxi back to a friend's house, where he had left his red Volkswagen.

Then, with alcohol still in his system, he got behind the wheel to go to a party. "We were going to a party but I wanted to go home after that," Tillman told the Huffington Post. "I stupidly thought I'd drive there so I could leave – it was five minutes from home."

Tillman lost control of his car on a bend along Lawrence Hargrave Drive at Austinmer, clipped the curb and rolled into a power pole. While his two passengers were unhurt and able to scramble out of the car, Tillman was trapped and had to be cut out of his mangled Volkswagen.

The accident damaged his spine, leaving him paralysed and in a Sydney hospital for months while trying to learn to walk again. His blood alcohol level was measured at three times the legal limit, which meant he had a court date a year later. In Wollongong court he pleaded guilty to high range drink-driving. He copped a $1000 fine and lost his licence for five years. "Having regard to what he's inflicted on himself," Magistrate Michael Stoddart said, "he's suffered far more [punishment] than what the court can give him."

A fundraising concert to help Tillman was held at Yours and Owls and the town hall on January 19, 2013 featuring music exhibitions and live art. Included on the bill were local acts Mother and Son, The Bungalows and The Walking Who. Owls co-owner Jones said more than 20 local bands and musicians had put their hands up to appear at the show to acknowledge Tillman's impact on the scene.

"Ben Tillman has been prolific in the upkeep of the Wollongong music scene since the demise of the Oxford Tavern," Jones said. "Through his commitment to live music and ongoing hard work, Ben has become an influential and respected figure in the Wollongong music scene."

Even the Wollongong Hospital colleagues of his mother Lesley Vining pitched in, deciding to get sponsors for their efforts at the Canberra running festival. "We're running because Ben can't," said organiser Michele Power. "We hope people will dig deep and sponsor us to fund medical costs for Ben."

By March 2013 his mother said Tillman was out of hospital and could be walking by November.

"He won't be walking like you and me, [he'll be] hobbling with walking sticks but walking all the same," she said. "He's pretty determined – he's amazed me really."

Tillman would end up getting out of a wheelchair and taking his first steps with the aid of a walking frame.

10

The plans to offload the Yours and Owls space continued during Tillman's recovery, and a farewell party for the venue was set up for August featuring the likes of Tumbleweed, Totally Unicorn, The Walking Who and Step-Panther. "We chose who we think are the best bands from the area and the ones we've had a good relationship with," Tillman said.

In September the Kembla Street venue was sold to former venue manager and Step-Panther drummer Daniel Radburn. The Yours and Owls guys were taking the name with them, so the venue was renamed Rad Bar.

"I want to follow in their footsteps, learn from what they've done and improve," Radburn said of his plans. "It would be too much of a loss to lose this place. I've loved it since it's been open, and being a musician myself, I wanted to keep it going."

The Yours and Owls brand in turn ditched making coffees and serving drinks and returned to the sort of band and venue booking that Tillman had done under the Liberteen Ranch moniker – albeit on a much bigger scale.

But first, they had to change the city a little more. The newly elected council had put a focus on what it called the "night-time economy" of the CBD. Work on the multi-storey Wollongong Central development along Keira Street had started, after the GPT group delayed works due to the global financial crisis and the tumult caused by the council's ICAC woes. That was seen as the starting gun for other developers, who had been waiting to see whether the big guy would move forward or not.

When it did, the skyline in and around the city CBD started to change. Cranes seemed to forever be in the sky, building apartments (which caused locals to wonder where developers were expecting to find all the people to live in them). With more people expected to call the CBD area home, council recognised they would need things to do at night and so the focus on keeping the city going after the sun went down began.

A key component of a night-time economy is bands playing gigs, so in 2013, the council launched its Live Music Taskforce. The taskforce itself fed into the earlier work done by State of the Music Scene forums that had been held for several years and which brought together bands, venue owners and other stakeholders. The aim of the taskforce was to improve the council regulations to make it easier for existing venues to book bands and for new ones to open. "We'll look at regulatory issues with venues like noise and licencing," said taskforce chair and city councillor Ann Martin. "But it's not just about making sure performances don't get shut down, it's also how we can make it easy for people to do their work."

In August, just before Yours and Owls morphed into Rad Bar, the Illawarra music community members of the taskforce were named, including Tillman and Taylor. They took the role seriously – Taylor attended all six meetings, with Tillman only missing one. "That they even put the taskforce together means they recognise live music as important to city life," Tillman said. "Live music has always had its supporters, but now it's in the face of town leaders. It's only a matter of time before it filters to the rest of the community."

Even before the taskforce had handed down its report, there were signs the vibe of the city was changing. In the 18 months to November 2013, 20 venues had applied for a liquor licence, from small bars and restaurants to art galleries and cafes. "What great initiative," Cr Martin said. "They're actually taking the bit between their teeth and setting up fabbo little bars and, for me, that's a real sign of their confidence in their city, and the fact they want the city to be cool."

Council economic manager Mark Grimson had also noticed the change. "For a period of time, Wollongong's lagged in this space," he said. "There hasn't been a real diversity on offer. But, now it's started to grow, it's demonstrated that demand is there – which is in turn attracting a much more diverse demographic."

The taskforce report was released in January 2014 and offered a range of recommendations, many of which council later adopted. A crucial one dealt with the bane of music venues; people buying a residential property next door and then complaining about the noise. Council altered the Section 149 certificates – which notify residents of issues relating to their property such as land uses or heritage information – to include a statement that they can expect some loud music.

Those certificates now mention the drive to create "greater activation and investment beyond 5pm through an evening economy. Future residents should be aware that these uses may generate noise, odour, traffic and have longer hours of operation, which is part of living in/near a commercial centre".

As well as bands, venues and the punters who go to one to see the other, the change found a surprising pocket of support – real estate agents. "If you are moving into the city," said MMJ Real Estate's Daniel Hastings, "you have to accept it will be noisy sometimes and there will be live entertainment at night – that's city living."

***

The changing face of the city wouldn't come without a few growing pains. Some of those were experienced by Adam Murphy, owner of Humber Bar, located right next door to the new Wollongong Central development. A three-storey building, it had a café on the ground floor, a bar on the second and another on the roof overlooking the CBD.

Murphy ended up with a fight on his hands to get a liquor licence, for which he applied in May 2014. In October the NSW Office of Liquor, Gaming and Racing said it felt Humber's application should be refused because there were too many bars in the city fuelling an already high level of alcohol-related violence.

Before the body made its final ruling, it opted to hold a community forum in Wollongong to gauge the level of support. And there was plenty of that. Local music historian Warren Wheeler came out all guns blazing, pointing out the new bar scene was helping to change the city's "insidious drinking culture". To him, the established drinking venues were "little more than meat markets frequented by cashed-up bogans whose primary goal on a Saturday night is to pre-fuel, hit the nightclubs and either provoke a fight or conquer a sexual desire (or both) sufficient enough to be able to regale their gym buddies with their tales of unsurpassed machismo the following morning."

Yours and Owls' Tillman was a bit more restrained, noting that "it just seems obvious the small bars and smaller licenced venues are something positive, because every good city in the world has a massive night culture and that's often focused around these types of venues."

Even the city's Lord Mayor Gordon Bradbery was in favour of Humber being granted a liquor licence, saying places like that were a departure from "beer swilling halls" and in line with council's push to develop a sophisticated night-time economy.

Almost a year after applying, Murphy finally got his licence. "It has been a long road to get to this point but we have always felt supported by the people of the city in our journey," Murphy said. "From the start we have felt that Wollongong City Council, the local licencing police and the community have understood implicitly what we are trying to do and feel we have a legitimate place in the urban centre."

***

In 2013, the Live Music Taskforce wasn't the only thing Taylor and Tillman were teaming up to do. They were also planning the very first Farmer and the Owl festival to be held at the university on November 23. With plans to make it an annual event, the festival was headlined by The Drones and featured Dappled Cities and local acts Los Tones, The Walking Who, Mother and Son, Shining Bird and Machine Translations.

"The event is an extension of the culture Yours and Owls/Music Farmers have been trying to create for the past few years," read the statement on the event's Facebook page, "and the overall vibe and feel of the event will reflect that."

"It was something we've been talking about for a few years," Taylor explained. "It's meant to be something a bit different to the usual. We wanted to create an event, not just a concert, with the art and market side as well."

They came up with a marketing ploy that was a bit different to the usual – and a bit scary for uni students too. Around 500 students returned to their cars parked on the campus to find a brown envelope stuck under their windscreen wipers. Normally a parking fine was inside, but not this time. "Warning!!! A music and arts festival ticket must be purchased," the letter read. "It will be a real criminal offence to miss out."

Tillman said the aim was to spread news of the festival to more than just the live music fans. "No-one likes a parking ticket," he said. "But they have a look at it."

The pair followed up the first Farmer and the Owl show with a King Gizzard and the Lizard Wizard show at MacCabe Park a block south of the city mall. It was initially intended as a laneway show but was moved to the bigger venue of the park. The event actually came about with the help of that Live Music Taskforce; among its recommendations was one to look at creating special entertainment areas, which made it easier to hold outdoor events.

"They are getting more supportive," Tillman said of council. "We've been plugging away for a while and they are taking notice. We're showing we're trying to do something good, and not just kids causing trouble."

Taylor later described the King Gizzard show as "really chaotic" and noted it "was a pre-cursor to a lot of what has followed".

The third key part of the music scene's fourth golden age had been making a name for themselves with gigs at Yours and Owls/Rad Bar – which started when an underage Billy Fleming and Zach Stephenson tried to sneak into a 2012 Hunting Grounds show at Owls.

11

It doesn't take long to drive through Windang, a suburb huddled on a peninsula jutting into Lake Illawarra. And that's what most people do, drive past and onto the bridge that links Wollongong to the suburbs of Shellharbour. Following the six-lane road that cuts through the centre of the Windang, from its northern end to the bridge over the lake will take you less than two minutes. Maybe longer if you get held up at one of the two sets of traffic lights in the CBD.

That CBD includes a few takeaway food places and cafes, an "express" (ie small) supermarket, a bottle shop, tattoo parlour and the Computer Town store that locals of a certain vintage will always remember because of its jingle (a jingle that has been mentioned in a number of Hockey Dad stories even though it's doubtful some of the authors have ever heard it). Behind the main drag there is a handful of streets full of houses.

The feel of the place is more like a sleepy coastal town

where you went for summer holidays as a kid than a suburb of a major regional city. And that's evidenced by the presence of a bait and tackle shop in the main street.

Like a number of suburbs in Wollongong, there's an Indigenous influence in the name Windang. It comes from an Aboriginal word meaning "place of a fight". Though, these days it's hard to see just who would be doing the fighting, given the suburb's population skews heavily towards the over-60s (thanks to the two retirement villages). Seniors make up 41 per cent of the suburb's population of 2656, according to the 2016 Census, while those 19 and under account for just 17 per cent.

Which probably goes some way to explaining how the age gap between the two members of Hockey Dad, which put Stephenson two grades ahead of Fleming at school, was never an issue. With relatively few young people, kids couldn't afford to be picky about hanging out with someone who wasn't their own age.

"We had a bunch of mates who were older than us by far," Fleming said. "So when I got into Year Seven, Zach was in Year Nine and we had mates who were in Year 12. The reason was we all surfed together, it broke down the barriers. It meant the whole age difference thing didn't matter."

One of the handful of streets that go to make up Windang is Boronia Avenue. It runs east-west, sliced in the middle by the main drag. At the western end is a footy oval, while the eastern side ends with a sandy pathway through some coastal bush leading to the beach.

The Hockey Dad story starts on the beach side of Boronia Ave, just over a block from that sandy path. When he was a kid, Stephenson and his dad Ross were playing footy in their front yard on Boronia Ave. "Billy walked past and joined in," Stephenson said. "He lived down the road and after that he never left, he was there every day." Incidentally, Fleming was quite a sportsman in his pre-band years – as a kid he was pretty good at cricket and admired some guy named Don Bradman.

"We were just little groms," Fleming remembered, "playing heaps of sport, but then we started surfing heaps and everything else went out the window. From then it was just surfing and music."

By the time Fleming entered high school, music had become the focus. "We first started getting into music in Year Nine and [Billy was] in Year Seven," Stephenson said. "I'd been playing guitar for a little bit and it was me, Billy and another friend of ours had gotten together. We all played guitar and Billy jumped on drums because no-one else wanted to."

This garage band became Abstract Classic, who had an early gig at the Lake Illawarra High School Battle of the Bands in May 2010, where Stephenson remembered they played a cover of The Living End's *All Torn Down*. It wasn't good enough for them to win – Abstract Classic ended up finishing third.

Despite only one member (singer/guitarist Kyle Willoughby at 18) being old enough to buy a drink at a bar, the band scored a few pub gigs here and there including the local Lake Illawarra Hotel. If you head over to YouTube you'll find a short video of them performing *All Torn Down* at the Lake hotel in February that year. Stephenson handles the lead break well and Fleming – who looks even younger than his 14 years – is already pretty impressive behind the kit for someone who never took a lesson.

After falling short at the school band comp, Abstract Classic set their sights on a bigger prize – the *Mercury* BlueScope band competition. The popular event ran from 2007 to 2011 where bands could win a $5000 cash prize and recording sessions. "It's a prestigious competition and we want to get out there and get noticed," Willoughby told the *Mercury*. "We're hoping to surprise ourselves and at least get through a few heats. We're confident but we want to take it one gig at a time."

They did get a surprise of sorts, making it to the final at Waves through a wild card online vote. They'd actually finished second in that vote but winner Loud Whisper were unavailable, so Abstract Classic was one of the 10 bands in the final. They fared worse than the school band comp, not even making the top three.

But they'd be back in 2011, having recorded five new songs. "We've been doing heaps of gigs since then," Willoughby said, "and we've entered more band comps and hopefully we can come back and make it to the finals again."

This time out, they won their heat – playing tunes like *Yes, We're Pirates*. That win took them to the finals, and their 15-minute set is on YouTube for those interested souls. It's hard to find any pieces of the Hockey Dad sound in Abstract Classic – the dominant characteristic is a ska/reggae-pop feel. Stephenson only takes lead vocals on the last song – *Skank*.

Abstract Classic did better this time around – finishing

third while Tommy M and the Mastersounds took out top spot. Still, the Windang fourpiece took home $1500. The band continued for another two years, planning to record an EP and playing what was one of their last shows – a January 2013 all-ages gig at The Patch in Fairy Meadow underneath headliners Tumbleweed.

In early 2013 Abstract Classic "fizzled out", in part because Willoughby and bassplayer Kurtis Train had left school and now had jobs. So Stephenson decided to record some of his own tunes. Fleming offered to play drums on the tracks and that was pretty much the start of what soon became Hockey Dad.

By this time, Stephenson and Fleming had already formed a connection with Yours and Owls, having gone down there in mid-2012 to stand outside and listen.

"We were both underage, we were still in school," Stephenson told *Coal Coast* magazine. "We might have been about 16, so we hung out at the front door and listened to all the support bands. Then by the end they finally let us in just to watch Hunting Grounds. It was really good, they put on an awesome show. I think that was like the first set I saw there and it had me hooked on the place."

Radburn – the bar manager at the time – remembered the night slightly differently. He said the pair were "begging to be let in" . 'We're not gonna drink or anything, we just want to see the show', Radburn remembered them saying. At any rate, Stephenson and Fleming did get in for the headliners and it was a visit that led to a strong connection between the pair and Radburn, and with the Yours and Owls team – both of whom soon played a significant part in their rise that started a year later.

But before that could happen – before they could play a gig even – they needed a name. That came from an episode of *The Simpsons*, where Bart and Milhouse are playing a video game called *Hockey Dad*. It featured two fathers beating each other up after one ridiculed the other's child. The eventual winner is named Chuck Shadowski and Bart's line of "feel the drunken wrath of Chuck Shadowski" ended up as the band's bio on its BandCamp page. "We thought it was hilarious then," Stephenson said of the Hockey Dad name, "and now we're stuck with it forever."

The first time Hockey Dad appeared in the *Mercury*'s gig guide was for a Yours Owls slot in August 2013, supporting Melbourne band The Stiffys. But there was a gig before that at the uni in May. With Stephenson studying at the University of Wollongong, Hockey Dad were eligible for the UniBar band comp. The new duo performed in their heat, finishing second, which meant they missed out on the final. Though history would show that loss really didn't mean too much in the bigger scheme of things.

12

For the next 12 months, Hockey Dad honed their stage act, largely with shows at what was now known as Rad Bar. "That's where we played a show pretty much once or twice a week for about for about a year and a half," Stephenson said. "We kind of figured out what we were doing as a band in that venue and got to work on our craft. So if it wasn't for that venue, we wouldn't be a band."

There were other gigs too, including that first Farmer and the Owl show at the university – a sign the band were making the right sort of connections. And that was about to pay off.

Those taskforce meetings Taylor and Tillman went to didn't just lead to the pair of them working on a festival here and there. "After those meetings," Taylor said. "we'd just come out and say to each other 'people just need to do stuff if anything is going to help develop Wollongong in those areas'. So after a few different ideas we settled on kicking off a label."

It was an area Taylor was already quite familiar with. As well as having run the High Beam Music label, he and Music Farmers co-owner Nick Irwin had been releasing local bands on their Impedance and Music Farmers imprints.

In May 2014 Tillman and Taylor announced the launch of the Farmer and the Owl label. It fit in with what the pair had already been doing – preferring to stay in Wollongong and help build a scene rather that moving to Sydney or Melbourne and trying their luck. "There are so many good bands in our area so the label is a way for us to help them get some wider, national attention," Tillman explained. "Wollongong music is as good as anywhere in the country, it's just that we don't have that supportive infrastructure to help bands make the jump out of the Gong."

The label's first signing ended up being a band that had played their first gig just 12 months earlier – Hockey Dad. Taylor had seen the band play at Rad and was impressed, even though there was only a handful of people at the show. "The first time I saw them, they'd probably only played less than five shows," he said. "They were pretty rough and young but there was something behind the roughness in the songs. Zach's vocals really stood out a lot back then, even though they were pretty undeveloped and raw.

"You probably don't see it that early with a lot of bands, where you can look through that rawness and feel there is some potential there."

Taylor had met Fleming and Stephenson because they were regulars at the Music Farmers store. On one visit they gave him some of their tunes, but Taylor didn't like them much.

"At some point they gave me demos, which didn't really capture them that well," he said. "I think I told them that – 'oh, this is really not you guys'." Right there is an important moment in the Hockey Dad story. Plenty of Wollongong bands at that point would have either given up or decided Taylor didn't know what he was talking about.

What Hockey Dad did was go away, record some more tunes and bring them back to Taylor. Those demos ended up becoming the first EP *Dreamin'*. The significance of that wasn't lost on Taylor. "That was a hugely important thing – a lot of bands you'll say that to and that's it. They took a lot early feedback on board from Dan [Radburn], myself and Ben. A lot of bands are 'this is what we want and this is how we want it'. They won't take any advice."

Tillman didn't need too much convincing to go with Hockey Dad as the first band on the label. "The guys are like everyone's little brothers," Tillman said. "They were new, they were exciting and they were really good. It made sense to start the label with them."

Technically speaking Hockey Dad wasn't the start of the label. They may have been the first signing but – despite what the *Dreamin'* catalogue number states – it wasn't the first Farmer and the Owl release. That honour went to a compilation CD called *Beached Friends* – released with the assistance of some cash from Culture Bank (a local funding group where people pay a regular subscription and, several times a year, the money is divvied up between a few creative endeavours).

The first of several volumes over the years, it featured a song from Hockey Dad's upcoming EP, as well as tunes from future label signings TEES, Tropical Strength and The Pinheads, one or two bands who ended up on the Music Farmers label as well as a number of other local acts across its 17 tracks.

Taylor said it was hard to pick the tracks for the comp. "[It's] people we've worked with for a long time, people we have good relationships with. We've tried to pick the best; stuff that's coming up that people may not have heard of yet, even in our local area, and the ones that have been around for a bit longer that people should be more familiar with."

Tillman explained that every band on the disc had some sort of connection to Wollongong. "The album is an introduction to the rest of the country, a reflection of what we hope to achieve and a concept for the way we want the label to be." The label co-owner also felt it was a sign of what you could achieve if you got off your backside and did it (which seemed to be a stumbling block for many). "If you want to be involved in a creative industry in Wollongong, you have to do it off your own steam," he said. "It's pretty difficult, so hopefully people will see this as proof you can actually do stuff like this in Wollongong."

The first Hockey Dad release – the *Lull City* single – had come out in December. It was a song that described a state of mind when the ocean is flat, the waves aren't breaking and there's nothing to do – you're stuck in lull city, man. The video was shot at Rad Bar, with the opening scene an out-of-focus shot looking out across Kembla Street. Fleming and Stephenson look absurdly young, like the high school kids they still were at the time. Musically it was the right first release – it nailed the jangly surf-pop style the band became known for in their first year or so.

A month after the *Beached Friends* comp and label launch at the University of Wollongong – where Hockey Dad was on the bill with Jenny Broke the Window, The Walking Who and Shining Bird – *Dreamin'* hit the record store shelves.

With a name drawn from Daryl Kerrigan's favourite phrase in the film *The Castle* ('tell'em they're dreamin'!'), the EP boasted five tracks including the already-released *Lull City*. The songs had been written at various stages since the band formed, with some, like *Seaweed*, among the older tunes.

The cover featured an old photo Fleming's parents took in 1985 from the front yard of their Windang home, looking in the direction of the Stephensons' place.

"I went through my parents' old film photos back when they were first coming down here," Fleming remembered. "Originally they would come down in holidays – that was their holiday home."

At the time of the launch, the Hockey Dad pair sat down for what may well have been their first interview, with the *Illawarra Mercury*. In a Q&A, they chose to describe themselves as "two Leisure Coast lady killers" and listed a whole lot of other bands they were in – some of which may not have been real.

"We are both in a desert salt rock band called Batrays featuring some other local legends [Vulpes Vulpes], and also our first band Wedgetails from Windang, which is a psych-surf outfit. Billy does some solo electrical dance music under the alias of SURF and Zach plays bass in Step-Panther, under the alias of Graeme Anderson."

When asked to describe the sound on *Dreamin'* they said

it was "a dreamy experience of dirty surf pop". The June release of *Dreamin'* saw the band undertake a short national tour and the follow-up single *I Need a Woman* was released. Musically it followed on from the path set by *Lull City* – summery, jangly surf pop.

Having no cash for a video, they tooled around Windang on pushies and skateboards and got a friend to film it. "We just did a lap of our hometown, pretty much," Fleming said. "You can do a lap of our hometown in three minutes." And he wasn't kidding; pretty much every single shop in the main drag makes an appearance in the video as well as a few other landmarks.

Years later, listening back at *Dreamin'*, Fleming heard two guys "so excited about being in a band." "We were writing whatever the first thing that came to us was," he said. "We were writing songs in half-an-hour, 45 minutes at that point. It captured a very small timeframe of how we were doing things."

But it got things rolling for the band in a big way. In August they were named as a finalist in the Triple J Unearthed High competition – thanks to Fleming still being at Lake Illawarra High School. "It was definitely a surprise," he said. "Entering was a good opportunity for exposure but we didn't expect to come this far." They also picked up a local support slot for The Living End when they swung into town.

Hockey Dad was also picked as the Unearthed winner to play at the Byron Bay Falls Festival. Even though they had to play at midday and "everyone was hungover as fuck", according to Fleming, they still had a good time.

Things were getting so serious the band decided they needed to get a manager. And they found one at Rad Bar – owner Daniel Radburn. "It had never even crossed my mind to try and manage a band," Radburn told David James Young. "I guess, after years of playing music and working around it, I felt like a new challenge. I loved the band – both musically and as people – and so I wanted to help with it."

And then there was the big talk Fleming and Stephenson had to have with their parents. The year *Dreamin'* was released was Fleming's HSC year, which made for a few problems. He was able to sit some of the exams at school but found himself on the road for a few. "The Bad//Dreems tour, the boys got me absolutely hammered and we were on shots," Fleming said. "I like half-died that night! The next day I had to sit my English HSC test in Adelaide hungover as fuck."

He must have done okay, Fleming managed to get early entry into the University of Wollongong. And Stephenson was already there – but this Hockey Dad thing was starting to kick off. "That's when he sat us down," Fleming's dad Bill told Young, "and said that he and Zach wanted to give the band thing a proper go. We told him to go for it – you can go back to uni any time you want, if you want. If this is what you want to do, then we're behind you."

And around this time they were also in line to play at a new festival that would soon really put the city on the map.

13

Let me tell you about the time The Rolling Stones were going to play at Berkeley. It all started in 1974, with a plan from Sydney bookie Bill Waterhouse to build a resort and casino on an artificial island in Lake Illawarra, off Currungoba Point. No, I am not making this up.

Waterhouse planned to spend $50 million on the project, which included a casino if the state government went ahead and legalized them. But that's not all; he wanted to add a 400-bed hotel, nine-hole golf course, shopping area, health club and top it all off with a monorail to ferry visitors around. He tried to sell the council on the idea by claiming every resort needed a casino, because it would attract 100,000 overseas tourists. But council was not as keen, especially when they heard from Illawarra Natural History Society's Mr N Robinson about the site's propensity for flooding. "The area where they are planning all this development in my memory has flooded at least a half-dozen times – about three times in the last 12-13 years," he said.

Despite no development application being lodged, Waterhouse wanted the council to give it the green light. But they didn't – though he gave the dream up slowly. In 1978, he told the *Mercury* the plan was still a possibility.

At the end of 1975, Sydney-based promoter Panama Developments got the nod from Waterhouse to hold a music festival at the site of the planned resort. To be called the Sunray Farm festival, Panama's managing director Mr G Kron said he had already signed up The Rolling Stones and Neil Diamond, and had plans to telecast the concert around the world. With the festival slated to start on January 31, 1976, Kron was still chasing council approval in mid-December – not surprisingly, they were concerned about the flood risk.

Some of the council aldermen were supportive, particularly an Alderman Hall, who noted the council "has done little in fostering good relations with the youth of this city".

"Let's put Wollongong on the map as far as the pop festival is concerned," Alderman Hall said. "We owe it to the youth of the community to provide something like this."

Yet he was in a minority, with the bulk of the council following a health and building committee recommendation to knock it back on environmental grounds. Lord Mayor Frank Arkell objected to the location, suggesting West Dapto was more suitable.

While Arkell was granted authority to find an alternate site, nothing came of that. "The Lord Mayor said he would come up with a suitable site but he didn't," Kron said. These comments came after he'd rejected a suggested site at Shellharbour as "swampy and useless" and a farm at West Dapto was not available.

Other festivals were more successful in getting off the ground. The longest running is the Illawarra Folk Festival. The volunteer-run festival started in 1985 at Jamberoo, a small village a half-hour drive from Wollongong. The festival grew to sprawl over three days and effectively take over the town, with stages and campgrounds set up on the sporting ovals and gigs taking place in several venues on the main drag. In 2007 the festival's growth saw it move to the greyhound racing track at Bulli in Wollongong's north.

In 2000 Marty Doyle organised the first Kemblastock festival in the hills of Mt Kembla. Held as a fundraiser for the American Creek Regeneration Group, entry was free but people were encouraged to fling a gold coin or two in the donation buckets. While the list of bands playing on the back of a semi-trailer parked at Mt Kembla Oval were mainly local over the years (including Babymachine, FUgG, Richie and the Creeps and Monstrous Blues) the occasional out-of-towners – like Darling Downs, featuring indie icons Kim Salmon and Ron Peno – made an appearance.

"Kemblastock is a chance to put on a big outdoor concert and do some fundraising," Doyle said. "I like music and bush regeneration so I decided to combine the two."

The festival ended up a victim of its own success. Over the years crowds grew to more than 2000, which caught the attention of Wollongong City Council in 2008. The council said the Doyles had to lodge a development application, which included third-party insurance, security and traffic management. The cost was prohibitive and so Kemblastock was no more.

In 2002 Peter Conran started the HOPE Festival, in memory of his girlfriend, Unheard bassplayer Belinda Deane, who committed suicide in July 2001. Deane started playing keyboards in a garage band in 1981 as a 17-year-old but switched to bass after being inspired by the likes of female bassists like Talking Heads' Tina Weymouth, Suzi Quatro and Sunday Painters' Kerrie Erwin. She joined The Unheard in 1991. Pat Lyons, who was also in the band, remembered Deane as "cool and funny and smart, and a great bassplayer".

Deane's problems started with the onset of rheumatoid arthritis in her hands, hips and feet, when she was 28. It meant she had to give up the bass, which had a crushing impact. Over time, the constant pain and side-effects of painkillers took their toll. That along with bouts of depression led to the decision to take her life in 2001.

The first HOPE show at the Oxford Tavern in 2002 featured four bands – The Unheard, Bracode, Pancake Day and FUgG – Deane had been a member of or liked to dance to. Soon enough, HOPE grew into an annual event held in July each year to raise awareness and funds for suicide prevention, helping groups like Lifeline (13 11 14).

As part of a promotional mailout for the 2005 show Conran wrote of the pain caused by Deane's death. "It still feels like a dream," he wrote. "I opened the garage door to find that Belinda had hanged herself. I reached up gently stroked her on the cheek and said 'Oh Binni, what have you done?'."

When the Oxford closed, HOPE moved to The Patch at Fairy Meadow for a few years before heading to Dicey Rileys at the top end of Wollongong and was still going strong almost 20 years later.

"I thought I'd still do it every year," Conran said, "but I didn't realise that it would become such a necessary thing or such a well-loved thing throughout the community.

"A lot of people who go there who still remember Belinda don't go out very much anyway – they're older people. But they tend to turn up for this. It's become part of their social calendar and they run into people they haven't seen for years. In a sense it brings people together."

Another annual festival throughout the early 2010s started out as a way for the organiser to celebrate his birthday. Hy-Test bassplayer and singer Luke Armstrong kicked off HyFest in 2011, convincing more than 20 of his favourite bands to turn up at The Patch and charged punters $10 to see the lot.

"The idea was that it would be a one-off thing," Armstrong said ahead of the fifth HyFest show, "but it just seems to have snowballed every year. By the third year we did it we didn't even have to try and pick the line-up and call and ask them to play – we had so many people hassling us to play."

With life gradually taking over, by 2017 HyFest was too much of hassle for Armstrong, so Warren Wheeler from Helter Smelter Booking and Promotions stepped in for what was the last time the festival was held.

"I offered to help because I love loud rock, punk and metal music and know plenty of others do too," Wheeler said. "HyFest is as much about that community as it is about getting your eardrums shattered into a million pieces. Not that this compares with the Yours & Owls festival at all, and look, I love those guys and they've got a good thing going.

"But there's another demographic that gets left out of that scene a bit. HyFest caters for those that love their rock 'n' roll a little louder, a whole lot uglier."

***

But in terms of duration and size, no festival in Wollongong would be bigger than Yours and Owls. Their first festival at Stuart Park – which became the event's home – was set up for October 2014. As well as Hockey Dad, Safia, Dune Rats, Bootleg Rascal and Sticky Fingers were on the bill for what was just a one-day festival.

Held on Saturday, October 4, in the coastside park, around 2000 punters paid their $37 (plus booking fee, of course) for a ticket to get inside the festival's fenced-off area at the south-western side of the park. Tillman said it was surprisingly easy to book the bands – in fact they were keen to sign on. "It's not like bands didn't want to play in Wollongong," he said, "they just didn't trust that it could happen down here."

The day before the festival – the biggest thing the three guys had organised to date – the atmosphere was chilled. Maybe because it was too late to make any wholesale changes. "It will be good to kick back and watch it happen," Tillman told the *Mercury*. "We have been pretty organised so we haven't been too stressed in the lead-up, but this has taken up the majority of my brain space in the last few months."

A few years later, with the benefit of hindsight and the understanding that a year's planning went into the other festivals, Tillman recognised the 2014 version might have been a bit of a rush. "The first year, we banged the festival together in a few months," Tillman said, "between deciding when we were going to do it and show day." That could have contributed to why he remembered that first festival as "a fucking shambles" and made a mental note to "get more toilet paper" for future festivals.

With that first festival, they also opted not to wait for approval before getting to work. "Within a couple of months we had pretty much fully committed to the idea, begun booking and promoting the thing, locking in logistics and tickets on sale," Tillman told Tone Deaf. "We may or may not have had approvals back at this stage but luckily we had a bit of beginners' luck and it all played out well in the end."

"It was ridiculous," he later told *Brag* magazine of that first festival. "But people still had fun. I guess what made it okay is that we're honest. We don't pretend to be Splendour in the Grass or some professional festival. We were just like 'fuck it, we'll see how this goes'."

It seemed to go well, with people coming up to the organisers stoked that there was a real, live music festival in town. "This has never happened before in Wollongong, not a festival of this size," one punter said. "It's great that we're not on a train to Sydney – we're in our home town."

Tillman himself rated the performance of a certain Windang duo among the highlights. "When Hockey Dad came on and the crowd just turned on and went wild – it all felt like a 'real thing'."

Even the cops liked it, Wollongong police Inspector Jim Fryday said the punters were well-behaved. "It went well, he said. "We didn't have any issues." But that would change as the festival got bigger and bigger.

14

In the 2010s, Music Farmers and Yours and Owls weren't the only signs of a growing local music scene. Writers, artists and film-makers were also doing their bit to focus attention on the city's sounds. At the start of that decade Warren Wheeler founded the website Steel City Sound, which featured biographies of Wollongong bands from the 1960s onwards. Among the bands profiled were locally popular 1960s band Earl's Court, the (overtly left-wing) politically-focused '90s act Nabilone, stoner rockers Thumlock as well as the various iteration's of the city's street press over the years.

A local music fan, Wheeler got to a point in time where he'd realised the bands he loved had all quietly faded away – they weren't repressing their albums, they weren't posting their old songs online. In a way, it was like they hadn't existed.

"Some of that stuff is really difficult to get your hands on,"

Wheeler said. "Not just the recordings but the history of the bands. The idea was to put all this in one central place, not only for the people who have come through the scene to reminisce but also to show people around the world that Wollongong has had and continues to have a thriving independent music scene."

Also in 2010, a group of musicians and artists got together on the *5x5x5* project, which was both an exhibition at Project Contemporary Artspace in town and a gig at Waves in the northern suburbs.

Five Wollongong artists each created five posters for five bands playing at the gig – Babymachine, Ye Luddites, Bulldoze All Bowlos, Leadfinger and The Nice Folk. Among the artists were Tumbleweed's Lenny Curley and Steve O'Brien, organisers Shane Kenning and Trina Collins.

"We wanted to give the local talent, both musically and artistically, a showcase," Collins said. "Venues are dying off in Wollongong and also we can't put posters up on poles or the places we used to. Even the uni, we can't put posters up there any more without paying a gigantic fee to put them on noticeboards."

As if Wheeler wasn't already busy enough, he founded the online stress press site Helter Smelter in January 2011. The aim was to fill a gap – while the local scene was growing, the coverage of it wasn't. "Independent music and art scenes in Wollongong have always struggled to be heard above the din in mainstream media," Wheeler said. "If we can encourage your typical mainstream radio listener to check out our site, we may get more people to shows and thus, breathe new life into an already healthy scene."

Later that year, Wheeler acknowledged he had enough on his plate and handed over the running of the site to Collins, who had already been writing for the site as well as using her artistic and graphic design skills.

A highlight of the site and something which went a long way to raising awareness of the scene were the regular compilations Helter Smelter put together. Created as downloads (which are sadly no longer available) six volumes were released in around 18 months – including cover art.

Well-known acts of the time like Dropping Honey, HyTest, Babymachine, Bennie James and the Hesitant Few and Bulldoze All Bowlos appeared on the comps. Along with them were other bands whose memory has faded over time – Feick's Device, Gym Instructors, The Wesley Snipers and Vennsquidink. Though this is the value of a local compilation – it catches a moment in time that might otherwise fade from people's memories.

In 2012 Wheeler and Collins worked on a two-week festival showcasing the city's talents, called Unscene. The festival, included music, a zine fair, work by artist Shane Kenning and an exhibition of gig posters at Yours and Owls.

"There are always so many events happening in Wollongong," Collins said, "but a lot of time people never know about them until after they've occurred. So we thought, let's look at two weeks and try and advertise as many events as we can locally in that time. There's a history of music and art in Wollongong. There's a whole history here and people should value that and look at what people have done in the past."

In that year, Nabilone frontman Nathan Burling released

The Occy, a short documentary of the demise of the Oxford Tavern. Burling first picked up his camera and started filming in 2007, before it became obvious the writing was on the wall for the Oxford. Though he saw the way the wind was blowing soon enough, when new management told him to stop singing political songs while on the Oxford stage. The doco included footage of a number of bands and interviews with the various booking agents over the years.

The high point in marking the city's musical history came in late 2014 in the form of the *Steel City Sound* exhibition at Wollongong Art Gallery. Curated by Wheeler, it covered 50 years of music in the city. Showing band posters, T-shirts, hours of live footage and recordings and a special section on Tumbleweed, it was the pay-off for his years of research into what had been the ignored musical history of Wollongong.

"I love going through old newspapers and finding stories about a little band from the 1960s that disappeared," he said. "It is a snapshot of what people were thinking at that time and it's put to a song, even better.

"Nowadays you can just jump on the internet and hear a band that might have only got together last week. Going back to the 1960s, the way the music came into the country was quite unique. People on the ships coming into Port Kembla would bring records from all over the world. They'd bring The Beatles or Rolling Stones and introduce it to their family before any of the radio stations picked it up."

The opening night of the *Steel City Sound* exhibition saw the gallery crowded with people, almost as if it were a gig. It was proof that people still cared about this stuff; they cared about the bands they liked, the gigs they saw, the singles, CDs or cassette demoes they once owned. It was a message Wheeler had already learned while collecting various items for *Steel City Sound*. "I have found that people, their eyes light up when they talk about their youth or young adulthood, and they remember the bands that they went and saw. They remember the venues and the people they met, the people they fell in love with.

"They also remember the tragedies, people they've lost along the way, people they haven't seen for 20 or 30 years. So it's been a very beautiful experience, meeting new people and hearing their stories."

Ironically for an exhibition about bands, Wheeler found the hardest thing was tracking down copies of local recordings. "Recorded music, as powerful as it is, it can also be very disposable," he said. "So people do just get rid of it, especially in the digital age. People say 'why do I still need CDs, why do I still need records? Everything's digitised'. So they get rid of it."

Fortunately he was able to track down enough music to create a compilation CD, which was inserted in the exhibition booklet. The 23-track CD started with a 1961 tune by The Wanderers and ended with Hockey Dad's first single from the *Dreamin'* debut, *I Need a Woman*. Also on the CD were The Proton Energy Pills, metal act Segression, '60s pop stars The Executives, Babymachine and the theatrical rock of Bracode.

But there was one act missing – probably the first local band to release a recording. "Wollongong's first rock and roll recording that I'm aware of was by a group called Johnny Johnson and the Rebels," Wheeler said. "This would have been in the late '50s, just after Little Richard toured. These guys went down to Victoria and recorded an album's worth of material. Unfortunately, no known copies are still in existence – which is a real shame."

Taylor got Music Farmers involved in the exhibition, releasing a limited run of three vinyl singles, each featuring two Wollongong bands. The first paired Sunday Painters with The Unheard, the second combined Evol and Mojo Hands while HyTest and Thumlock were the final pairing. Musicians Lenny Curley, Rebecca Mayhew and Nate Clark designed the single covers.

Taylor had been to the exhibition on opening night and saw its worth as being beyond a nostalgia trip for those who were there. "I think it's also really good for a lot of younger bands that are coming through now and they can see what came before them," he said. "It's good to be able to go back and have a good look at what was around before any of us started doing stuff in the music scene."

One of the bands on the singles had been an eye-opener for Taylor. While he had heard about Sunday Painters here and there, he'd not heard any of their music until Wheeler played him a few tracks. "They're so ahead of their time and to actually be doing that here in Wollongong in the 1980s is actually really crazy," he said. "Some of that stuff is on par with a lot of stuff that's going on now. You can understand why, especially in Wollongong back then, it didn't really get much traction."

***

After it had taken a back seat to the Yours and Owls Festival for just over a year, the Farmer and the Owl festival made a return over a weekend in March 2015. The festival over four stages – one of which was in a car park – back at the University of Wollongong hadn't yet developed the "boutique" feeling it would later be known for, but the list of bands on the bill was still impressive. It included DZ Deathrays, Bad//Dreems, Jebediah, The Mess Hall, US act Bass Drum of Death and South African rapper PHFAT. Local acts made the line-up too – of course Hockey Dad was there, as were HyTest, The Pinheads, Shining Bird and Step-Panther.

For something a little bit unusual, the organisers borrowed a trick from Radiohead's 2007 release of *In Rainbows* and priced tickets at "pay what you like". (Well, for the first release, at least. And there was a minimum spend of $5. And the second and third release cost $69 and $79 respectively).

"We're appealing to people's goodwill," Tillman said. "We're hoping people don't take advantage of the $5 minimum. We hope they pay what they feel the bands are worth and if people are being genuine then we'll keep it rolling – otherwise we might have to cut it off on the first day."

He didn't get that chance – the 'pay what you like' allocation sold out in about five minutes. Tillman wouldn't be drawn on just how many cheapskates paid just the $5 but implied some did. "Obviously people were taking advantage but a lot of people did the right thing."

15

The man, dressed in a dark suit with a red and blue tie, strode across the stage of an upmarket Sydney hotel in August 2015. The CEO of BlueScope, Paul O'Malley was there to announce a $136 million profit, which was an improvement on the previous year, where the steelmaker was in an $82 million hole.

Despite the business being in the black, there was a kicker coming for Wollongong. There were two choices – either work out how to cut $200 million a year out of the Port Kembla steelworks or close the joint altogether. Both options would cost jobs, either 500 or 4500. Oh, and it had to be figured out in three months, in time for the BlueScope annual general meeting in November.

There had been rumours swirling around for a month or two that the steelmaker was looking to get the razor out at Port Kembla. The fears weren't helped by the company accidentally emailing a private cost-cutting plan to the workers. But the announcement on that Sydney hotel stage was the first time the steelmaker had confirmed what they were planning and how deep the razor would be cutting.

Just as the city's music scene was getting back on its feet, the news of the steelworks' potential closure was a kick in the teeth. There was no doubt the two were linked – despite Wollongong's gradual diversification meant the "steel city" tag was making less and less sense, the loss of the steelworks would smash the economy. A study by economic modellers from the university found that the closure of the steelworks would blow a $3.3 billion hole in the region's economy with unemployment hitting 16 per cent. It wasn't just those who worked at Port Kembla who would be affected. Businesses who supplied goods to the steelworks would go under. Also, cafes, restaurants, bars and anywhere else steelworkers and their families spent money would be hit – and that included the city's music scene and its venues.

"You can't take $3 billion out of the region's total economic output every year and expect the region to carry on as normal," South Coast Labour Council's Arthur Rorris said. "This is not business as usual, that's 21 per cent of the gross regional product of the region. Twenty-one per cent with one industry, that's not an adjustment, that's carnage. And that is what we're likely to see in this region if we don't do something and do it quickly to save this industry."

The unions and the company ended up finding the cost cuts to save the steelworks by the deadline. It created the awful situation of workers at a union meeting voting to accept a package of cuts that would see some of them out of a job. No wonder union official Wayne Phillips told the meeting it was a "shit sandwich" but they had to eat it.

"I know a few of my good mates who are going to lose their jobs out of this," steelworker Lance Turner said. "Even they had to put their hands up because most people saw the bigger picture. If we voted 'no' it wasn't just going to be those of us in the room who has to pay the price, it would be a lot of other people."

The gates stayed open, Port Kembla kept making steel and the business was in good enough shape to manage to post a record-setting $1.7 billion profit just six years later. And the region avoided the recession and years of struggle that came in the early '80s when the steelworks offloaded hundreds of jobs. While that period led to an uptick in the local music scene, this time around it was already healthy enough. Also, the image of the city itself had changed – it was becoming a place people chose to stay in rather than feeling compelled to pack up and move elsewhere in search of opportunities.

***

For a long time, bands from Wollongong opted to hide that fact whenever they were out of town. It was just easier to get gigs if they said they were a Sydney band; venue bookers wouldn't take a punt on booking a Wollongong band because, obviously, their local fans weren't going to travel to Sydney. Besides, no-one really thought of Wollongong as a place where bands came from. That snobbishness started to change around the time Hockey Dad were coming through; indeed they were one of the drivers, proudly wearing their Leisure Coast credentials. "Even now, we don't say we're from Sydney, we tell people we're from

Wollongong," Stephenson said a year after the release of *Dreamin'*, "and people are surprised that anyone would start a band here. What's happening here is still almost under the radar."

The idea of moving to the big smoke never crossed their minds. "Everything we wanted was in Wollongong," Stephenson said. "It just made no sense – we could drive there [Sydney] in an hour and a half."

Things were happening for Hockey Dad; there was a national tour and the recording for a new album. And then they were spotted by a US label. Kanine Records owner Lio Cerezo was at BIGSOUND in Brisbane and already had his eye on the two dudes from Windang. "Sifting through hundreds of bands before I arrived, there was one in particular that I kept coming back to," Cerezo explained on the Kanine website.

"Their name, Hockey Dad, was intriguing, and their single *Can't Have Them* simply wouldn't leave my head. Upon seeing them live in Brisbane, I was pleasantly surprised to find two young artists having a good time above all else. Their energy was infectious, and their ace songwriting didn't hurt either."

At BIGSOUND he offered to get them to the US for CMJ and South by Southwest, which was a big deal. But Taylor said people back home thought the kids were too young for that opportunity. "Pretty much me and Dan [Radburn] were the only ones who thought we should do it," Taylor told writer David James Young. "Everyone else was saying that it was too early for the band to go over to America, and that going next year would be better. We decided to take the risk."

It paid off – Cerezo signed the band to his label. Though

that also meant local fans had to wait another six months for the release of their debut album. Recorded in June, 2015, they had planned to release it in the second half of the year. But once they signed to Kanine, it made sense to release it here and there at the same time – even though that saw the release come out around a year after they recorded it.

Hockey Dad weren't the only ones busy at the back end of 2015. The Pinheads, a new signing to the Farmer and Owl label, put out their first release – a six-track EP named after the lead song *I Want to be a Girl* and recorded in a shed at Stanwell Park. A '60s garage rock-punk hybrid, the seven-piece band formed in the northern suburbs in early 2013 after going bowling, apparently.

"We all go ten-pin bowling every week as a team and started calling the loser of each game Pinhead," they told the *Mercury*. "Later a pal lent us a mysterious eight-track karaoke machine from the '80s and we started making some songs for fun. Our mate James Kates heard we were recording songs and he asked to hear some of them, and liked them so much he used three songs in his surf film and also joined The Pinheads, playing drums."

Jones, Smith and Tillman were busy in late 2015. They had another festival to run – one that would be bigger than the previous year's.

16

Stuart Park is an example of what can happen when someone pays back political favours. The park on the northern fringe of Wollongong city that hosted the first run of Yours and Owls festivals was officially declared in 1885 and came into being through the bold actions of one Archibald Campbell.

Archie was a fan of the idea of acquiring the land that makes up Stuart Park and paid for a survey of the area to be undertaken. He then brought it to the notice of Illawarra MP and State Premier Sir Alexander Stuart. Now Stuart, knowing Campbell was such a strong supporter of his, asked the man to find out what the cost was.

Campbell went one step further. Finding the price to be reasonable, he whacked down a deposit using his own money. The Premier then had little choice but to complete the purchase, lest his ardent supporter be left in a tight spot.

Since that time it has been used for a range of purposes,

including a campground. In 1958 Wollongong Council accepted a tender from EJ Barker to turn a decent section of the park into a camping area. The idea behind the strategy was that the private sector could build the facilities while at the same time paying council for the privilege.

As part of the deal Barker agreed to make improvements to the park – including a kiosk and amenities block with toilets and a laundry – that one alderman expected would see Stuart Park "rank as one of the foremost tourist attractions in NSW".

Things must have gone pear-shaped for Mr Barker because in 1963 he did a runner. At a Wollongong court hearing, it was reported that he owed council £5000. His partner Alice Barker was called before the court; she admitted he was nervous about financial problems but had no idea where her husband had gone.

Barker was ultimately evicted in his absence and council decided in June 1964 to close the park to camping just a few years after *opening* it to camping. Both holidaymakers and permanent residents had until July 1 to pack up and leave.

Just two years later the council flip-flopped again, opening Stuart Park to campers for a trial between March and May. One alderman was smart enough to notice the idea of holding a trial in the colder months and not summer was pretty dumb. "Any people on the road with caravans will be heading north now," he said. A few years later, as expected, camping was again banned at Stuart Park.

The battle to ban camping at the park returned in the 2010s. This time the problem was unofficial campers – people from out of the area who came to the beach on

Australia Day or New Year's Day, set up a tent in the park and stayed the night. The following mornings, the area looked like a tent city and, after visitors left, a dump as they declined to take their rubbish with them. After a few years of council rangers warning people to pull down their tents by sundown and then dishing out a few fines, campers got the message.

The Stuart Park area was also a home for hoons of an evening. In the early 1990s, those with hotted-up cars and those who liked to look at them had been hanging around Marine Drive, just to the south, doing laps of the road, helpfully assisted by the roundabout at either end. To try and stop that, council put up barriers of an evening, before deciding traffic-calming measures were a better option.

While Marine Drive was out of action, the revheads made the road along Stuart Park towards the Lagoon Restaurant their new home. In what may have been a slight overstatement the restaurant owner claimed the car owners had made the nearby area look "like LA under siege". But it was a problem; the long line of cars with owners enjoying pouring oil on the road to then conduct burnouts, were scaring away customers.

The police didn't like it either, with Senior Constable Dave Carroll suggesting someone could be killed. "It only takes one high-powered burnout on smooth tyres in oil, to lose traction and then get it back again and fly off into the crowd," he said. Incidentally, in 1995, a man was booked for losing control of his car during a burnout and crashing into another vehicle.

As part of a crackdown, police regularly headed down to

Stuart Park at night, handing out hundreds of defect notices, which tended to rile up the revheads. In October 1993 police were pelted with rocks and a bag of left-over McDonald's take-away as they tried to get a crowd of 1000 car enthusiasts to leave. In March 1994, the revheads pelted police with tomatoes when an officer tried to book a driver. Surprisingly, the driver drove away from the mass of revheads to a quieter spot to allow the officer to continue booking him.

In time, traffic calming measures like speed humps and requirements that cars park front to kerb (to stop revheads from sitting in their cars and watching the action on the road) did much to deter the hoons. Lord Mayor David Campbell said trying to fix the hoon problem had proved a headache for council.

"We have thought of different things," he said. "The speed humps were put there to stop drivers being able to pick up speed. But you can't close the area down so no-one goes there.

"It is a public area and a beautiful one at that and other people who don't break the law should be free to drive near Stuart Park if and whenever they like."

***

As well as drive, they should feel free to rock there as well. For three days if they wanted, for that was how long the second Yours and Owls Festival would be. The length of the festival meant camping was once again welcome at Stuart Park.

Of course a three-day show means you need to find more bands to fill up the schedule. So coming to town for that long weekend in October 2015 were Gang of Youths, The Smith Street Band, The Preatures and Samonella Dub.

The big day was Sunday, where the top names were playing, so Yours and Owls decided to do something different. They made Sunday an all-ages day, allowing teens who otherwise had the options of trying to sneak in or sitting on the grass outside the festival fencing and listening the chance to get inside. "This is by far the biggest all-ages event to happen in the Illawarra region for as long as we can remember," Tillman said. It probably wasn't — a fundraising festival at Stuart Park in the 1990s (more on that show later) likely drew in more punters. But the bands on the Yours and Owls bill were certainly a whole lot cooler.

Local bands weren't left out in the cold either. The Pinheads, Gerringong's Bungalows and Shining Bird were on the bill (Hockey Dad missed the 2015 show). In between sets, the Parkside DJs spun some tracks — they'd started up in much the same way as Tillman's Liberteen Ranch shows. Sick of playing at home, they set up their own parties so they could DJ them. "We would get together every Friday night and share music, because the music we liked was only really played in Sydney clubs," said DJ Ben Beverley. "We got sick of the music scene here because it didn't cater to what we wanted to hear, so we started doing our own events."

Also slated to play at Yours and Owls, was Triple J contest winner Bec Sandridge. She won the 2015 version of the annual contest that saw one local band get a slot on the Yours and Owls bill. Around a year later, she released an EP on the Farmer and the Owl label.

The decision to triple in size from one day to three saw

the Yours and Owls team biting off more than they could chew. As Jones later told the *Telegraph*'s Kathy McCabe, it was a jump in size that almost backfired on them. That started with almost losing the sound system, which is never a good thing to happen at a festival.

"It was a big expansion with 5000 people and big bands like the Preatures," he said. "We pretty much had this homemade sound system brought in and a wooden stage built there on the day.

"And during the Preatures set there was this huge crackle. They were not happy." Neither were other people in the industry, Jones said. The Wollongong trio were sent the message that, unless they grew their festival properly, out-of-town bands weren't going to come.

At the end of 2015, Farmer and the Owl organised a smaller-scale show for Christmas in Globe Lane, just off the mall. This time, Hockey Dad were back in town and available to play at the free show, alongside fellow locals Shining Bird. The Pinheads, The Escarpment and future label signing TEES.

It was also the launch of the second *Beached Friends* compilation, with the first 500 people to RSVP for the Christmas show scoring a free CD copy of the compilation. Made up of 22 tracks, it included tunes from Sandridge, The Walking Who, Shining Bird and Hockey Dad. That CD became a bit of a collector's item for those in the Wollongong scene – to date only a handful of the 22 tracks have ever been released digitally. So if you wanted to hear the release, you had to have the CD.

In terms of other releases from Farmer and the Owl, 2016

was their busiest year to date with two albums, an EP and a handful of singles hitting the racks.

17

In the annals of rock music, there are only a tiny number of bands that have a food dish named after them. One of that tiny number is Totally Unicorn (a band apparently named for a horse of a former drummer, who was heavily involved in a local medieval society), originally made up of ex-members of Wollongong bands Hospital The Musical and Ohana.

The 2009 *MasterChef* runner-up Poh Ling Yeow released a cookbook called *Same Same But Different* and, in that book was a recipe called Totally Unicorn Beetroot Cake. "If you're turning up your nose at what seems an unlikely marriage, try it first" she said. "The combination of earthy beets, bitter, smoky dark chocolate and slightly salty cream cheese is heavenly."

The connection with the band came from the fact Poh's brother-in-law was drummer Michael Bennett (he of the medieval society). "Whenever they go on tour and stay with us, this is what they get for supper after a night of intense head banging."

The band name is somewhat misleading, suggesting some sort of glittery pop sound rather than hardcore. And the live shows aren't sedate affairs either, largely due to the efforts of the hirsute bear of a lead singer Drew Gardner, who is prone to disrobing. An early gig at the Novotel Northbeach, not long after their 2010 debut, saw the band get kicked out of their own show. "While we were playing Drew de-robed to his underwear, ran out the back and dived onto a patron's table, knocking their beers to the ground," Bennett told online site Radar Illawarra. "Then he fell off the table, rolling around in broken glass. From memory then he ran back inside and was bleeding on people and swinging on this balcony thing. Security's all 'put your clothes back on and stop goosing around' or words to that effect. I think he refused, or the set ended or something."

In 2010 the band released their first EP *Horse Hugger*, which included the single *Daddy's Stabby Surprise* (which was quickly banned from YouTube due to the nudity of some band members). Two years later, they released *7 Inches*, with two songs, *Street Hugz* and the wonderfully named *Lets Spice Things Up With Laser Swords*. The 250-run vinyl single sold out in days, in part because it was pink and penis-shaped. They'd revisit the joke a year later, releasing a slightly bigger version called *9 Inches* – with the extra track *Inner Tube*.

The band's line-up chopped and changed over its first five years, with the suggestion they may have broken up at various points. In 2015 they'd come together to sign with Farmer and the Owl, with the band's first release on the label coming out for Record Store Day in April of that year. The single *Sometimes I Sit and Drink, and Sometimes I Just Drink* and its cover were inspired by Courtney Barnett's debut album *Sometimes I Sit and Think, and Sometimes I Just Sit*. It featured two songs – *Customer Service Station* and *Convict Brick* – which turned up on their album release more than a year later.

In April 2015, Farmer and the Owl re-released the *Horse Hugger* EP. Four months later, their first full-length album, *Dream Life* hit the racks. It was real life that so often got in the way of recording the album, with three band members married and/or with kids. On top of that, guitarists Aaron Streatfield and Kerim Erkin listened back to what the band had initially recorded and figured they could do things better.

"We came to the conclusion that we weren't entirely happy with where things were headed," Streatfield told street press *Forte*. "We proposed rewriting and arranging the songs using the drum tracks that we had already recorded. The other guys didn't like that idea at first, they were happy with the songs the way they were.

"We pushed to let them see what we could come up with on our own though, and I ended up writing two new songs out of the incomplete drums. Kerim did the same, and we're pretty happy with what we came up with."

The critics were as well, with *Dream Life* scoring a wealth of favourable reviews. "It's been crazy overwhelming – people loved it," Gardner told the Scenestr website. "It's just surprised the shit out of us really. The process to write the album was such a long and shit thing, so to finally get it out, we were so unsure, and the responses and reviews have been fucking great."

Meanwhile, the label's first signing, Hockey Dad, was travelling the world in the first half of 2016. There was the US for South by Southwest and a few shows in March and then a run of 16 shows in the UK, Netherland, France and Germany in May.

Then it was back to Australia for the release of that album they'd been sitting on for almost a year, having been delayed due to the Kanine signing.

The 11-track album was named *Boronia* – after the street the pair grew up on. That, combined with the photo on the *Dreamin'* EP cover, made it a bit easy for intrepid fans to work out where they lived. But it seems the fans give the boys some space. "We don't get anything too intense," Stephenson said. "We're actually pretty lucky. We just have people saying 'hi' and that we make good tunes, so you can't really complain about that at all."

The cover of *Boronia* featured a photo Fleming took of his niece while on a family holiday in Western Australia. "I wasn't fully going, 'I'm going to take a photo of my niece on a beach' or whatever," he said. "That wasn't the sole purpose of it. It was just one of those photos I took and it was like, 'I'm going to use that one day, for something'. I just love the photo."

As for the content of *Boronia*, it showed the band had grown from the days of *Dreamin'*. There was more depth to the tunes. That was likely a reflection of the fact the songs were all written at the same time, giving the album a clearer focus than the EP. And that focus gave added meaning to naming the album after the street they grew up on.

"I think a lot of the album lyrically is based around being

at home and what it was like living there," Stephenson told *Paste*. "The album has a lot more homey vibe. So I guess it just stuck with us. It gives people a reference point of where we're coming from and what built up to the release of the record. Where we came from and where we're headed."

That idea might not seem to gel with the words in *Jump the Gun*, singing about not wanting to go home. But the song is about surfing, not longing to be away from someone or somewhere. "That song was written in my room while staring at my *Endless Summer II* poster, one of our favorite surf movies of all time," Fleming explained. "The lyrics spiraled off the line, 'on any day of the year it's summer somewhere in the world'."

The song was one of four singles spun off from *Boronia* and the video – directed by Fleming – showing the band, their dads and friends surfing their local break helps explain the feeling behind the song. It also contains echoes of the clip for *I Need a Woman*, as it revisits some of the same spots in Windang.

The first single from the album was *Can't Have Them*, which had been released as a teaser late in the previous year (with non-album track *Girl with Two Hearts* on the B-side). It's about pining for girls who are just too pretty for you. It was one of several relationship songs written while Stephenson was single, though he'd be hooked up by the time the album was released. The video was filmed at the visually stunning Bombo Quarry, which had previously been used by Tumbleweed for their *Mountain* video and the unforgettable (not really) 1995 film *Mighty Morphin Power Rangers*.

It starts with Stephenson plugging his guitar into his amp,

even though he's in the middle of a quarry and the amp is not plugged into anything. And then, once he's plugged in, the amp is never seen in the video again. With all the jump cuts in the video as the band move around the quarry, it looks like hard work for Fleming, who would have had to pick up and move his bass drum and snare so many times for a video running just three minute and 25 seconds.

The video for the *So Tired* single saw them back at the seaside, this time to create a parody of a 1950s beach party film complete with dancing bikini girls and Stephenson dressed up as the bad guy greaser in a leather jacket. And there's also some weird shark attack-zombie action going on too.

The final single was *A Night Out With*, with a video shoot in a suburban backyard in front of an audience of one sitting in an inflatable pool. Hidden up the back of *Boronia* was the lyrically deceptive *Two Forever*. From the title it sounds like a song sung to a lover, and the first two verses and the languid pace of the song certainly give you that impression. But then comes a mention of always being a friend of mine, and then not needing a woman because "I got you man".

Then it becomes clear Stephenson wrote it about his and Fleming's close friendship. Some have called it a "bromance" but, given the emotion on display in the song, that's too flippant a term. It's undeniable from the words – and the fact Stephenson wrote the song, and the band recorded it – that there is a deep bond between the pair. It could be taken as a sign of Stephenson's growing confidence as a songwriter to pen such an open love letter to the guy he knew ever since he walked past Stephenson's house and joined in on that game of footy

And if you didn't pick up on what the song was really about at first, don't worry, Fleming didn't get it either. Some of the demoes for *Boronia* were recorded in the coastal Adelaide suburb of Grange (yes, that's where the final song on the album got its title from). Stephenson pulled out the tune *Two Forever* and after they recorded it, Fleming asked what the song was about.

"And he's like 'oh, I was waiting for you to ask me that'," Fleming told Yasmine Shemesh from On The A.Side website. "And then I'm like, 'wait, who's it about?' and he's like 'it's about you, dickhead!' I'm like, 'Oh! Okay!' It was just the funniest thing, because I was expecting it to be about some girl that I didn't know about, then he drops that bromance on me."

The album climbed to No55 on the Australian charts and picked up some decent reviews, with most outlets giving it a 3-3.5 stars out of five. "There are few people that could soundtrack summer better than two Aussie beach-punks," wrote Paste Magazine, "and Hockey Dad fulfills the position entirely". Consequence website found "the 11 tracks within are a tide of charmingly messy guitar hooks and remembrances of endless summers past". In the US, National Public Radio (kind of like the ABC and Triple J mixed together) just loved *Boronia*. "Messy and fun, the Australian duo's pop-punk bursts with chunky guitars and big riffs as they collide with yowling vocals and firecracker drumming," Mike Katzif wrote. "It's the perfect sun-streaked soundtrack for skinned-knee skate videos and beach bonfires at dusk; for staying out late and sleeping in later, only to do it all over again the next day."

After the release of *Boronia*, it was back to the US and Canada in August to plug the album in the first real tour of both places. "It's exciting to be driving the whole way across the country and get the chance to check everything out and play the shows and keep on doing it," Stephenson said. "It's exciting to drive around in the car and make a big road trip."

On that road trip, there was the obligatory playlist for the drive. That list included a surprise – the '80s pub rock classic from The Radiators, *Gimme Head*. "This one's an absolute banger," they told Alex Underwood from Pilerats. "We were having a piss-up around the fire before we left for the States and we were throwing around old classic songs to listen to. Been copping it daily ever since we revisited it."

While they hit the obvious spots like LA, San Francisco and New York, being from a regional town themselves, Hockey Dad didn't forget the other places, so the likes of Boise, Idaho and Omaha, Nebraska also got a visit from Windang's finest. Though Fleming had a few problems with America's higher drinking age limit.

He was 20 at the time, which made him legal for two years in Australia. But in the US he was still underage, which can be a hassle when you have to get into a venue to play. "I've found a couple of sneaky ways to get around the whole 20-plus thing," Fleming said. "I can't reveal as to how I did it but I've been doing it pretty well."

***

The duo were back in time for the Yours and Owl festival in October. In 2016, gender balance for festival acts became a hot-button issue via the list of performers Spilt Milk booked for their Canberra show in December. Released in June, there were 15 male acts with Vera Blue the only female representation.

After copping a serve via social media, Spilt Milk organisers realised their error and responded. "Opportunities for female artists in the music industry ARE less than those for men," they said. "We have an opportunity to do something and that is what we are doing with our second round announcement this week.

"Expect to see announced more female artists that we are really excited to have as part of Spilt Milk; some of whom we had booked prior to our first announcement, some of whom we were considering booking and now have, and some of whom we discovered and booked as a result of the discussion around this issue."

Yours and Owls managed to avoid any conflict by having a 50-50 male/female split in the line-up released around the same time. Though Tillman said it was by accident rather than design – it was simply the case that there were so many good female acts to choose from.

"Our process is I go out and hunt around for a line-up and come back to everyone with what I've got and one of the guys pointed out it was half girls," Tillman told the *Telegraph*'s Kathy McCabe.

"I was just trying to get the best line-up, these were the acts that were available and this is a testament to how much great music there is being made by women. I know a lot of festivals are copping a bit of flak for never having girls on the line-up.

"I think I will definitely be conscious of it in the future but you don't want to put constraints on yourself when it comes to choosing acts."

In general, when booking Yours and Owls, Tillman described it as a "balancing act", where a few big drawcards needed to be booked while also making sure the bill features unknowns that deserve to be seen.

"If you book entirely based on the idea of statistical analysis and what's getting played on the radio right now, then I think that's a pretty soulless venture," he told *The Industry Observer*'s Joseph Earp. "That doesn't really interest me. If you wanted to get into music to earn money go work in a fucking bank.

"There's stuff that you know isn't going to turn many heads, but it's the stuff you want people to see. And you know it's going to be good on the day and people are going to enjoy it when they're there – but you also need those acts you know people are going to go for."

Among the female artists on the bill were Ladyhawke, Vera Blue, Sampa The Great, Thelma Plum, Tired Lion, Tkay Maidza and Washington's Chastity Belt.

Another female onstage at the 2016 festival was Bec Sandridge, who was playing Yours and Owls for the second year in a row. Her 2015 slot came as a prize for winning a Triple J Unearthed comp where Illawarra and South Coast bands vied for a chance to join the festival.

Sandridge's musical story started via eBay. In Year Nine, the Stanwell Park local bought a bright blue acoustic guitar on the auction site. While her family figured it was the next fad – having seen her go for horse-riding, soccer and surfing in the past – this one stuck. "I fell completely head over heels in love with the instrument," she told *Coal Coast* magazine.

"I'd literally walk from my living room to the bathroom with my guitar firmly attached."

A neighbour taught her some Blink-182 songs before she decided to move in more of a Missy Higgins-Waifs direction. After she and friend Mel Creaghan finished Year 12, they formed the acoustic duo Mad Polly. "We had our first gig in the CWA Hall just after we finished the HSC," she said.

"It was really nerve-wracking. Me and Mel were the first band up and we were shaking, but the crowd was mostly made up of families - and was really supportive."

Her first solo show came after a booking agent heard she could sing and offered her the spot at the Otis Bar. Though her family had to push her to get onstage, using the reverse psychology of betting her cold hard cash that she wouldn't do it.

She did – and soon went overseas and spent time in Glasgow, where she further honed her performance skills by busking. Sandridge also started to change her sound, using an electric guitar after realising what sort of music she really loved listening to. When she returned to Australia and toured, she carried on busking during the day – both for the money and the exposure.

"I think the biggest compliment in the world is when someone stops in the middle of their day and listens to you in the street, because no-one is asking you to perform," she told the *Newcastle Herald*. "I think it's completely different. I get more nervous when I'm busking than at my own shows because anything can happen when you're busking in the street."

Sandridge had already released a few EPs herself, including *Lyons and Bees* and *Wild Heart*, and had already garnered some praise by the time she signed with Farmer and the Owl. "I met up with Ben and Jeb and their love for the local scene was infectious," Sandridge said. "As someone who has danced between Glasgow and Australia for the past few years, it's nice to have such direct and overwhelming support from my home town."

The first release was the single *You're a Fucking Joke*, which is quite a direct break-up song about a person in Glasgow. "For the first time in a long time I wanted to be as direct as possible in my writing," she said, "and I felt that this title was the most honest set of words to describe the situation that went down."

The quavering theatrical vocal delivery called to mind Kate Bush – which wasn't a coincidence. "I listen to artists like Kate Bush who aren't afraid to step into that theatrical realm," she said. In December Sandridge's five-track EP came out – including *Joke* and the other side of that single, *In the Fog, In the Flame*. "I was just buzzing, waiting to release this EP," she said. "When I got back from Glasgow I'd been sitting on those songs for probably six months to a year."

Just in time for Christmas, in December 2016 Farmer and the Owl released the third instalment of the *Beached Friends* compilation series. Pilerats used the release as a chance to talk about how much Wollongong's art and culture scene had changed in recent years.

"There has been a huge change in culture in Wollongong over the last few years so there are people doing great things across many areas," Taylor said.

"The annual Wonderwalls street art festival has become something pretty amazing, the crew behind that also run a great little gallery called Moving Mountains. There are an endless number of great cafes, restaurants and bars popping up and there are also way more artists, photographers, filmmakers, designers etc staying in the area rather than leaving for Sydney or Melbourne."

Tillman felt it was still a work in progress and there were more things that needed to be done, but admitted the city was on the right path. "It feels what we're doing is actually working, and there is real tangible evidence of that, that you can see in the city every day," he said.

"You know when all the mainstream shops, and pubs/restaurants start getting interested in live music, and asking how to get bands in at their venues that something is happening."

That third volume of *Beached Friends* featured Sandridge as well as Hockey Dad (obviously) and The Pinheads. White Blanks, the 2016 Unearthed 'play at Yours and Owls' winner, was there as was northern Illawarra's Solid Effort.

Also there was a mysterious brand new band with a fondness for the 1982 teen film *Fast Times at Ridgemont High*. Called Geoff & The Spicolis, after the Sean Penn character in the film, they offered the one-and-a-half minute song *Lincoln Sux*. The song was about the vandalism of the car of Ridgemont High's star football player Charles Jefferson, seemingly done by cross-town rivals.

The band was actually Hockey Dad hiding under an assumed name (though they did play a gig or two as Geoff & The Spicolis). The track *Lincoln Sux* came from the seven-track digital release *No Shirt, No Shoes, No Dice*, which was recorded by Stephenson and Fleming purely as an exercise to get the creative juices flowing while writing the follow-up to *Boronia*.

"When we had a dry streak, we started a joke punk band just to get it out of our system," Fleming said. "We wrote some pretty great songs though. We were just meant to be writing songs that were jokes." Stephenson agrees that they "ended up turning out good".

They're right too. The seven-track release clocks in at barely over 15 minutes and it's a raucous pop-punk gem that doesn't feel like something that was dashed off in a hurry. What you hear is a tight, fast duo who have really gelled over the years – to the extent they can make what was supposed to be a "joke" band sound so damned good.

All the songs are based on *Fast Times at Ridgemont High*, from an ode to Geoff Spicoli's hated teacher (*Mr Hand*) to Brad Hamilton fantasising about his sister's friend taking off her red bikini (*Linda*) and the title track which is a reference to the sign stuck in the window of the fast-food restaurant where Brad works.

As Wollongong albums go, this one is an undiscovered gem and it's a little surprising Hockey Dad seem happy to let it fly under the radar.

18

Early 2017 saw Hockey Dad out on their 'Benefit of the Doubt' tour, which involved quite a bit of shooey-drinking and stage-diving, if promo videos of the tour are any indication. One shooey saw someone take a girl's boot over to the bar, where they filled it straight from the tap. As for the stage-divers, one of the more notable ones was Stephenson's mother Julie at the University of Wollongong show.

"I remember my mum stage-dived and she smacked her shins on the barrier," he said. Sadly for Julie, the catchers in the crowd missed her – once she cleared the punter barrier, she sunk beneath the crowd. "I thought I was going good and the boys said to me 'just run, just run'," Julie said. "So I did, I ran from the corner, I ran and boom, straight on the floor."

The Australian tour was when they discovered just how

popular they were – people had tattooed the band's name on their skin. "We've found two," Fleming said, "which is two too many. It's a spin-out when you're looking at them because it's like that's in your skin forever, your kids are going to see it." He said the quality didn't seem the best – "I don't think they booked into a tattoo shop that's for sure." For the record, Fleming himself has a Hockey Dad tatt – a thumb-sized "HD" scrawled on the underside of his upper arm.

After that tour, it was over to the US and Canada – the latter with Dune Rats – where everyone understands the meaning of the name Hockey Dad. Back home at the Farmer and the Owl label, The Pinheads released their self-titled debut album in May.

The cover showed the band parked outside a bowling alley in Bellambi, the same location that was home to the music venue Wonderland Ballroom/Capitol Hall in the 1960s and 1970s.

The band wrote the songs for their debut at The Pinshed in northern Illawarra as well as a stint in coastal Murwillumbah. "We definitely didn't want to do what people expected of us," Player told The Music website. "We took into consideration that it was our first album and we wanted to make something that was true to ourselves and honest. Music that we want to hear.

" We value capturing the energy of our live show in our recordings, even if it means the takes aren't perfect. We have no producer and no sound engineer – we like to have complete creative control over our work. We actually have no idea what we're doing."

The back half of 2017 saw Yours and Owls branch out with another festival – Last Frost held at Innovation Campus (tagged by those who work there as 'Isolation Campus' because it's not in walking distance of anything). Headlined by Violent Soho, the bill also included Cloud Control and Cub Sport.

"If there was an award for 'city that punches above their weight, has sick music festivals and is the definition of the lucky country' – Wollongong would be winning by a mile," Pilerats reviewer Liam Apter said.

Tillman said they sold around 4000 tickets to the single-stage show and it all went well despite strong winds in the days before causing headaches when setting up the facilities. He was hopeful the success of the event would see more shows at Innovation Campus.

"We set the capacity ourselves, but I think we were being a little bit conservative and we could probably fit a bit more in there to be honest," he said.

"We got the numbers that we were looking for … Hopefully that means there'll be some more stuff happening at this site."

There would be, because Yours and Owls decided to do "more stuff". The following winter there was a Big Top festival at the site.

Meanwhile, after Hockey Dad returned home from their overseas tours, they had some big gigs, including a slot on the main stage at Splendour in the Grass and at the Fairgrounds festival in Berry. In between was a three-month stint supporting Grinspoon on their tour marking the 20th anniversary of their *Guide to Better Living* debut album.

***

In late 2017, Australia got caught up in a rather acrimonious debate over whether same-sex couples should be able to marry. Despite the obvious answer being "Of course they bloody should. Why hasn't it happened already?" plenty of people got upset that if we let gay people get married it would cheapen the value of their own marriage. Though if the concept of their own marriage was that fragile, then perhaps they had bigger problems they should have been worried about.

Rather than do their damn job and pass the legislation, the government foisted it onto the people in the form of a same-sex marriage survey. To encourage a yes vote Inertia Music's Meg Williams and Gab Ryan created the *30 Days of Yes* mixtape. With all of the profits going to LGBTQI+ youth organisations Minus18 and Twenty10, the digital album available on Bandcamp featured 30 bands with a song a day released through October (though in the end the album had 49 tracks).

"It's the music industry's way of saying 'we're supporting you guys'," Williams told SBS. "What we want to do is change the dialogue around it and say, 'we're all here, we're all standing by you, we're not tired yet, we'll still be here when we have marriage equality."

On the mixtape were The Jezebels, Beaches, Jen Cloher and Courtney Barnett, Ali Barter, Karnivool, TEES, Shining Bird and Hockey Dad.

The Windang pair contributed a cover of You Am I's *Purple Sneakers* to the tape (a song that also later appeared as the B-side to the *Join the Club* single and on the Farmer and the Owl comp *Family Values*.

"We are so grateful to be able to contribute to the *30 Days of Yes* campaign with our very sub-par cover of a great Australian rock song," the pair posted on Bandcamp when their tune was released on October 17. "Let's band together with the power of shitty covers to give every Australian the basic right we all take advantage of. 'Cause everyone needs somebody, to feel somebody."

Fleming said it was a song they'd wanted to get around to covering for quite a while. And it made Stephenson's dad happy too – it's his favourite song of all time.

"I think he liked it – he seems happy enough," Stephenson told Triple J's Richard Kingsmill. "I'm sure he doesn't like it as much as the original, but that's fine."

The *Purple Sneakers* tune wasn't the only one Hockey Dad released around this time. Fans also got a taste of the forthcoming album *Blend Inn* through the release of the single *Homely Feeling*. Similar to the situation with *Boronia*, the band had recorded the album around a year ago and had spent all this time sitting on it.

The first taste of *Blend Inn* highlighted a new maturity in the band's songwriting. They'd ditched the straight-forward surfy-pop of the earlier releases in favour of a rockier direction with darker undertones.

The song – and the album it came from – was the first where Stephenson drew inspiration while on tour rather than sitting home in Windang. So it made sense that there was less of the beachy surf vibes of *Boronia* and in their place a deeper understanding of the world spawned by actually seeing more of it.

The single was drawn from life on the road but, unlike most "touring" songs written by bands, Hockey Dad distills it down to the feeling of isolation and loneliness that set in once the fun and novelty of being on tour wears off. The song may still have its roots in hanging around Windang, like much of their earlier efforts, but the tyranny of distance allowed them to look at their home town with new and different emotions.

"It's sort of about [how] you get the feeling of home," Stephenson told Triple J, "and when you're not actually at home you just want to be at home, and having sorta semi-freakouts in the street of some city. Just like, I just gotta get home."

Fleming gave his own spin on the song to the lunchboxtv website. "When you wake up hungover as fuck in a town you've never been to before and you sit there – you just close your eyes and you imagine yourself at the beach with a choccy milk in hand, you've got your board, it's just pumping, but no-one's there. You're just by yourself on the beach.

"*That* is the homely feeling. That's all I dream about. When I'm away, I just want to get home."

Speaking of home, the video for the song is set in the backyard of Stephenson's parents. Fleming arrives with a pump, drains the pool and then the gang turns up with their skateboards and beers and makes a party of it. Eagle-eyed viewers may spot Stephenson wearing a Grinspoon T-shirt he picked up while on tour with them earlier in the year.

The video of them skating in the pool inspired a few

cheeky neighbourhood kids. "We were on tour," Stephenson said, "and my girlfriend messaged me saying random kids just turned up wanting to skate in the pool. But it was already filled with water by then."

19

It was a Monday night, August 17, 1998, when the heavens opened up and the rain started to fall over the Illawarra. And it kept falling all day on Tuesday. The rain gauges filled up – 375 millimetres was the official reading though some suburban gauges up north were pushing 400 millimetres.

And there was nowhere really for all that rain to go; except through people's houses. Water, at thigh level in some places, washed under front doors and through neighbourhood streets, bringing mud and debris with it. The wild weather knocked down fences, pushed parked cars off bridges, flipped them over and left them resting on their sides up against houses, washed others out into the surf, closed roads and put most of the northern suburbs under water.

Two people died in the storms. Seventy-one year old John Thompson was trapped in his car as waters rose near his Bellambi home, while Unanderra's Joanne Doyle fell from the balcony at the Bulli Family Hotel. She had sought refuge there after her Sydney-bound train was cancelled. Many Wollongong residents working in Sydney were stranded at clubs and hotels as the rains cut the rail lines and their only route home.

Emergency services saved plenty of other people caught out in the deluge as suburban streets turned into oceans and seas, sometimes piggybacking them to safety. Others had to leave their cars behind on Bulli Pass as a landslide buried them. As the rains eased, people were able to return to their homes to try and salvage what was left. In many cases there wasn't much worth keeping; in the days after the storms, mud-splattered household goods like fridges, washing machines, cupboards, closets and lounges were stacked up on nature strips all over Wollongong. Homes and streets had been inundated with mud and water, yards destroyed, roofs collapsed – some houses were unlivable.

But, unbelievably, more despair was to come, thanks to some hard-hearted insurance companies. Looking to avoid a payout, the likes of NRMA, GIO, VACC and QBE decided the damage to their customers' homes was caused by flood and not storm – therefore they weren't covered. The NRMA waited just two days to drop that bombshell, GIO following suit a day later. It was a devastating blow for many who were already on their knees. One of those was Figtree's Nada Srbinovska who, on the night of the storm was swept away with her two children when water rushed into their home. In the darkness, they were swept in different directions, each spending hours believing the others to be dead. Days after that horror, she found the NRMA knocked back her $65,000 claim.

There were odd situations where one resident in Balgownie got their claim rejected because the insurer claimed it was flood damage, while their next-door neighbour – affected by the very same water – got a payout when their insurer decided it *was* stormwater. Or a homeowner at Mt Ousley getting a payout for stormwater damage, but the tenant who was living in the house had their contents claim rejected.

Sometimes the claims were rejected before they were even lodged – a worried policyholder calling the insurance company was enough to see the company fire off a letter denying liability.

But if the insurance companies thought they were going to get away with it, they were wrong. The residents banded together to form the Storm Water Action Group (SWAG). "It was a time of drive-by assessments," said group spokesman Richard Nederkoorn. "Assessors claim they went onto premises to get information but it appears in a lot of cases they did it without the homeowner being aware of it. We've had reports of hydrologists making their reports after talking to children."

Solicitor Mark McDonald from local firm Maguire and McInerney also came on board to fight the insurers. In October, he helped people lodge as many as 250 claims with the General Insurance Claims Review Panel. At the end of that month SWAG protesters stormed into the NRMA annual general meeting – and a day later the insurer caved in. Days after that GIO also decided to pay all claims.

The likes of QBE, VACC and Suncorp wouldn't come to

the party. Peter and Coral Roil from the northern Illawarra suburb of Towradgi had been fighting with VACC for almost a year, before capitulating and accepting a portion of their $50,000 contents claim after water a metre-high washed through their home.

"We're not getting the full monty, but we're sick of fighting," Mr Roil said. "I offered them a chance for a 'serious' settlement and they offered to pay for the entire cost of our contents to the water level of 0.5 metres."

As part of the relief effort a Sydney company by the name of Cool Change announced plans to hold a three-day music festival at Stuart Park. Storm Aid was held over the weekend of November 20-22. It boasted a strong line-up of 1998-era talent, including The Angels, Mental as Anything, Wendy Matthews, Marie Wilson, Eric Burdon, James Reyne, The Whitlams, Jenny Morris, Richard Clapton, Billy Thorpe and John Paul Young. Local acts like David Beniuk and Erika's Jive also scored slots on the bill.

The free festival raised money through donations on the day as well as cash coming from the market stalls and rides. But the organisers would fall well short of their $750,000 target; four weeks after the concert just $40,000 was added to the Lord Mayor's Relief Fund.

However, Cool Change's Mark Filby said that target could still be reached, announcing plans to develop a documentary to air nationwide in the new year – where further donations would be sought.

"We are very optimistic about the TV special," he said. "The footage is sensational. It'll be shown in prime time on WIN and maybe another network."

That TV special was never made. Filby's Cool Change partner Steve White said in June (almost a year after the storm) that there had been problems with sourcing the $40,000 to $100,000 needed to put the special together. White admitted it was now too late to get to work on the doco anyway.

"To be frank, now it's old news and nobody would be interested in airing it," he said. "But I am not disappointed by the effort we put in, and I am not disappointed by the support given by the rock industry."

Lord Mayor David Campbell wasn't surprised by the fact that $750,000 target wasn't reached – he said he never expected anything to come of it right from the start. "They certainly came and created high expectations and made rather large statements," he said. "They came onto the scene very late when most of the contributions had been made. So many people had already given small amounts and large organisations had made their donations."

***

The Storm Aid festival vies with Yours and Owls for the title of 'biggest concert ever held in Stuart Park'. But in terms of the calibre of artists, the Yours and Owls festival has it beat. The 2017 show – which sold a record 14,000 tickets – featured US act At The Drive-In as headliners along with big names like The Presets, A.B. Original, Safia, Alex Lahey, Dune Rats and The Preatures. Local acts got a look-in in the form of Totally Unicorn, Bec Sandridge and The Pinheads. They even organised live screenings of the NRL and AFL grand finals, that were also held that weekend.

Tillman said there was a gap of about a week between when the festival line-up was locked in and when the public heard about it. And that week could be quite stressful indeed.

"You can't really tell anyone, so you just send yourself a little bit mad, over-analysing it," he told Joseph Earp from the Industry Observer. "You're going 'are people even going to like this anymore?' Then you start second-guessing yourself – 'why did I book that band? Oh God, this will be a mistake'.

"But it was such a relief when the line-up did get such a good reaction, and people started buying tickets. That's the ultimate encouragement."

After trialling things during the first three years of the festival, Tillman felt they'd now figured out what worked and what didn't. "Last year we got to a set-up we were happy with but there were still a few little things that weren't as tight as they could be," he told the *Mercury*. "This year was about consolidating and refining."

The 2017 festival was also when Tillman really saw the change taking place in his city – a change he helped create.

"The local thing has always been important," Tillman told Josh Butler. "We've always prided ourselves on nurturing and fostering the stuff going on here. That's a bit of a different mentality to the Wollongong of yesteryear, where everyone was looking outside of the area, so we went the other way and said there's lots of good stuff already here so let's get that out there.

"We're proud to be from Wollongong. There's a rising sentiment of Gong pride, whatever you want to call it. It's pretty cool. Wollongong used to be a dirty word, people looked down on you but now it's a positive thing. You don't have to convince or explain why it's a good thing, it is a good place and a cool place."

20

Back in 2016, Farmer and the Owl released *Got The Feeling*, the debut single for Sydney via Wollongong duo TEES, on clear vinyl. Made up of Lizzie Tillman and Sean Duarte, the pair got together at her house in Redfern after he drank a cup of tea she'd made as a condition of entry. Duarte had already been writing pop house music with a female vocalist in mind and, despite Tillman already being in a band at the time, he decided to poach her.

They released a few singles themselves before signing with Farmer and the Owl. That label debut tune had impressed Taylor, even when he heard it on FBi radio after its release at the end of one of his Wollongong DJ sessions. "It really made me feel like continuing my night instead of just heading home," he said. "At that moment I realised how much of a party starter these guys are."

After a gap of a few years, the duo released their first EP, a five-tracker called *Flow*. Three years in the making, the songs explored the complexities of relationships present and past. "This EP encapsulates exploring and experimenting, trying not to be suffocated into a space of expectation and rigidity," the pair explained. "Each of the songs explore the concept of striving to become self-determined and seek independence however there are differences in how each song aims to get to that point."

The first single from the EP, *Boy*, was inspired by a friend of Tillman's who was going through a break-up at the time. "It's a story of ambivalence toward ending a relationship and then finally taking the leap," she explained. "It speaks to feeling consumed with your partner, losing the joy in the relationship, realising you can't keep forcing it anymore … finding independence again, redefining yourself, and being free."

***

Aside from the sound system almost collapsing at the 2015 festival – prompting people in the industry to tell them to get serious or forget about it, the Yours and Owls team hadn't had any great problems with festivals. That charmed run ended in February 2018, when they decided to branch out from their usual 'Triple J' music crowd and chose to work with an icon of commercial radio airplay in Jimmy Barnes.

The Barnesy show was at MacCabe Park – with Cold Chisel bandmate Ian Moss also on the bill, along with icons of yesteryear like Mental as Anything, Diesel and Daryl Braithwaite. The attempt to broaden the focus of the local promoter made sense, as there was still a decent chunk of the city's population who liked to go to the occasional gig but wouldn't be bothered with that 'weird' music they played at a Yours and Owls festival.

Maybe it was that the Barnesy crowd had higher expectations than the average Yours and Owls punter, maybe it was because they were older and figured they wouldn't be able to last the whole festival and so got there early – who knows. But some of those who turned up at the show weren't very impressed at all.

And they vented on the Yours and Owls Facebook page, complaining about having to wait more than an hour to get in after the gates opened at 2pm, long waits for beers at the bar, food stalls closing at 6.30pm as well as sound issues and obstructed views of the stage (given the uneven topography of MacCabe Park, that last one should have come as no surprise).

"Worst-run event I've ever been to," fumed ticket-holder Melanie Grant. "Yours and Owls should be ashamed of themselves. Bands were great but sound quality was appalling. Poor Mental As Anything played to half an audience as everyone was still lined up outside waiting to get in."

With 6000 tickets sold, that was around 1000 more than Yours and Owls had expected. And with a lot of those queuing up to get in right on the 2pm start time, it was a cascade of problems after that point. "We had 90 per cent of the entire capacity of the event (around 6000 people) turn up bang on 2pm, which is unheard of," Tillman said in a statement.

"Usually crowds will filter in over the first three hours of the event, not all at once, right on doors [opening], so yes, we were unfortunately unprepared for that, which really sucks, and essentially is what led to most of the other issues. Everyone came in at once, went to the bar at once and it was chaos."

Tillman said he'd spent the entire day after the festival contacting people who'd complained to resolve their issues as much as possible. "We are disappointed that everybody didn't have as good a time as they could have, the vibe in the park did feel good, with majority of people having fun, dancing and having a good time, but the negativity of the social media did gain a bit of momentum throughout the day, which is a shame," Tillman said.

"We have taken into account the feedback, been in touch with the people who made comments, and any emails that came through."

The early months of 2018 were a bit better for the first Farmer and the Owl label signing. *Homely Feeling*, the teaser single from Hockey Dad's forthcoming album, gave the band their first Hottest 100 appearance (the first year the event moved away from Australia Day, in response to the Change the Date movement – a decision which angered people who didn't even listen to Triple J in the first place).

Coming in at No54, the Windang duo finished ahead of the likes of tunes by The Presets, Flume, Lorde and Arcade Fire. The honour meant Hockey Dad was the first Wollongong band in 20 years to make the Hottest 100 – Tumbleweed reached No59 in 1996 with *Silver Lizard*. Also, at 2:21, *Homely Feeling* was the shortest song in that year's list.

Just before the Hottest 100 announcement, the second

single from the new album hit the decks. *I Wanna Be Everybody* includes a riff that bore some strong similarities with a certain well-known song from Nirvana. "To be honest it wasn't a direct inspiration at all," Stephenson said. "It just ended up sounding that way."

The tune continued the theme of discomfort with your surroundings started by *Homely Feeling*. The video, largely shot on the streets of Los Angeles, saw Stephenson go through a lot of costume changes – goth, skater, footy player, surfer, fisher, priest and businessman among them – placing a light-hearted take on the lyrics that speak of feeling out of place. It also made Hockey Dad seem like a solo project, with Fleming barely appearing in the video.

The Hottest 100 debut for *Homely Feeling* gave the first hint that things were about to change for Hockey Dad. It was clear that a lot of people were waiting for the new album. On February 9, they got it – with *Blend Inn* hitting the record store racks (and the digital sites, if that was your thing). It performed better than 2016's *Boronia*, reaching No6 on the charts (the first Wollongong band to enter the top 10 since Tumbleweed's *Galactaphonic* in 1996), compared to the former's top placing of No55.

The band had been sitting on the album for almost a year, having recorded it at Robert Lang Studios in Shoreline, just north of Seattle, in March 2017. Nirvana, Foo Fighters, Presidents of the United States of America, Macklemore, Alice in Chains and Death Cab for Cutie are among the bands to use the studio. "There was a lot of ancient artifacts of bands who have been through there, and also the last mic that Kurt Cobain recorded through, which was very cool,"

Fleming said. "A bit humbling and daunting at the same time. We actually used one of Death Cab for Cutie's bass drums for the recording, so that's on there."

The eclectic interior of the studio can be seen in the second-last episode of the Foo Fighters' *Sonic Highway* series. The exterior, well that's it in the photo on the *Blend Inn* cover taken by Fleming.

"It looks like an old haunted house converted into a mansion-dungeon thing," Fleming said of the studio.

"Robert Lang built it himself. There was a little house at the front on a grass hill. He thought 'I want a studio, so I'm going to just dig into this grass mound' and so he dug it out and concreted it.

"It's so bizarre but it makes it truly good for recording. It's made out of marble and stone. He's done a great job but I don't know how he did it."

The 12 tracks on the album showed the band had taken a step up in terms of songwriting. Gone for the most part was the surf-pop sound of *Dreamin'* and *Boronia*, replaced with a grungey rock feel and lyrics showing more depth and introspection. That was likely prompted by a change in the songwriting approach. The earlier tunes were worked out with the two of them playing together but the outlines for songs on *Blend Inn* were created by Stephenson alone.

"A lot of it I was writing at home on my computer, demoing rather than jamming it out and playing it live first," he said. "I'd send it to Billy and then we'd talk about it later on when we finally picked up our instruments."

The only songs that would make it to that stage were those Stephenson was really into; he wasn't the type to sit and sweat on a song for days. "The feeling's gotta be there from the start," he told The Brag. " You've gotta be stoked to be playing it. If you're writing it and it just feels like pushing shit uphill, you're never gonna get it anywhere."

The moods expressed in *Homely Feeling* and *I Wanna Be Everybody*, are indicative of what was going on across the whole album. It found the pair looking at their situation and realising they weren't those two kids from Windang any more. And if that's who they weren't, well then, who were they? "It's an ode to living this sort of lifestyle whilst growing up and not really growing up the same way as everyone else," Stephenson said. "Having a weird experience in your early 20s and not really knowing what's going on.

"That's probably what it's all sort of aimed at and all the songs that were written on it were all written with that sort of mindset. Trying to get a hold of what's happening around us. Finding your feet while you're also travelling around and not staying in one place at the same time."

With that in mind, it makes sense that the album title should reflect that sense of displacement and confusion as well. "Blend Inn is the part of your head that you want to go to when you're overseas and wishing you were back home, it's within," Fleming explained to Consequence.net. "We're always just trying to be comfortable and semi-blending in, so it's the name we gave to that place you zone out to."

It wasn't all serious questioning of their place in the world on *Blend Inn*. One of the tunes that acts as a bridge of sorts to *Boronia* is *Sweet Release*, which marked Fleming's first effort at singing. It only happened because Stephenson was sick of Fleming giving him grief. "It was sort of a joke song,"

Stephenson said. "And I was just yelling the lyrics, you know, spitting them out. He was giving me shit, saying 'that's not it, you're not getting it', so I said, 'well, you go and do it then'.

"And he did! And he did it pretty good. Yeah, he was heckling me and I got sick of it. He showed me – I think he liked the idea of a fun, stupid song, and that's how he wanted to make his debut."

The *Blend Inn* album saw the band gain a new level of attention – so much so that some Brisbane shows had to be switched to a different venue after moshing teens bent the floor. During a matinee show at The Woolly Mammoth – where the gig room is on the first floor – people underneath could see the roof bowing and bouncing alarmingly just three songs into the set. That night's show had to be rescheduled due to structural issues caused by the passionate moshpit.

A structural engineer had to be called in to inspect the venue for damages, a Woolly Mammoth spokesman told Triple J. He said the room was given the all-clear, with just a fissure found in a beam that didn't directly support the main floor structure.

"The damage, as small as it was, is already getting fixed as of this morning," he said the day after, "and will be followed by reinforcing the existing structure to make sure it withstands at least double the previously prescribed capacity. All future show will go as planned."

April saw Triple J broadcast the band's March 22 set from Melbourne's Corner Hotel for *Live at the Wireless*. The show included a cover of The Vines' *Get Free* with special guest Ecca Vandal (the track would be added to a re-released version of the *Dreamin'* EP the following year).

In November *Blend Inn* was nominated for album of the year in the J Awards at Triple J. "Once checked-in to *Blend Inn*, it's hard to leave," the nomination read. "Hockey Dad's youthful and summery spirit oozes out of the record." They were up against Tash Sultana, Amy Shark, Courtney Barnett, Camp Cope and the DMA's but would lose out to Middle Kids' *Lost Friends*. In December *Blend Inn* also made the longlist for the prestigious Australian Music Prize; though there were 84 other albums on that list. "We're both very honoured to be nominated," Stephenson said. "Many of our favourite bands have won it before and we are just happy to be out there in the running." Ultimately, the band's album was among the 76 that didn't make the shortlist – the prize eventually taken out by Gurrumal's *Djarimirri* album.

Still, the year saw Fleming tick off the last two boxes on a wishlist he'd created when he was just 14. The one he'd already accomplished – several times over, in fact – was to play at a music festival. Also on the list was to sing a song onstage and have the crowd singing along; that box was ticked thanks to *Sweet Release*. And the final box was ticked in March, when the band headlined at the Metro in Sydney. They actually played there over two nights and managed to sell out months ahead of taking the stage. But 2018 had a little more in store for the band.

21

It should be stated that Farmer and the Owl wasn't the only record label in town during this resurgence of the Wollongong music scene, nor were Hockey Dad and the stable of bands on that label the only ones playing in town. And nor was Rad Bar the only venue of note. For the scene to really grow, there had to be others doing their things.

In terms of record labels, one in the northern suburb of Thirroul actually pre-dated Farmer and the Owl. Spunk Records started out as a fanzine of the same name put together by Aaron Curnow and a friend in Sydney. Sometime after starting the label, Curnow chose to move the operation down to Thirroul – a place in the city where there were more "indie kids" than further south in the Wollongong city area.

"I've always had a fascination with the place," he told Vice, "but it wasn't until my wife became pregnant that we came here. And by inviting people to play shows here I thought I could help vitalise the scene."

The label had been putting out releases since 1999, including albums by international acts such as Sleater-Kinney, The Yeah Yeah Yeahs, Antony and the Johnsons and Bonnie "Prince" Billy. Curnow was also behind a number of northern suburbs shows, including Coalchella at the Wombarra Bowling Club.

Also up north for a while was Urge Records, which also had a short-lived shopfront at Thirroul before closing due to issues with council about staging live music events. The label's running is now split between Sydney and Los Angeles. There's also Third Eye Stimuli, "devoted to bringing you far-out sounds from Australia, New Zealand and beyond", which is run by the founders from Wollongong and Sydney bases via a lot of Facebook Messenger.

On an even smaller scale, is Wreckless Enterprise, putting out seven-inchers. Started in 2019 by Ronny Van Dyk to release something by his band The Leftards, it's trundled along on a hand-to-mouth basis. "There's not a bean in it," he said. "We just started off with a bit of redraw money. Whenever we do get a sale, we get pretty excited because in very small doses it chips away a bit of the debt. We're always just trying to recoup losses and break even so we can put out the next thing."

The most notable releases on the label are the *Short Fuse* compilations – seven-inch punk singles featuring up to 15 artists all playing songs less than a minute long. "We came up with the idea that the ideal quality volume and playing time for a seven-inch single is around five minutes a side," Van Dyk said. "It's as many songs as we could fit into five minutes while making sure it would still sound good and not lose the quality of the music."

Also released on Wreckless was one of the many bands Van Dyk has been in – The BotBots' seven-track EP *Stoneage Scomeos*. The name and cover art was a pastiche of the Hoodoo Gurus' *Stoneage Romeos*, and some tunes took swipes at Scott Morrison and his government – especially the track *Engadine Maccas*.

One of the local bands signed to Curnow's Spunk label is Shining Bird, based in the northern suburb of Austinmer. Given the laid-back, beach location it's not surprising the seven-piece band's sound is laid-back with tinges of surf music and a focus on instrumentation that makes you sit and immerse yourself in the sounds. Their album covers feature art from the likes of painters Paul Ryan and Ben Quilty

When members Russell Webster (also cranking music out under the names of Russell W and A Ruffian) and Dane Taylor started playing together in the early 2010s, it wasn't really with a band in mind. The music was a way to deal with depression and other problems. "We started making music as a bit of a distraction and to give us more of a direction in life," Taylor told the Lunchboxtv website. "It all happened really organically. At the time most of us didn't have that much experience in bands or making music, so we put out an album before we'd even played a live show. We just recruited a bunch of mates and a few housemates ended up being in the band – for a lot of the members Shining Bird is the only band they've ever been in."

When it comes to metal – which tends to be a musical genre that sits very much by itself in the Wollongong scene

– the best-known name is Segression. Though they weren't always known by that name. The foursome started out as Eezee, releasing their first EP way back in 1992. In 1996, after realising that name wasn't the greatest (and maybe because of a musical change of direction), they became Segression.

Under that name, the band had their greatest success with support slots for the likes of Ozzy Osbourne, Pantera and Slipknot. In 2003, they decided to park Segression for a while and pursued more melodic heavy rock as Side Effect X ("I needed a break from doing all the heavy stuff," bassist and singer Chris Rand said). By 2009 they decided it was time to bring back Segression – the reunited act releasing two more albums and counting.

It's usually a good idea to run a mile from a band releasing a concept album. They tend to be bloated, self-absorbed, faux-clever messes. Except in the case of You Beauty, who got part of their line up from Wollongong band Ohana. In 2014, they put out the album *Jersey Flegg*, which tells the story of a star rugby league player in 1998 who finds love (in the form of Ann-Marie Biggar from *Agro's Cartoon Connection*), loses it and then wonders if it's worth picking himself back up again. It is likely to be the only album to reference both *Whispering Jack* and Ray Warren.

A year later, they followed it up with another concept album – *Illywhacka* – about an online scammer who reels in lonely women and then fleeces them of cash. But things take a surprising turn when the scammer realises he has a connection with Dee, his latest victim. The storylines are in the background; you can ignore them and just enjoy the You

Beauty sound – Australian pub pop that you might hear on an early '80s movie soundtrack. Others have drawn comparisons to very early INXS, which makes sense too.

The band's Will Farrier is responsible for the concept album approach. "My life is boring and I can't think of anything worse than writing about my personal experiences – to put it simply," he told Mixdown website. "It's also just fun to get deep in a subject and pull all the strands out. Some people can find interesting detail in their everyday life that they want to explore. I have to make it up."

A book about the Wollongong music scene can't really leave out a band called Wollongong. They've managed to record more than 80 albums, which isn't all that difficult when you discover they make up the songs as they go along.

The songs on each album are improvised on the spot and recorded. Live shows follow the same format, with the crowd suggesting song titles to inspire the band. "It's an interactive project by its nature," said bassplayer Michael Manzini. "We try to include people in the community as much as possible. It's a bit like karaoke, but not compromised by bad singing."

In 2018, Rock-funk fusion act Ruby Tuesdays was one local act that got international attention – just not of the right kind. A band who'd only had a few videos posted on YouTube managed to raise the ire of US fast food chain Ruby Tuesday. Bizarrely concerned with the thought there was someone on the planet dumb enough to confuse the two, the burger chain launched a $2 million lawsuit.

The suit demanded the band surrender its name, destroy all its merchandise and transfer their web domain to the burger business – and also compensate them for past lost sales. Guitarist Shaun Snider wasn't having a bar of it and refused to relinquish the name. "The nature of trademark is that you're trying to sell something similar under the guise that it's [the same thing]," he told the *Mercury*.

"It's ridiculous that someone would rock up to a gig in Wollongong under the guise that they were going to get a burger. That's what they're trying to sue us over – it's just that silly." The burger chain – who were obviously trying it on to see what would happen – ended up blinking and dropped the lawsuit.

It's the nature of bands that many of them stick it out for a few years before breaking up. Maybe they hated each other, maybe someone had to go get a proper job, start uni, or maybe Jodie got married (bonus points for getting that reference). One of those bands who shone for a short while before calling it quits was Spit Chewy. Three of the members met while in high school and had their first single – *Grunge is my Religion* – out in mid-2018.

"Influences for *Grunge Is my Religion* range from the sameness of coastal suburbia to the celebration of being an outsider amongst it, I suppose," singer Annabelle Scobie said. "As well as finding joy in '90s music and other simple pleasures in life. That's where the lyrics come from and as for the music, a mix of happy, sad and not too bad is the aim really."

Two years later, they pulled the pin, releasing the five-track *Home Movies* EP containing the last songs the band ever recorded. Scobie moved onto the solo electronic project Yen Strange, while other members Liam Jordan and Josh Fogarty went over to Ok Hotel.

Kelly Jansch started in bands at 16 after older brother Chris steered her to the drums and they started jamming. Things changed when Chris ended up joining Dune Rats, so Jansch had to find a new band. Ultimately, that ended up being the grungy guitar-driven three-piece Totty, with Jansch on vocals and guitar.

"We're definitely a loud rock band first and foremost," she said. "Being from Wollongong, we've taken as much from bands like Tumbleweed as we have from bands like Hockey Dad."

They released the singles *Riff* (inspired by friends' R.I.F.F tatt – Remember It's For Fun) and *Sigh* in 2017 before signing to the Dune Rats' Ratbag Records (Jansch doesn't think their mum pressured Chris into it). The label debut was *Cut the Poppies*, which brought the band to the attention of those outside Wollongong – something Jansch had to come to terms with.

"I think we're a good band," she told the *Sydney Morning Herald*, "but I'm still shocked when people who've never seen us before actually like our gigs. In Wollongong everyone knows everyone in the band scene. We just did this so we could hang out together, but now other people are invested in it."

In 2020 came the band's second EP *Garden*, including the single *Lucky*. The video of that tune, which sees Jansch get sacked from her job, is set in Wollongong and features a scene of her drowning her sorrows at Rad Bar.

Now based in Melbourne, Heather Riley and Jonathon Tooke were University of Wollongong students when they met on the plane flight, leading to the creation of the duo Cry Club. "We met on a uni trip to Japan – we were sitting next to each other on the plane," Tooke explained to the *Mercury*.

"I was watching a show on my laptop, Heather was like, 'I love that show', and we bonded over how when we first watched it we were crying our eyes out. So when we landed on the name Cry Club, it was like, 'wow, this is perfect'."

That was in January 2018 and, a year later, they headed south to Melbourne – where things were happening for the band. That year saw the self-described "queer bubble-gum punk duo" become 2019's most played artist on Triple J's Unearthed digital platform.

A year later, they had released their full-length debut *God I'm Such a Mess*, which opened with *DFTM* – a song calling out guys who grope people at gigs (it stands for Don't Fucking Touch Me). Tied into the music is a strong sense of theatricality – the album cover sees them dressed up as glam members of the French aristocracy and many of their videos feature some fabulously outrageous costumes. It's something that creates a complete Cry Club package but also means they can take ownership of their own identities, silencing those clowns who might otherwise choose to take issue with it.

"It's about purposefully putting yourself – and things like your queerness – out there, so people can't use it as a way to attack you or drag you down," Riley told Pilerats' Hayden Davies. "It's about wearing your insecurities on your sleeve, like holding a big sign saying that you're this particular thing, because then people can't attack you for that particular thing – you've claimed it for yourself."

The wife-and-husband duo that make up Chimers has quite a history in the local scene. Drummer Binx was in Wollongong's Unearthed-winning band Evol and, more recently, The Fangin' Felines. Guitarist Padraic played in a Dublin hardcore band before heading to Wollongong, where he joined The Pink Fits (as the drummer), the band started by Lenny Curley after Tumbleweed's break-up. They're also both drummers in The Drop Offs – yeah, the band has two drumkits onstage.

Binx was reluctant to be in a band with just the husband, wanting to keep the music and the relationship separate. But that changed during the 2020 COVID lockdown when neither could have anyone over, so if they wanted to play music, it had to be with each other. And living with your bandmate does come with some advantages.

"We can jam pretty regularly," Padraic told Vox FM's Ben Hession. "It doesn't have to be a full, organised thing. If we've got an hour of downtime we can just go out to the band room and everything's set up ready to go."

They've released a few singles and a self-titled album, full of tunes that certainly call to mind the likes of Joy Division – especially *Surrounds*, the first release from the album. The video features their son Charlie walking around the Wollongong area and the first thing he does is buy a record from Taylor at Music Farmers, before walking past Nathan Stratton setting up at CBD music venue La La La's and gradually making his way home to where the grown-ups are in the band room out the back.

That single was on the band's debut self-titled album released in September 2021, the COVID-related vinyl pressing issues delayed the physical release until early 2022. Somehow Henry Rollins found out and pre-ordered it, which is not bad for a little old duo from Wollongong.

In terms of new venues, perhaps the most noteworthy isn't even in the Wollongong CBD. To see a gig at The Servo you have to drive all the way to Port Kembla – which people are tipping to soon become the hip, cool, bohemian suburb of Wollongong. Though they've been saying that for more than 20 years and it still hasn't happened yet. The name derives from what it once was – a service station with a UFO-like canopy in the middle where the pumps once stood. With a forecourt with enough space for food trucks to park, it was opened in 2018 by a collective of 11 friends – including Wollongong city councillor Ann Martin and local music stalwart Warren Wheeler. "At the moment in Port Kembla, there's nowhere to get a meal in the evening," Martin said. "So this way, even if you don't want to have a beer or listen to music, you could pop down and grab something to eat."

The venue kicked off on March 1 with a folk and gypsy night – and a huge turnout. "The purpose behind the venue is to provide a diverse program of food and entertainment," Wheeler said, "and that's because we are a diverse community. We're looking to foster unity through diversity."

During the 2020 COVID outbreak, the venue took advantage of what was the petrol station's forecourt. With a small band room, the social distancing requirement would mean fewer than 10 people watching the gig. So they put a stage outside and off they went.

22

Before Hockey Dad came along, the only big band flying the flag for Wollongong was Tumbleweed. The band from Tarrawanna started out after the demise of the Proton Energy Pills and, capitalising on that band's early success, soon found themselves riding high in the indie charts.

Then, when Nirvana broke and every record label needed a loud independent band, Tumbleweed got signed up by Atlantic. That should have been a great thing but it wasn't. By the band's own admission, they weren't as professional as they should have been – and the label didn't really need them anyway. They'd signed up a bunch of acts for very little cash in the hopes that one of them would be a winner. And that winner wasn't Tumbleweed.

The big release while signed to Atlantic was their self-titled debut, which the label liked so little they cut the guts out of it and turned it into an EP. The band didn't like it either, figuring it didn't sound like them. The fans enjoyed it however, pushing the debut to No48 on the charts shortly after its December 1992 release.

Tumbleweed ended in 2000 with a whimper, after sacking three members and replacing them with hired hands and then watching what would be their last album get caught up in record company takeovers.

There was a lot of lingering animosity between the various members for years before they patched things up and reformed in 2009. They released a new album, *Sounds from the Other Side*, in 2013 and of course there were the obligatory re-releases of earlier material. That included a collection of their early Waterfront Records recordings in 2010, followed by an expanded release of their second album *Galactaphonic* (because the band liked it more than their debut) in 2015.

Then on Record Store Day in April 2018, Farmer and the Owl released the *Tumbleweed* debut on limited edition blue vinyl – along with a seven-inch of the *Daddy Long Legs* single (a black vinyl version was released in June).

"We've been talking about this re-issue for the band over the last couple of years and finally the timing made sense to do it," Taylor said. "I've always felt these are important records to be re-issued on vinyl as they were released in a period where vinyl was scarce so they never made it to vinyl."

There was also a personal reason for the re-release; Tumbleweed was the inspiration for Taylor to make a career out of the music biz. "As a very young teenager I discovered a couple of songs from the band," he said. "When I realised they were a bunch of guys from a few suburbs down the road doing well on the national stage, it was an inspiration first to start a high school band and play shows and from doing that, it led me into the music scene and with booking venues, managing bands, opening a record shop and starting a record label."

Tumbleweed's Richie Lewis found it humbling that people were still interested in the band after all these years. "I'm very grateful for that," he said. "For me it's like a lot of people have been asking for it to be on vinyl for a long time so I'm very happy that we've finally got the opportunity to deliver it to them."

Lewis remembered the recording of the album as a bit of a struggle because they'd cranked out two EPs earlier that year and the songwriting well was a bit dry. "We put all our great songs into those two EPs and we had a few left over, like *God*, *Atomic*, *Sundial* and I think *Healer* was left over too," he said. "So we had to come up with some more songs, so there's a couple I think we rushed into, like *Starseed*.

At least one song was actually changed by the recording process – which was done on tape. The producer grabbed a chorus from one take, a solo from another and intro from somewhere else, cut the tape with a razor and then connected them to make a 'completed' song. In the case of *Acid Rain*, the razor process led to the song being longer than when the band wrote it, so they had to re-learn the tune from the recorded version.

After the 2018 re-release, the band played the album at live shows, which meant they had to go back and listen to the whole record to remember how to play songs they hadn't tackled in well over 20 years. "Time is an amazing thing and looking back on it from 26 years on, you can hear it with fresh ears," Lewis said. "You can almost view it as if it's not really you; you listen to it as if it's someone else."

Two months later, another Farmer and the Owl album saw the light of day. That was *Zutti* by Tropical Strength, a band made up of Shining Bird's Alastair and Russell Webster (though their Tropical Strength nom-de-plumes were Al Foil and Sir Dinsington). The brothers had been working together under the band name since at least 2013, when they released the ambient experimental pop of *Wake In Fright*.

Taking its name from a novel and cult movie of the same name set in the Australian outback, that song was inspired by all things Aussie. "At the time I was collecting and surrounding myself with everything Australian – which I still do," Foil said. "I'm trying to find the best sides of this country, from the kitsch Australian to the cheesy larrikinism to the spiritual history. So duly these themes found their own way into the song."

Five years later, that song would turn up as the opening track on *Zutti* – even though there wasn't initially any plan for an album at all. "When I first started recording I had no intention of releasing an album," Foil said. "The songs were more like musical diary entries and ambient sound collage experiments than anything else. I guess that's why the final product is so anomalous and genre-fluid."

It wasn't until Foil's brother got involved that these aural diary entries became something more. "With my brother's input we became more involved in developing the ideas into songs," he said. "A lot of the time he would mishear me singing from my room and what he had heard would be better than what I was actually singing."

As can be expected when songwriters spread themselves

across a number of bands, songs end up finding their way to bands they weren't initially written for. Such was the case with *Let's Take A Walk*, which the pair wrote with Shining Bird in mind. That band knocked it back because it "was a bit too '60s" so the brothers took it for Tropical Strength.

Meanwhile, Hockey Dad had spent the middle of the year travelling to the US and Europe on tour, before heading back home for an all-conquering moment in September. Following on from their Metro success earlier in the year the duo had managed to sell out the 1600-seat Enmore Theatre for two nights running as part of their *Join The Club* tour. "It was a venue we've always grown up going to and been like 'that would be insane to play one day'," Fleming said. "To do that by ourselves was pretty wild."

The shows, as they say, went off – kids were jumping from the balcony to join the heaving moshpit down below. The show impressed *Sydney Morning Herald* reviewer George Palathingal so much he gave it 4.5 stars. He caught the down-to-earth nature of a band still shocked at their level of success. "They're as surprised as anyone to be playing this sizeable venue (twice, no less – the second is on Sunday) but don't let it show, musically speaking at least, over an hour-and-a-half so apocalyptically exciting that by the end of *I Wanna Be Everybody* fans are jumping off the balcony to join the mosh downstairs."

The sight of a packed Enmore left Stephenson amazed. "I don't know what else to say – they were epic," he said of the shows. "They were definitely the biggest thing we've ever done."

A few weeks later, the band was back at Stuart Park for

the 2018 version of the Yours and Owls Festival. Hockey Dad's name didn't appear at the top of the bill; this year's headliners were Angus and Julia Stone as well as Peking Duk and Alison Wonderland. Other names included Cub Sport, Methyl Ethel, The Jungle Giants and Ocean Alley.

As well as Hockey Dad a stack of Illawarra bands got a slot, including Tumbleweed, The Vanns, Babymachine, Good Lekker, Enfant Terrible, Spit Chewy and Homewrecker.

With the league and AFL grand finals on the same weekend, the organisers created The Jeb Taylor Hotel ("think of your favourite watering hole minus your nanna on the pokies") where the games were shown live.

The annual festival had by this time well and truly passed through its growing pains phase and had become an anticipated event on the music calendar – for those outside of Wollongong as well as local music lovers.

It had even started pulling in some rave reviews. The Savage Thrills site called it "one of the best bloody festivals in Australia".

"From the smallest of stages to of course the biggest, the festival works to create an open dynamic line-up that is filled with an assortment of sweets!" the Savage Thrills reviewer said. "Whether you are going to catch your favourite band, solo artist, DJ, or catch up on some unknown acts, you are guaranteed to have a blast of a weekend."

Scenestr's Cassidy Chapman had nice things to say about the 2018 festival too. "A once-industrial uni town, Wollongong is home to a predictably young and active music scene," Chapman wrote. "Its beachfront Stuart Park location sets a serendipitous scene for just the kind of music festival that sees you not stop for two days and still return home glowing. Not that you would want to stop."

There were around 150 people who perhaps didn't have a great time over the weekend. With the help of drug detection dogs 43 revellers were pinged by the puppies, had their drug seized and were kicked out of the festival. Oh, and they got a notice to attend court too. Outside the festival gates, Greens members were campaigning against the use of sniffer dogs at festivals.

"Last year [at Yours and Owls] there were a few prosecutions," said Greens city councillor Cath Blakey, "and mostly it's users. It's people with small amounts just for recreational use that are being targeted by sniffer dogs."

Tillman didn't come out in support of the sniffer dogs at the festival, taking the approach of whatever keeps the punters safe. "We don't want anyone to get hurt; we want it to be as safe for everyone as it can be. If there are preventative measures that can be done and that are proven to work then we want to be able to do it."

As well as the 43 found with drugs, 36 were thrown out for being absolutely smashed, while more than 100 people were busted trying to scale the fences – caught by event security and the police. "We had quite a lot of police down," said Wollongong's Chief Inspector Darren Brown, "and [the mounted unit] mainly outside, just to give us a bit of operational support considering it's such a large crowd. The crowd was reasonably well-behaved on both nights and both days."

While music was the obvious focus of the festival, Yours

and Owls had been increasing its eco-friendly element over the years as well. "We were always taught that when you leave a campground, you leave it exactly how you found it," Balunn Jones said. "It's one of the most important things that we can advocate, that we can have a good time but no harm comes to the environment because of that. I can't imagine running Yours and Owls and not thinking about how we can have a positive impact on the local environment."

The push had started the previous year, when they brought in biodegradable cardboard tents for campers that could absorb up to 400 per cent of their own weight in water. "It's a hassle-free, environmentally friendly accommodation option for music festival punters," Jones said. The approach was designed to reduce the practice of punters who bought a cheap tent for the weekend and left it behind when the festival was over.

The stakes were raised at the 2018 festival; single-use plastics got the chop – so no bottled water, straws, cutlery and food containers. In their place, punters were encouraged to buy reusable cups and bottles – which people could take home or return at the end for a refund – and compostable food containers would be used. After the show the rubbish was sorted into recyclable and compostable piles rather than chucking it all in landfill.

Tillman knew the green push had the potential to cause gripes from the festival goers, but they weren't going to change anything. "It's about education," he said. "If people don't like that they have to spend an extra five minutes learning a new process, maybe they shouldn't be coming to the festival. We feel the festival is such a positive thing to have in the community and it's important that we minimise any negative impact we might have."

That year, they also teamed up with Wollongong council to help regenerate Puckeys Estate Reserve just north of the festival site. Volunteers who helped dig in the 500 plants were rewarded with a free festival ticket, which would be an ongoing initiative.

"The younger audience do have environmental awareness, and providing this opportunity allows them to do a practice like bush regeneration but with peers who have a combined interest in music," Yours and Owls bush revegetation officer Lyle Hunt said.

"On the day itself you've got very like-mined people that enjoy music, arts and culture but are also concerned about the bush. I feel like it is attracting more intrigue to bush care and environmental awareness."

23

Wollongong has long had a bit of an inferiority complex; locals have looked at other places – most notably Sydney and fellow "steel city" Newcastle – as better than where they're living. Whatever's happening here, the self-deprecating logic went, can't be equal to let alone better than what's going on somewhere else.

So it would have been a surprise to find others felt what was going on in the Wollongong music scene was worthy of taking a closer look, and perhaps emulating. Those in the know saw the worth – both culturally and economically – of events like the Yours and Owls festival.

University of Wollongong Professor of Human Geography Chris Gibson has made a study of music festivals, finding that they offer a surprising economic boost for rural and regional areas. "Agriculture is obviously really important to rural Australia," Gibson said. "But it turns out, regional festivals and events are more significant than agriculture in terms of the economic benefit."

The Yours and Owl team had estimated that for every dollar spent on the festival there was a three-fold economic impact for Wollongong. With the festival itself costing between $2-3 million to stage, that's a boost of more than $7 million.

Gibson's study also found that Yours and Owls had gone about things the right way. They started local and kept growing – but never got too big. "It's often a mistake made in other regional areas for promoters, music festivals and events to parachute into town," he said. "Yours and Owls has grown out of this place. It's become a genuine homegrown treasure for the region.

"Music festivals are often not taken as seriously as they should be as drivers of regional transformation. The mistaken thinking being that they're ephemeral or, worse, merely noisy youth activities."

The festival also helped give the city a positive makeover, particularly among out-of-town music fans in their teens and 20s. They came to the city for the festival – located right on the coast – and had a great time. They left with positive images of the city, which may well be better than the way locals see their own place.

People outside the city saw what had been happening in Wollongong music scene in the 2010s and figured they should start taking a few notes. In 2018 a NSW Parliamentary Committee investigating the state's music and art economy held a hearing in Wollongong to find out what had been going on, and what Sydney could learn from the city.

Among the people called to speak at the hearing were

Taylor and Adam Smith from Yours and Owls. Smith told the hearing they were lucky to open up the café/venue right at the point people were looking for new options like small bars. Still, he felt like the trio had bitten off more than they could chew.

"We just kind of opened the doors up to all different types of performances," he said. "We had everything from poetry readings to music. We tried to really open up and that probably ended up to our detriment. We probably tried to do too much.

"It is pretty hard to run a small venue – the overheads are huge. We just kind of relied on our willingness to do it for free to be honest."

Smith also noted there was no quick fix to build a local music scene; that suddenly creating a load of music venues wasn't going to work. "If there was nothing before and all of a sudden you install these great new facilities and say to everyone 'start going to venues', it is probably not going to happen," he said.

"It takes time for the culture to change. Places that have had iconic venues for a long time will have that captive audience already. With Wollongong we felt like we had to build it, not from scratch, as there was a rich history of bands here, but certainly venue wise, there was not a lot."

Taylor felt there had been a big change in the scene in his time. "When I first started working in music in Wollongong you could probably go out and see bands like two or three nights a week at the most," Taylor said. "And I think now there is something on every single night."

He also noted the importance of a small venue like Yours

and Owls/Rad where a band like Hockey Dad could start small and build up a following. "I first saw them on a Wednesday night playing to three people or something like that, and they have just sold out two shows at the Enmore."

Both Taylor and Smith noted that the city had changed so much that people from Sydney were now choosing to move to Wollongong – which is what can happen when people identify a new, cool music scene. "I know for sure that we have seen a lot of musicians, promoters, industry people from Sydney move down here," Smith said.

"That is probably not something widely discussed but Mr Taylor and I have definitely come across it a lot – pretty established people who are just leaving Sydney."

Taylor felt it was partly driven by lifestyle and economics – they can sell up in Sydney and buy something nicer in Wollongong (at least they could before prices skyrocketed). But the move was also a sign that there was value in a music industry person being in Wollongong. "There is more stuff happening here so they can actually do some of their work down here as well," he said.

One thing the committee focused on was the eternal problem of people moving in near a music venue and complaining about the noise. Taylor had experienced that first-hand back when he and Nick Irwin had been booking bands at The Patch at Fairy Meadow. He told the Helter Smelter website that he'd never experienced this level of noise complaints with any other venue they'd booked. "I'd never had to have meetings with licencing police and council in that time," he said, "but in the last six months I've had several."

At the time, Taylor and Irwin were working in their space at 5 Crown Lane, with construction of Wollongong Central going on literally across the road. And there was a lot of noise – they had to drill 16 metres down through some of the hardest bedrock in Australia. They managed to break at least 20 drill bits in the process and even planted explosives to try and fracture the rock. That tactic wasn't repeated after the first explosion sent chunks of rocks out of the site and sailing over the CBD.

Taylor made the excellent point that there was nothing to be gained from lodging a noise complaint because they were just doing their job. "They don't seem to treat live music as a job for people," he said of noise regulations, "but in reality it is many people's jobs; the artist, the tour manager, sound engineer, door person, venue booker, bar staff and hotel manager. Then there is flow-on to merchandise companies, booking agencies, the people who work at the bistro and alcohol suppliers."

The situation at The Patch got so bad that, in 2012 they organised two-day benefit to raise the cash to help pay for the soundproofing of the venue. It didn't help – less than a year later the Office of Liquor Gaming and Racing banned amplified live music after a noise complaint (the publican reckoned the complaints were coming from the hotel next door).

Taylor told the committee about the problems created by the noise complaint regulations. He said the process wasn't clear; sometimes the police dealt with it, sometimes council did. "This has got better over the last few years," Taylor said, "but a lot of venues still do not know what the process is for noise complaints. Everyone is very scared of noise complaints, because they are not sure how they are going to be dealt with."

When the committee headed to Newcastle, they found noise was an issue for venues up there as well. Owner of the Wickham hotel the Lass O'Gowrie, Ian Lobb said it was "the cradle of Newcastle original music". He was very concerned about a two-tower, 206-unit going in next door to the pub. "I did put a submission in when the plans went in with my concerns about the live music venue and the noise," he said. "I did ask them to do a sound check and to double glaze the windows."

He said he saw the woman doing that sound check – in the middle of the day when no bands were playing. "I said, 'why don't you come back when the bands are on? This is crap. You are taking the sound of the leaves falling. You need to be here when the noise is on.' We finish our music around about 12 o'clock with the bands. She said, 'No, everything is okay. This is what we are here to do'."

He told the committee he saw the writing on the wall for the future of the venue once people moved in next door and started complaining about the noise. "I think you will find if that happens the hotel will probably have to be gentrified and that would change its dynamics, Lobb said. "You would lose the music venue; it would go as it is now. It still might have a soloist or whatever."

He was right – of course. He sold the pub two years later and not too long after that, the new owners had to cancel the bands. Why? Because residents of the apartments next-door complained about the noise.

A change was coming, but it arrived too late for the Lass O'Gowrie. In 2018, Newcastle council decided to take what they referred to as "the Wollongong approach", creating their own version of the live music taskforce. "From this process, a range of better regulation approaches were delivered quickly," Newcastle city councillors wrote of Wollongong in their 2018 motion, "that also supported associated actions items in preparation at that time, and has been a solid foundation from which the music industry and events are doing well in Wollongong."

In time that led to the adoption of Wollongong council's strategy of noting on planning certificates that purchasers of a new apartment in the CBD could expect to be dealing with noise from music and other forms of nightlife.

"We forewarned people, that yes, there are advantages to living here in the city, but also some challenges," Wollongong Lord Mayor Gordon Bradbery said, "namely that you're entering a space where there's likely to be entertainment on at all hours of the night."

Academics too were interested in what was going on in Wollongong, speaking of the scene in the same breath as those in Detroit and Birmingham. A trio of academics from Griffith University – Zelmarie Cantillon, Sarah Baker and Raphael Nowak – were studying the music heritage initiatives in cities that had gone through industrial decline. In 2018, they visited Wollongong for a week and discovered "the importance of passionate, committed individuals in the community who were taking a grassroots, do-it-yourself, do-it-together approach to telling stories about popular music's past."

With extra funding, the researchers were able to expand their study to include Detroit and Manchester – meaning Wollongong had been first on their list.

"We're looking at places that have, number one, a very rich musical history, and that is the case with Wollongong," Nowak explained, "and two, which had known a de-industrialising trajectory over the last 20 or 30 years. What we are talking about here is the steelworks and it is not what it used to be in the '80s. So we're comparing places that have similar trajectories economically and socially and culturally."

With a friend in Wollongong, Nowak had visited over the years; he was sure he'd gone to the Oxford Tavern during a few of those visits. So when the idea for a study into music heritage came up, Wollongong was fresh in his mind.

As an outsider Nowak noticed that the usual trajectory for a town so close to a capital city of heading to the 'big smoke' to be a success wasn't being followed in Wollongong. As far as the creative industries were concerned, the flow was so often in the other direction. "There are many people who choose to stay in Wollongong and clearly that's saying something," Nowak said. "People want to stay here and creative people want to stay here. We found there's a lot of people who have stayed in Wollongong who are interested in doing something along the lines of cultural and creative activities in Wollongong."

YouTube also noticed something was happening in the city. The music arm of the online behemoth launched Neighbourhood Sounds in late 2019, asking so-called "local heroes" in 13 cities across the country to curate a playlist. Among the lucky 13 were Adelaide, Bondi, Canberra,

Newtown – and Wollongong. That city's local hero was Taylor, who had 37 songs on his playlist.

"I picked out what were key artists that came from Wollongong, or based here, or had an influence or a strong connection," Taylor said. "It got trimmed down but I probably submitted about 60 songs."

There were some obvious inclusions, such as Hockey Dad and other Farmer and the Owl acts like The Pinheads, Bec Sandridge and Totally Unicorn. Midnight Oil songwriter and northern suburbs resident Jim Moginie made the cut, as did Shining Bird and the now Melbourne-based Cry Club.

But there were also a few surprises, such as Radio Birdman's *Aloha Steve and Danno* and The Saints' *(I'm) Stranded*. The local connection with the latter, Taylor said, was that the video was directed by Russell Mulcahy – who directed numerous music videos before moving onto movies like *Highlander* – who lived in Corrimal for a while. As for Radio Birdman, they had local connections via Deniz Tek's old band TV Jones and the fact Wollongong was a regular stop on their touring schedule.

Taylor saw the fact that YouTube had come to town as an acknowledgement that something was definitely happening in Wollongong. "Just having people like that noticing that there's stuff going on in Wollongong now is a positive thing," he said. "Because we all live here we kind of get used to what it is and don't really see it as a destination."

24

At 2pm on the last day of July 1902, an almighty boom was heard to the west of the city. People in Wollongong rushed to their windows or out into the street and saw a large plume of smoke rising into the air in the area of the Mt Kembla coal mine.

Fearing the worst, people started making their way out to the mine. "In a short space of time the road to Kembla was dotted with men hurrying forward – on horseback, on bicycles or in vehicles," the *South Coast Times* reported. "Distressed women, dragging children after them, were passed but nothing authentic was learnt until arrival at Kembla Heights.

"The whole hillside was covered with anxious miners' wives, children and friends, concentrating towards the tunnel mouth, and seeking information about their loved ones. A glance around the pit mouth was sufficient to disclose the terrible nature of the explosion.

"The main entrance was completely blocked up, and the engine-house wrecked. Huge pieces of timber and bars of iron were respectively splintered or twisted into every variety of fantastic shape. Sheets of galvanised iron were suspended from tops of trees several hundred yards away."

A tunnel south of the entrance was still accessible and rescuers entered through it to hunt for injured and trapped survivors, while those who could make their way out stumbled dazed into the daylight.

The explosion ended up killing 96 men and boys, created 33 widows and took the fathers of 120 children. The explosion was the result of a large section of the unsupported roof collapsing, pushing air and methane gas into the main tunnel, where it stirred up coal dust. That dust made contact with the exposed flames lighting the tunnel and ignited. A series of explosions followed after the first, giving miners no forewarning.

However it wasn't the explosions that were the most deadly; that would be the odourless carbon monoxide gas that filled the tunnels. The gas also accounted for the deaths of two rescuers, William McMurray and Henry Osbourne MacCabe (who had also helped in the rescue effort at Bulli mine in 1887). The pair were among the first rescuers who ran into the tunnel entrance, heading in several times to bring out survivors.

On their last trip in, former military man MacCabe started to feel the effects of the gas and warned the rescue party to turn back. He was soon overcome by the fumes and collapsed, two other men trying to drag him to safety, before he told them "it is no use boys, get away and save yourselves". When they reached the outside world, they realised McMurray was no longer with them. He had succumbed to the fumes at the same time as MacCabe.

Several decades later, in 1929, Wollongong council decided to rename a paddock just south of the city's main street MacCabe Park, in honour of the Mt Kembla rescuer. Though the gesture would be tarnished by pretty much everyone – including later councils – misspelling it as 'McCabe' Park.

For the first 40-odd years of its life, the park looked very different to how it does now. Back then it was primarily used for sport, with a cricket oval, rugby league/soccer field, tennis courts and bike track. In 1948 a visionary engineer at council named RE Glastonbury said the sporting infrastructure should be ripped up and the place turned into a garden park. At the time, the city was full of residences but he felt, in time, it would become the home of businesses and sporting fields should be located closer to where people live. But no-one really listened and, in the 1950s, council looked to increase the sporting facilities by adding an Olympic pool.

By the 1960s the council had come around to Glastonbury's way of thinking, and so began the long process of making changes. While they figured out what they were doing, council cleared the northern section and turned it into a car park (at one stage there was a plan to build a car park underneath MacCabe Park).

That car park remained open for more than a decade before council in 1974 finally decided to close it and develop the area as parkland. An aerial photo of the park from 1977 shows the hill in the centre, with a pathway leading south to the as-yet-unconstructed amphitheatre. The location of that amphitheatre, hidden away at the southern end of the park, has prompted rumours the construction team had the plans upside down and placed it at the wrong end. It is possibly true; the amphitheatre's location does seem strange tucked away from the rest of the park.

The park as we know it now became the home of city festivals, with Carnivale '78 taking place there in 1978 and on New Year's Eve 2OO (now i98fm) launched their arrival in the city with a concert in the park featuring Jon English and Doug Parkinson. The park was also home to the Festival of Wollongong's Teen Queen beauty pageant in 1980 and the safe-sex promoting Condofest, featuring Tumbleweed.

Over the years, the park had also become associated with anti-social behaviour, a by-product of initially being surrounded by houses with bored teens in them, and later a CBD with plenty of pubs that drew in those bored teens from suburbia. In 1931, kids were in trouble for using "filthy language" while playing cricket in the park and, in the 1940s, complaints began surfacing of vandalism of the sporting facilities. By the 1980s, drunkenness in the park was the problem – both with late-night vandals destroying things and underage teens carrying in a bottle of spirits or a case of beer and hiding in dark corners getting drunk. That issue reached a peak in the 1990s, with the park bearing the name of a Mt Kembla hero then labelled a "black spot" of the city.

More recently the green space in the CBD has improved, in part due to the efforts of council. The park has buildings surrounding it on three sides and, whenever one comes on the market, council snaps it up and then knocks it down. The result is that it opens up the park and provides more entry points from the street.

The other reason for the improvement is the return to the park being used as a place to hold festivals and events. Among those was the Yours and Owls team, who would learn from that Jimmy Barnes show a year earlier. The city space would become a home for the boutique Farmer and the Owl festival, taking advantage of the nooks and crannies offered by the topography and occasional space left by a demolished building to place a stage or create a performance space.

The last Farmer and the Owl festival had been held at the university in 2015 but put to the side while the team worked on building the image of the annual Yours and Owls festival

"Farmer and The Owl started, basically when we had no idea what we were doing, at the uni," Tillman said. "We did that two years in a row, then stopped it and did Yours and Owls and that built up to what it's become.

"Now we've decided that with Yours and Owls establishing itself, we are looking at doing something a bit more experimental, a little bit different. We wanted to keep it separate from Yours and Owls so we looked for a new park that fit the vibe we were going for and MacCabe Park made sense."

That led to a different approach in terms of booking the acts. With the Yours and Owls festival, the bands' profiles came into the mix – if you want to pull a big crowd, then you need to book a few bands that will draw a big crowd. Farmer and the Owl, however, had different criteria.

"We're programming acts purely on their merits as a musician and we're not factoring in all those other things; how many tickets is this band going to sell? How much radio play is this band getting? It's more 'do we like this band – yes or no?'."

The people making that decision were the bands on the Farmer and the Owl label. Hockey Dad, Totally Unicorn, The Pinheads, TEES and Tropical Strength got to curate the festival. "It was a pretty awesome experience to be part of," Totally Unicorn's Drew Gardner told Double J. "The label hit us up about a year ago. They said 'pick some internationals and some locals that you love and we'll see if we can make it happen'. Most of it did, which is amazing."

Among the bands they chose were Ed Kuepper's The Aints, Dinosaur Jr's J Mascis, Beachhouse, Deafhaven, Amyl and the Sniffers and Stella Donnelly.

"We're not targeting young people, or 18-24s – we're targeting music lovers," Tillman said. "I don't think that necessarily has to have an age demographic, because good bands will stand the test of time."

Gardner felt a boutique festival featuring indie bands perhaps not familiar to the general Triple J listener was a sign of the changing face of the music scene in Wollongong. A few years earlier, he couldn't see Wollongong being able to sustain a festival with such an eclectic, obscure line-up but now the city could "definitely" do it.

"The venue Rad Bar, a lot of more obscure Aussie bands can play there and fill it out," he told Double J, "and I think that has built up the appetite. I think the live music scene there is going really well. People are going to shows, even if they don't know who's playing. It's getting good."

But the NSW government seemed set on ensuring the end of Farmer and the Owl – and just about every other music festival in the state – by imposing a set of regulations that would mean promoters had to shell out thousands of dollars for the show to go ahead. Of course, they couldn't afford to do that and so several festivals – including Mountain Sounds and Psyfari – had no choice but to cancel; an action for which the state government did not see itself responsible.

The drama started to unfold in mid-September – a good six months after planning for the Farmer and the Owl festival had started. On the weekend of September 15-16, 21-year-old Diana Nguyen and 23-year-old Joseph Pham died of overdoses of MDMA at the Defqon.1 dance festival in Castlereagh, near Penrith. Nguyen, who had recently become engaged, came up from Melbourne for the festival, while Pham – an ambassador for the Castlereagh festival – lived in Sydney's west. It brought the total number of deaths at Defqon events in the past five years to four.

Police said up to 700 people sought medical attention for drug-related issues, 15 of whom were hospitalised. "It was a very traumatic scene," said NSW Ambulance liaison officer Katherine Rallings. "We had three patients in cardiac arrest simultaneously. It's so hard when you lose anybody, particularly young people. This is a senseless waste of life. No party is worth risking your life for."

The deaths saw NSW Premier Gladys Berejiklian go on the attack against the festival. "I never want to see this event held in Sydney or NSW ever again," she said. "We will do everything we can to shut this down. I don't want to see this ever happen again – young lives lost for no reason."

Right from the start, the Premier ruled out the sensible option of allowing pill testing to take place, claiming people who supported the idea were "giving the green light to drugs".

"There is no such thing as safe drug and, unfortunately, when young people think there is, it has tragic consequences.

It was a stance that was opposite that of the ACT Police, where the Groovin' the Moo festival had introduced pill testing. At a 2019 inquest into the deaths of six people at NSW music festivals between December 2017 and January 2019, Detective Superintendent Rohan Smith told the coroner that "the co-existence of pill testing and ACT policing at the two Groovin' the Moo festivals has been a success".

Dr David Caldicott from Pill Testing Australia (the group working at the Groovin' the Moo testing tent) found the claim they were giving the green light to drug use a headscratcher. He said the very fact they were there testing drugs signalled the opposite of "safety". The punters who queue up outside the tent (and there is really a queue) are told about the risks of drug use and, once the pill is tested they are given straightforward information about what was in it. They're also given that information on a personalised card so that, if they still chose to take it and overdosed, medical professionals would be able to see exactly what they took.

"This is the opportunity to reiterate to young consumers the hazardous nature of the undertaking that they're about to embark upon," Dr Caldicott told Deputy State Coroner Magistrate Harriet Grahame. "The idea that is frequently put to us that this is in some way a green light or reassuring, we're still puzzled as to how that is translated in that way." He added that there was nothing particularly reassuring about the need to have doctors and chemists on site to test substances. It was an indication of risk, he said, even to those who don't use the service.

Pill Testing Australia's Gino Vumbaca pointed out that, if someone's child had purchased drugs before a music festival, the parents would feel it was better that the last person they spoke to before using the drug was someone at the testing tent, rather than the person they bought the drugs from.

At the 2019 Groovin' The Moo festival pill testing may well have saved the lives of seven people, who threw their MDMA away after discovering it contained lethal substances (though one person was dudded when he discovered the pill he'd bought was actually a breath mint).

Nguyen and Pham's deaths brought the total number of festivalgoers who had died at Defqon events in the past five years to four. One of those was Nigel Pauljevic, 26, and his father Mita said closing down the festival wasn't the answer. "This is normal for kids to get together," he said. "Get rid of the dealers. When these guys commit several murders, it's mass murder. They should get life."

Paul Dillon from Drug and Alcohol Research and Training Australia said shutting down the festival was just "a vote-winner" and wouldn't solve the problem. "Do we really want to go back to the days of the early '90s with underground events held in warehouses and police raiding them and people doing more dangerous things?". The Australian Medical Association was also an advocate for pill testing. "It's an opportunity to try and inform," president Tony Bartone told the *Sydney Morning Herald*, "about the dangerous consequences and try to get an opportunity to give them education and access to rehabilitation in terms of trying to reduce their drug dependency."

Rather than outlaw the Defqon festival, Berejiklian set up a panel to work out ways to make festivals safer – with pill testing not to be considered. That panel did not include any representatives from the music industry. Among their findings were recommendations to make dealers responsible for the death of anyone to whom they supplied pills, and on-the-spot fines for those found at festivals with drugs for personal use.

One recommendation would cause problems for festivals – a plan to set up a new licensing regime from March 1. That included a "high risk" category, where such festivals would have to pay for the presence of emergency medical staff. Not long after the announcement, Mountain Sounds organisers cancelled a week before the festival, citing the extra $200,000 they would have to pay for a police presence. Psyfari was cancelled for similar reasons and Bluesfest organisers said they would consider moving the festival to Queensland.

"This will cost us hundreds of thousands of dollars to comply with a policy where we and every other event in this state have had zero opportunity to have any consultation or input," Bluesfest promoter Peter Noble said.

While the coroner's report into the six music festival deaths, released in late 2019, noted that five of them occurred at dance music events (the genre most associated with MDMA), the NSW government licencing scheme threw all festivals into the same boat. Amazingly, the Illawarra Folk Festival – where it's hard to imagine anyone popping a pill that's not for high blood pressure – was also looking at the likelihood of forking out $550 an hour to have a NSW ambulance crew onsite for the entire four days.

In Wollongong, Lord Mayor Gordon Bradbery went into bat for the region's festivals, labelling the NSW government plans an "over-reaction". "The Premier needs to sit down with the stakeholders and look at a more robust way of dealing with live music events," he said. "A cookie-cutter approach is not going to work and it's going to damage the opportunities for our local music festivals. It's jeopardising tens of millions of dollars coming into the local economy."

The Lord Mayor even spoke out at the Don't Kill Live Music rally at Sydney's Hyde Park. "We are alive because of music, every generation including Gladys' needs to sing," he yelled to the crowd. "Live music brings people together … it's also an opportunity to celebrate our identity. It's not going to be wiped out, Gladys. It might go underground but it will still be there."

With their 2019 Farmer and the Owl festival due to take place literally a day after the new regulations came in, Tillman was justifiably concerned. "It's riddled with contradiction," he said just two weeks out from the festival. "It seems fundamentally flawed in the fact that they're on the one hand saying they want to promote festivals and culture. But then, at the same time, we've run different events through their risk categorisation matrix and its basically impossible for an event to come out with anything other than high or extreme risk."

The organisers also released a statement listing the hassles they had in getting across the line, under the tongue-in-cheek tag of "how to stress out and rapidly age your favourite festival team".

"Three weeks out from their event (which has taken months of meticulous planning) tell them that their current licence approval is no longer valid and they need to re-apply for a new licence," they said. The team had already gone through the approval process with Wollongong council – as had been the case with previous festivals – and gotten the okay but the government had changed the rules.

When that new application came back, Farmer and the Owl was classified as a high-risk event but with no explanation why or how this would impact the festival.

"One and a half weeks out from their event continue to not reveal what their high-risk classification means or how it is going to affect them or their operating budget," the statement continued.

"[Then] one week out from their event send them an email at 10pm on a Friday night to tell them they are no longer classified as a high-risk event and that their original licence approval has been reinstated."

Farmer and the Owl may not have been on the list of the 14 festivals declared "high-risk" by the government panel, but there were some odd inclusions. The Newcastle Up Down festival was one of the 14 festivals the government panel declared high-risk – even though it had never been staged before. Laneway Sydney was also on the list, despite having just two punters hospitalised across its 14-year history. "There was no consultation, no reason given. It was just simply you're on a list of high-risk festivals in NSW," organiser Danny Rogers told Triple J.

After all the tumult and stress, the Farmer and the Owl

festival went ahead as planned, with Double J's Dan Condon saying it "was an event unlike any other I have experienced in this country".

"If you think that every festival bill kinda looks the same in 2019, I'm not going to argue," Condon wrote. "The crossover of artists appearing at our country's music events – both beloved and burgeoning – is more pronounced than ever. It's like that because it works; logistically and commercially.

"But this is precisely why an event like Farmer and the Owl felt so utterly unique. Its scope was even broader than the admittedly still very cutting-edge Meredith and Golden Plains events. It took genuine risks in booking a line-up that deviates from what the average Australian music lover has come to expect."

As for the new system of regulations, they were ultimately rubbed out after Labor's music spokesman John Graham moved a motion in the NSW upper house later in the year. He said the aim was to send the government back to the drawing board and "come back with a regulatory regime that has been worked through collaboratively with industry".

Understandably Berejiklian was unimpressed. "This action will result in an immediate end to the regulations, putting thousands of lives at risk as we come into the summer music festival season," she said. "It is utterly reckless to throw out these regulations without having anything in their place as summer approaches".

A later government review of those high-risk festivals that had gone ahead under that legislation suggested it had little effect in dealing with the issues it was set up to address.

"While there is some evidence to suggest that there have been fewer adverse health outcomes," the review found, "and to a lesser extent assaults, at high-risk music festivals since the introduction of the Act, the number of serious drug-related presentations was consistent between 2018-19 and 2019-20 and a longer time series of data is required to draw any definitive conclusions." The review also found there were no breaches of the regulations by the organisers and the very term "high risk" caused "reputational damage" to the festival industry.

However, in September, the "high risk" requirements were re-instated by government legislation – albeit with a requirement that a music festivals roundtable was part of the discussion. "It's a victory for common sense," Graham said. "This means there'll be regulation in place for summer, but it means that the government won't be trying to do it all by itself."

Julia Robinson from the Australian Festival Association was pleased the industry would get input into the decision-making rather than having it foisted upon them. "Our members are really relieved that we've got somewhere to draw a line in the sand, we can just move on with the summer season," she said. "We'll see how the legislation pans out and we really just want to move forward and work together to make it as workable as possible."

25

While also looking for new music to release, Taylor also kept an eye to the past to pay tribute to the city's music heritage. That was evident in his decision to use the Music Farmers label to release three vinyl singles of bands past and present to tie in with the *Steel City Sound* exhibition in 2014. Via Farmer and the Owl, he brought back Tumbleweed's 1992 debut on vinyl.

He continued that trend by reaching back to 2010 to re-release a band from his old Impendence label – Mother and Son. The album – originally released in February 2011 and launched at Taylor's 5 Crown Lane store – got its second life in April 2019.

There was some present-day relevance to the release – the Wollongong duo served as the inspiration for Farmer and the Owl's most successful signing. "This was the band that started it all for us," Fleming told Tidal website.

"Sneaking into their show underage, going mental during their set and buying our first ever 12-inch record from the merch desk. It's a very swampy and waterlogged record, with harsh deliveries all throughout, giving it the perfect combination for a few grommets to lose their minds."

As well as inspiring the band to experiment with the surf rock sound, Mother and Son inspired Hockey Dad to *be* a band; the earlier act's lean guitar-and-drums set-up showed

Stephenson and Fleming they didn't need to find other members to form a band, the two friends could just do it themselves.

Mother and Son formed when singer-guitarist Bodie Jarman and drummer Mat Teudt met at uni in 2017 and boasted a dirty swamp-blues-surf sound – an amalgam of the stuff Jarman grew up on.

"I started out on the blues," Jarman said. "That's when I started playing, when I picked up a guitar, and just moved across to the old '50s rock and roll.

"Then I started listening to The Cramps and the punkier stuff. And that formed into the old '60s surf sound. We just took all those elements and put them together."

The band's debut album was very much a home-grown affair; the drums were recorded in a studio down the road from Jarman's place, while the rest was laid down in his bedroom and garage before mixing it himself too.

Jarman and Teudt had differing views of the Wollongong music scene when they were in it. During a European tour in 2012, Teudt told an interviewer that Jarman had chosen to move to Sydney because in part, they were making headway there and also the Wollongong scene wasn't quite cutting it. But Teudt stayed put, seemingly sensing that something was starting to happen.

"As a band from Wollongong, we have had far more opportunities to support bands than we would have had in Sydney," he said.

"Wollongong is a small place and bands always pull in for a show on their way to/from Sydney. So you can get great opportunities to play shows.

"People love to moan about the Gong, but you know there has always been somewhere to play, there has always been a bunch of great bands and a strong artistic community. We have places like Music Farmers, which is a great vinyl record store where you can play instores and have exhibitions.

"Then there's the guys from Yours and Owls who always support musicians either through their own small venue or larger shows at the town hall. Nothing wrong with the Gong."

Farmer and the Owl put out a new 12-incher at the same time – Totally Unicorn's *Sorry*. The album was a big step up from the *Dream Life* release; better songs, better production and songs that felt like they were there for a reason, songs that were really saying something.

That's something singer Gardner noticed too. "I feel like this album for us is a new beginning lineup-wise, the way we recorded it and just for myself lyrically," he told Mixdown. "We've taken a different approach to everything. So it's definitely a really exciting time for the band, but it feels like a whole new thing."

Gardner's vocal delivery was especially noticeable – switching from anger to what sounds very much like drunken misery, he sounds like he's working through something. And he was. Sometimes the best music comes from pain, from taking all the hurt and trouble inside and spraying the music with it, in the hunt for a cathartic release.

Among the issues he was dealing with was the divorce from his wife, which is the focus of album closer *Alley (Fucking) Cats*. (including the killer line "you're the wife of the party"). On top of that there was drug abuse, lost friendships, low self-esteem and body issues that flowed out in Gardner's lyrics.

"Lots of things have gone on in the past two years since the last record," Gardner told the *Mercury*. "Lots of substance abuse, losing friends due to relationships, dealing with my own sadness in myself and not being confident in who I am."

The emotional depth and pain of the lyrics cut against the grain of the band's live shows which are all about over-the-top fun. It places Gardner in the role of the sad clown; the guy who entertains others while feeling miserable inside.

That the exterior and the interior don't match up is on show in the album track *Prized Pig*. Gardner is a rather large man prone to taking his shirt off at gigs and giving everyone a gander at his belly. But that doesn't mean he's entirely comfortable with how he looks.

Which is exactly the subject of *Prized Pig*. "I have always struggled with my weight and appearance," he told LNYW website. "When I was younger I used to get super upset as not a day went past where I didn't get some smart-arse comment about my weight. It still gobsmacks me that still to this day, grown fucking adults feel the need to comment negatively on someone's appearance.

"This is a big fuck you to those people. Everyone is different and everyone is beautiful in their own way."

Playing songs that grew out of pain can be hard but it can also serve as a form of therapy. Then, over time, rather than serving as a reminder of that pain, the joy of the live performance attaches itself to them and changes the way they feel, which is what happened to Gardner.

"When you feel this way, sad and like there's nothing there, the best way to deal with it is to fucking talk to people," he said. "I am horrible at doing that. I always bottle my shit up. I have talked to friends about it, but this was another way of helping me get through it.

"Playing the newer songs, it's hard emotionally for me. But it's getting better and it's like therapy, so as we go through playing these songs it'll help me as well."

With the heavy subject matter, it could easily seem as though Gardner picked the album title of *Sorry* as a way to apologise to fans for the downbeat lyrics. But that stemmed from former bassist Lee Nielson's apologies after he and guitarist Aaron Streatfeild turned up to a Sunday rehearsal hungover and then started drinking again, which meant they wrecked every song. During the breaks, Nielson would blurt out apologies.

"It was a good reflection on all of us being sorry pieces of shit," Streatfeild said of the album title, "degenerates, at points in our lives when we really can't afford to be. Ideally we weren't many weeks away from recording and Lee and I had wasted an important session. I think metaphorically it was something we could all relate to."

The song of the same name was the last one written during the recording of the album, but it's also the one that encapsulates the excoriating nature of the record.

"As the other guys were tracking I walked down to the pub a block away and grabbed a feed," Gardner said.

"While I sat there watching some AFL game on TV and ate my schnitzel I thought about all the shit that had happened to me in the past couple of years.

"With all these emotions and stories of my life now for everyone to hear, I felt a large relief and the strength to be able to put things behind me. That's what this song is to me."

26

Record Store Day is always a big thing for the Music Farmers store. Vinyl fans queue up before the doors open to get a shot at the limited releases, while later in the day, racks and shelves are moved so as to fit in a band at the rear of the shop. For the 2019 Record Store Day, held on April 13, Rad Bar and the Music Farmers label joined up to create the first in a seasonal series of split seven-inch singles. The idea was that one side featured a Wollongong band, with an out-of-town act on the other side.

"With Rad Bar being the go-to venue for most artists starting out in the scene," the release blurb stated, "and likewise a first Wollongong show for many bands touring through the city, and Music Farmers being the equivalent for recorded music, the two entities are in a unique position to witness the best of what is coming through locally but also artists that are emerging on the national touring circuit."

The first single to kick off the series paired local doomrockers Velvet Elevator with Adelaide's Horror My Friend. That first release in the split-seven series also ended up being the last as a long-delayed aftershock of that council sex scandal from more than a decade ago led to the end of Rad. In the process, it became obvious the Wollongong music scene hadn't learned from what happened to the Oxford.

The building that housed Rad Bar was known as Lang's Corner, built in 1937. In 2003 the building on the corner of Crown and Kembla streets was bought by Frank Vellar's company Sebvell for $6.5 million. Five years later Vellar had been hauled through the corruption commission and seen council administrators run the red pen through much of his planned developments – including the controversial Quattro four-tower residential which was a centrepiece of the corruption enquiry, because he and lover Beth Morgan had engineered its approval.

So he needed to off-load a few properties, including Lang's Corner. There were no takers at an auction in 2008 but his company went into receivership two years later, prompting a fire sale of its assets. Later that year, several months before a cafe called Yours and Owls opened its doors, Lang's Corner sold for $4.37 million - more than $2 million less than what Vellar paid for it in 2003. It was bought by a Sydney developer who had ideas on knocking it down right from the start. "There are no immediate plans," selling estate agent Simon Kersten told the *Mercury*, "but the buyers will soon begin the process of getting a development application approved before developing the site."

But instead it went back on the market in 2013 – the same year Yours and Owls became Rad Bar – selling for $4.5 million. In 2017, the plans for the future of Lang's Corner became clear – knock it down and build a $45 million 11-storey office block. With the building changing hands, Daniel Radburn figured something bad was coming, but was still unhappy that Lang's Corner would be smashed to the ground.

"I'm very sentimental about the place, because I've seen lots of kids come through with aspirations to start a band, and then seeing their bands progress to have a tour around Australia," he told the *Mercury*.

"I think there needs to be more consideration for the heritage and life that is in those older buildings, and some sort of plan for culture."

He wasn't holding his breath that there may be some room in the tower for a "weird little place" like Rad. "They would definitely not have us on board, we make too much noise – in a good way."

More than 500 residents opposed the office tower, and the city council didn't like it either. "The proposed development will have unacceptable impacts in terms of urban design, heritage values, traffic and parking," the council said. "It is council's view that Lang's Building [sic] is significant in Wollongong and warrants some level of preservation."

A revised plan that included the requirement to save the facade of the old building and incorporate it in the design (though not before knocking it down and collecting the bricks) was approved by council.

Literally days after the release of the Rad Bar's Velvet Elevator/Horror My Friend single, Radburn told the local music scene via Facebook that he had been given his marching orders. He and the other tenants had two months to pack up and leave. "As soul-crushing as this news is," Radburn wrote on a post that got more than 500 comments, "there is absolutely nothing we can do at this point and we encourage you all to make the most of the last couple of months here."

The last show at Rad was on Sunday, August 16, with Sydney's Dear Seattle headlining over Wollongong bands Jacob and Raised as Wolves. Hockey Dad wasn't going to miss one last chance to play at Rad either; they had a sold-out show earlier that week with Step-Panther, Archy Punker and Los Pintar.

"It's really sad to see it come to an end," Stephenson told Triple J. "It's impossible to find another room with that atmosphere again. It's just iconic. The stairs are iconic – they're so ugly, so impractical!"

He also expressed a similar feeling as those who watched the end of the Oxford; it wasn't just the bands, it was a place you loved to go to. "It's just a sick bar that our friend owned and you could just go and party," Stephenson said.

"That's probably what we're going to miss the most, it was such a good place to hang out. Kept everyone together, kept everyone tight. It was the perfect place for all of us."

The parallels with the Oxford's downfall were strong. Both venues were lost to developers and, in both instances, the music scene had put all its eggs in the one basket. As was the case with the Oxford, Rad Bar was *the* music venue everyone went to. There was no real competition; and so when that venue disappeared, you could almost hear the sucking sound of the vacuum it left behind.

At least this time around, there was enough musical infrastructure in the form of a record label in town and a booking agency that the scene didn't founder for years looking for a new focus. "It's going to be a funny period once it does go," Tillman said, "in that interim between something else when that pops up, but we're working on that."

In October, that project was opened in the form of CBD venue La La La's, a partnership between Yours and Owls and former UniBar manager Nathan Stratton. Located in Globe Lane – a place the city council has long held out hopes of turning into a cool Melbourne-style laneway – it wasn't going to be Rad Bar Mark II. "Nothing could replace it, as Rad Bar's legacy will always be looked on fondly," Stratton said. "La La La's will have live music and will become its own scene."

***

In those last weeks of Rad Bar's existence, The Pinheads held a launch at the venue for their second album. With a title of *Is This Real*, it seemed a reflection on how people were feeling about Rad's impending closure. The band had made it over to South by Southwest earlier in the year and returned home to tour the new album in June, which bassist Tanya Avanu felt showed a growing maturity.

"Stylistically and also in terms of songwriting, I think we've come a long way," she said. "You know, initially, we were pretty heavy on the almost rockabilly, very low-fi sound and the songwriting was very simple, the structures were all very standard and by the book. I reckon the songs have definitely matured since we first started."

It opened with a bit of a surprise – a sprawling track that ran for more than eight minutes. Called *Pure Hate* it was a sign right off the bat that The Pinheads' sound had indeed matured. If, as frontman Jez Player had suggested, the band started without any musical experience, the moody build of *Pure Hate* showed they'd learned a whole lot since then.

"Looking back at this track, I have no real recollection as to what it means and how it came to be," Player told Tone Deaf. "It'd come from a four-chord progression [guitarists] Luke and Al were playing off. I was banging along on a floor tom and screaming atop (as per usual). That night, in a frenzy I wrote out a strange poem sort of thing and it turned out to fit the song."

It also felt darker and with more depth than their previous releases, which Player said was due to the deteriorating health of his and Luke's father, something that was taking place during the work on the album. He passed away just days before the band recorded the last track *Spread Your Love*. Dedicated to their father, the droning lullaby includes a mantra "Don't you cry, keep it cool" – the last words Player could remember hearing his father say.

The photo on the cover of *Is This Real* was taken at the Port Kembla steelworks and they'd be far from the only band to use the Wollongong landmark. The most notable use was Jimmy Barnes' *Working Class Man*; the first half of the video for that song was shot inside the steelworks. INXS also used the place as a video set – they just didn't tell the owners. Shooting the video for *Mediate* near the No6 blast furnace, they didn't ask permission, they just walked in.

The video is shot in a single take, which is what you have

to do when filming on the sly. They were able to get in two takes before being busted and told to leave.

More recently punk act SCABZ used the steelworks for the cover of their *Feel Good Summer* single and video – somewhat appropriate given the global warming theme in the tune.

27

In Wollongong in the 1990s, Tumbleweed weren't the only ones giving the fuzzy guitar sound a workout. While the Weed got incorrectly saddled with the 'stoner rock' label, it fit much better upon the back of northern suburbs act Thumlock. The band formed in 1994 when guitarist and singer Ben Lough, drummer Greg Eshman and bassplayer Wayne Stokes got together. Two years later, the trio became a four-piece when second guitarist Raf Iacurto joined. That's when things started happening, and when Jeb Taylor came on board.

The band was Taylor's first real foray into the music industry proper – as someone on the business side rather than playing onstage. The teenaged Taylor decided to manage the band and start up the High Beam Music label to release *Lunar Mountain Sunrise* on CD (because it's six tracks long, it gets called an EP in some places, but it's really the band's debut album). "They were the first band I ever managed," Taylor said. As a teenager I was straight out of school and I started managing those guys and that was the first release I ever put out."

For a few years in the 1990s, people had started to pay a bit of attention to Wollongong bands, due to Tumbleweed's success. One of those that caught the spotlight before it went off to shine somewhere else was Thumlock. "I feel like Tumbleweed had been that big Wollongong band that got out there," Taylor said. "That kind of opened the door for a few other bands to start coming through, and I guess Thumlock was one of those bands."

Three other releases followed *Lunar Mountain Sunrise* – two of them on the High Beam Music label – and the band gained a profile not only on the Australian indie scene but also in Europe. This was around the turn of the century, when the internet wasn't yet an ingrained part of our world. Back then, the idea of a Wollongong band having a profile in Europe was gob-smacking – that place was *so* far away. In an age before streaming, it meant someone over there had managed to get a hold of a Thumlock CD.

"It's so much easier now to release stuff internationally," Taylor said. "It's so easy to find and contact people. In '99 the internet was there but there was no Facebook or social media or YouTube. It was all email, so all the contact was really cold-calling via email and saying 'this is this band we've got in Australia, are you interested?'. In hindsight it's kind of crazy that a lot of little things happened with those releases."

While a European tour undoubtedly made sense, the band's finances didn't stretch that far. So Thumlock established a profile there without actually setting foot on the continent. The band ended up playing their last shows in

2002, with Eshman starting up El Sanchez, while the other three formed ROADS (Remnants Of A Dead Star). But Thumlock was never really forgotten. "It's kind of cool that people remember that," Taylor said. "I guess it's one of those things where, if a band doesn't play for a long time but their music's still out there, it creates this whole myth around the band as well."

For Iacurto to have this niche following decades later was both good and bad. "It's a double-edged sword," he said. "I play in these other bands so I know how hard it is to get that type of recognition and exposure and be able to play to audiences who want to lap up what you produce. It's great to have that fanbase and that acknowledgement but it's also a little disappointing that we can't follow through and deliver some live performances and feel that acknowledgement face-to-face." That would be because the four members are all in different places around the country, which obviously makes rehearsals hard enough, let alone actual shows.

To mark the 20th anniversary of *Lunar Mountain Sunrise*, Taylor and the band decided to give it a vinyl release it never had back in the day - complete with a gatefold sleeve and new artwork by award-winning artist Craig Phillips.

Taylor said they started talking about a release in 2018, when the band put the album on Spotify.

"From that a few people started asking about vinyl," he said. "Myself and the band started talking about it. It was 20 years since it was released, it never came out on vinyl at the time so now seemed like a pretty good chance to do it."

***

Between the Farmer and the Owl and Music Farmers labels, they released four albums by Wollongong bands in 2019. The Farmer and the Owl went in a different direction for the fifth album, released in October – it was from a band that didn't live in Wollongong.

In May 2019, the label signed up Adelaide five-piece Bad//Dreems, who Tillman had liked since they played at the Yours and Owls bar way back in 2011. "I thought they were laidback country lads who played good Aussie rock," he said. "We went on to book them at festivals. Their songs have always been good, and you could see them get more confident onstage."

Still, Tillman knew it was something different for the label to look outside of its home city. "Our label has always been Wollongong-centric in the artists we signed," he said. "So if we were going to step out of that and sign an Adelaide band, it needed to be a special one."

The band released two songs – the "Devo meets the Stones" of *Double Dreaming* and also *Morning Rain* – before the *Doomsday Ballet* album came out in mid-October. The band had an EP and two albums behind them but grew to find the "pub rock" category they'd been pigeonholed into a bit stifling. Part of that was because of a condescending perception that pub rock meant your songs were less worthy.

"I think the term is misleading and tainted," drummer Miles Wilson told Volume Media. "If by 'pub rock' you mean bands like Acca Dacca and Cold Chisel, then yeah great – happy to be in that category, of course. But it seems to label a band 'pub' is also to trivialise the songwriting and caliber of those bands, which seems a little unfair. That is my perception anyway. The term is synonymous with loutish, shit and basic music, whereas history would tell us that those very bands are successful as a result of the exact opposite of that."

When it came to record the album, the band had around 100 songs written and 40 at demo stage, thanks to an approach of having "immersive band weekends" where they'd churn out demo after demo. They headed into the studio with the motto of 'less pub, more art'. "The first two albums, we had basically gone into the studio, played the songs as we were playing them live in our rehearsal room, and recorded them," guitarist (and surgeon – really) Alex Cameron told *Stack*. "And even though we were happy with the results, what we realised is that a lot of the influences that were seminal to us – like Joy Division or Television - weren't being expressed as well as we might like."

The result was an album of light and shade, with slower songs like *Harry's Station*, *Sally's Place*, *Cannonball* and *Gallows* giving *Doomsday Ballet* some texture. Those songs were emblematic of the new approach to the album, where the songs got more attention, where they were pulled apart to see which bits were working and which weren't. "Songs were torn down and rebuilt over and over again to make sure each progression felt right," Wilson said. "I think that type of diligence, for Bad//Dreems, results in more ballads. We slowed songs down, we let them breathe. We gave life to the chords in new and exciting ways, with sparsity and sonics – whereas five years ago, we would have just flown into songs like one of those fire hoses on the loose you see on YouTube, and a song that could have been beautiful is instead pigeonholed as boorish pub rock."

The effort the band put into the songs didn't go unnoticed, with critics rating it as the fivepiece's best release to date – even if some of the reviewers couldn't quite let go of the 'pub rock' tag. Just after the album release, the band appeared on Triple J's *Like A Version*, playing their new single *Sonny* and a cover of The Warumpi Band's *Blackfella Whitefella*. For the latter tune, the band was bolstered by Emily Wurramara and Don Nunggarrgalu and Brad Bara from North East Arnhem Land band Mambali and some tall guy named Peter Garrett. The band got to know him earlier in the year when they played some support slots for Midnight Oil in the UK.

"I think I probably saw this song for the first time on *Rage*," Cameron said of the Warumpi Band tune. "I loved the clip and the song straight away. I discovered more about the band through Andrew McMillan book *Strict Rules*, which chronicled Midnight Oil's 1986 tour with the Warumpi Band through the centre of Australia and Arnhem Land. The Oils' support helped Warumpi Band get some national attention, although they never had the industry success they deserved."

Bad//Dreems also appeared on the bill for the 2019 Yours and Owls festival. Other bands from the Farmer and the Owl stable Totally Unicorn and The Pinheads were also playing but Hockey Dad would miss out due to their UK tour, which included a slot at the prestigious Reading Festival. The big names on the Yours and Owls bill included Amy Shark, Thundamentals, Vera Blue, Courtney Barnett and Baker Boy.

Way down the list were two bands that may well have not

made the must-see lists of many punters – due to a lower profile rather than their music. Sam Allen and his band played the Rad stage at 3pm on Saturday, while Husband Wants a Wife occupied that spot for a 20-minute slot at 1pm on Sunday. The unusual thing about the bands was a familial connection; Noah English played drums for Sam Allen, while his younger brother Luc was the singer/guitarist for Husband Wants a Wife (the band name comes from a member's mangling of the TV show *Farmer Wants a Wife*). It would be one of the few times brothers have been on the same Yours and Owls bill but in different bands.

In fact the brothers had only been in the same band once – for a primary school talent show. "That was before I started the guitar but just after singing lessons had started," Luc said. "We did an AC/DC song, where he just played the drums over a backing track. That was the band." The Yours and Owls gig was a big deal for Luc – at 16 he was underage so being a performer would be the only way he could get inside the festival.

After the festival, the Farmer and the Owl label took a step to secure its future – and that of the artists it had signed. Almost from the moment the alternative music world went mainstream in the 1990s, small labels got their pockets picked by the big boys. Those indie labels had signed bands hardly anyone outside the scene had either heard of or shown interest in. Then, after Nirvana changed everything, these bands had big record labels waving cash and the allure of fame under their noses – and off they went, leaving the small labels with nothing.

Since then, small labels looked for a way to counter that,

to avoid losing their big acts. In the case of Farmer and the Owl, that meant teaming up with one of them. In late 2019 the label signed a partnership deal with BMG, allowing the Wollongong label to release albums in Australia, while BMG had the rights for the rest of the world. It was a move obviously designed to keep Hockey Dad – the label's biggest act – in-house.

"If we kept it fully independent with independent distribution, it was probably going to get to a point where any of the bigger labels could swoop in and take them," Taylor explained. "We hit a point with the label where we needed to do a partnership with one of these bigger labels or just say 'we've done what we can, you guys need to go somewhere else'."

It worked out in Hockey Dad's favour – a large part of their image is the strong connection to Wollongong (and, of course, Windang). The BMG deal allowed them to stay on a Wollongong label while also having the weight and reach of a major.

28

One of the greatest things about Wollongong is that the beach and the bush are so close together. You can get out of the water, dry off, jump in the car and be walking through the bush in around 10 minutes – five in some areas. That's because the city is wedged in by the escarpment, which runs north-south for about 150 kilometres and turns the northern suburbs into a little strip of urban life between the blue of the ocean and the green of the bush.

But come summer time that bush can also be one of the worst things about living in Wollongong. Because it's been a long, long time since a bushfire tore through it and, when the heat rises, people start to wonder how much longer will their luck hold out. That last time was in October 1968, and today a lot more houses are a lot closer to the bush than they were in the 1960s.

That series of bushfires that hit the Illawarra have gone down in history as Black Monday – October 28.

That tag is misleading, as it makes appear as though the threat lasted a single day. A month earlier, there were fires in the south of the Illawarra at Albion Park and north in Scarborough.

In October, before Black Monday, fire crews battled blazes up north at Stanwell Park and Stanwell Tops, Waterfall and Appin. Some of those fires continued burning in inaccessible terrain for more than a week.

What became Black Monday started over the weekend with a fire heading towards Kembla Heights on Saturday. The village was protected but the fire made its way towards Dapto and Farmborough Heights.

Saturday also saw fires at Buttenshaw Drive at Coledale in the north, with the local bushfire brigade and residents battling the flames.

"It was an eerie sensation climbing the mountainside with the fire blazing," said firefighter Bill Rorison. "The whole hillside was alight."

The following day was Black Monday, where those fires kept burning and a fresh one started up, sweeping through Bellambi, Russell Vale, Woonona and Bulli.

"At midnight," the *Illawarra Mercury* wrote, "the whole coastal range from Unanderra to Coledale was still ablaze after a day of absolute disaster and chaos."

Gahans Avenue at Woonona was the location of one of many battles that day as fires tore through bushland near homes. Violent winds fanned the flames as high as 30 metres in the air and home owners in the-then sparsely populated street figured their homes were done for.

"By 1.30pm many residents had taken the complete

contents of their homes into the street," the *Mercury* reported. "They sat huddled on the footpath surrounded by armchairs, television sets, radios, bedding, tables and kitchenware. Many wept openly." With water running low, fire crews resorted to using sacks and branches to beat back the flames and save the homes before moving to the next fireground.

Twenty-five homes were lost that Monday, many of them along Bulli Pass, which was ablaze from top to bottom. "Ten homes were wiped out on Bulli Pass where flames cut a swathe down the mountain," the *Mercury* reported.

Photos showed the cruel randomness of the flames, with some houses razed while the neighbour's was left standing. At Bulli Hospital surgeons continued with an operation while hundreds of volunteers fought back a fire just outside.

Woonona-Bulli RSL was one of many institutions opening their doors to the homeless and emergency services. The club also sent food and several kegs of beer to the Woonona fireground.

In Coledale Heights 68-year-old Elizabeth Price suffered third-degree burns to her arms in a failed effort to save her house. "I know my attempts to try and stop the fire were feeble and useless," she said. "But I couldn't just stand there and do nothing. We did what we could but every time we put out one fire sparks started up another one."

Three aged care facilities – at Mt Keira, Thirroul and Figtree – were evacuated and hundreds of children in areas affected by fire were kept at school rather than sent home.

Barry and Nancy Weekes and their four children aged between one and eight – and a fifth due in November – lost almost everything when their Lachlan Street, Thirroul, rental property burned on Monday afternoon.

"I managed to get only one or two things before I could see the flames," Barry said from their temporary accommodation at the Fairy Meadow migrant hostel. "I ran like mad and when I looked back there was only a great sheet of flame. 'That's my home', I thought, and I felt like crying." WIN Television, which was broadcasting regular fire updates in several languages for the migrant community, lost its film library when embers from the Farmborough Heights fire set nearby grass alight.

"TV personalities Ron Ross, Terry Moore and Allan Hoy headed the studio firefighters," the *Mercury* reported. "Studio girls and office employees formed a bucket brigade to stop the burning grass from spreading to homes on the western side of Iris Avenue, Coniston."

By the end of the week, the threat had abated, except in the hard-to-reach bushland over the escarpment. That threatened the city in the first days of November when a two-kilometre firefront jumped Mt Ousley Road where weary firefighters had to again step up. No-one died in the Illawarra fires but 36 homes were lost, from Coledale down to Figtree.

Fundraising appeals were launched, with the Wollongong Mayor's appeal raising $34,000 in the 48 hours since it was launched the day after Black Monday. Sadly, some looked to take advantage of others' misfortune.

Brothers Kenneth and Cecil Puckeridge were caught looting homes in Bulli and Thirroul. Kenneth went to jail for a year, while his brother got a suspended sentence. Also, some employers threatened to sack volunteer firefighters or not pay their wages if they didn't return to work. The employers' stance quickly changed when it was impressed upon them how unpopular a decision that would be.

In the summer of 2019-20 it seemed like this had to be the time the escarpment would glow red. Hot, dry weather created the ideal conditions for bushfires across the state – and those fires came. That summer Illawarra residents who had been seeing the TV ads about bushfire plans finally decided it was time to organise one. Go-packs were stocked with vital supplies in the event they had to leave home in a hurry. On so-called Catastrophic fire danger days, where it felt like the air itself was about to combust, Wollongong people packed supplies, identification, insurance papers, photo albums and other sentimental items in their car before driving to work, because they didn't know if that day was to be the day when fires stopped them from going home. Every day people checked the RFS Fires Near Me app, hoping not to see some alert for a fire in the escarpment.

A massive firefront called the Currowan bushfire kept pushing its way up the coast from the holiday hamlets around Jervis Bay; by the time it was put out it had burned for 74 days. Coming in from the west was the Green Wattle Creek fire, another massive blaze that had been edging closer to the tinder-dry, long-unburnt Illawarra escarpment.

By the time the Black Summer fires were over, 18 million hectares of Australian bush had burned, 33 people had perished and nearly 6000 buildings had been destroyed. Yet somehow the Illawarra escarpment was left untouched, bushland to the south, west and up north was black and charred but the bush that hemmed in Wollongong remained green. That guilty feeling of being fortunate while others suffered fed into a desire to offer up whatever help people could.

One of those doing what they could was Hockey Dad, who set up a bushfire benefit concert at Windang's bowling club for January 24, On the bill were Tumbleweed, Totty, Shining Bird and Maddy Jane. "Billy's had a caravan down on the South Coast for a long time, and we grew up going down there a lot," said Stephenson, who used to holiday with Billy and his family. "It's a special place for us to go surfing and hang out and we've got a lot of friends down there so we really wanted to do something to lend a hand."

Their idea of a little concert soon got a whole lot bigger. Just a day after the announcement, ticket sales were so great they had to start hunting around for a bigger venue. "We wanted to do it at the bowling club," Fleming said. "We were keen to have it really low-budget and underground grass-roots style ... then we sold a lot of tickets, and Windang Bowling Club weren't really that excited to have more than 300 people."

That the show had to be moved came as no surprise to Tumbleweed singer Richie Lewis. "We're very proud to be involved in it," he said. "When we were asked to be involved with Hockey Dad, I knew it was going to be too big initially for Windang. Tickets flew out the window." The gig was moved to the North Gong Hotel because as Lewis said, it was about raising money for those affected. "We'd be doing them a disservice if we weren't able to get all those people in and get as much money as possible for them."

And bring the money in they did. In the end, Fire Fund

hit its $150,000 target, which went to the Rural Fire Service, NSW National Parks and Wildlife Service and the Red Cross Disaster Relief Fund. "The concert came together really well," Taylor said. "What started out as a conversation between Hockey Dad and us last month came together really well. It was great the other bands also agreed to donate their time."

29

When a band starts out, there aren't all that many people paying attention. But as their audience grows, as the album sales keep going up from one release to the next, as their songs get played on the radio, the number of plays on streaming services hit 10,000, then 100,000 and then a million, well then the pressure keeps building. Suddenly that band no-one really cared about once upon a time has everybody watching them to see what they do next.

That was where Hockey Dad found themselves in 2019. They had broken through to a new level with their *Blend Inn* album a year earlier, which barged into the top 10 and spawned a few classic singles. Three of them ended up in that year's Hottest 100 – a feat that put them on a par with Billie Eilish and Post Malone. *Join the Club* reached up to No18, with *I Wanna Be Everybody* coming in at No61 and *Sweet Release* at No73. On top of that *Blend Inn* was voted into third spot in that year's JJJ top albums poll.

Yes, there were a lot of eyes on them now, which caused no little stress when working on the next album. "I felt the pressure straight after we had some songs in the Hottest 100 and trying to write songs for [the next] record," Stephenson said. "I felt a bit of pressure from myself thinking 'Surely, I can't write a song as good as that one again'."

What helped overcome those nerves was a band trip out to Sofala, north of Bathurst. They stayed there for a few weeks in a house off a rough, dirt track – so rough that the band's van couldn't make it and they had to pile into Billy's 4WD to get there. Those weeks let Stephenson release the pressure valve.

"We went back to how we used to do it," he said. "We just played live and mucked around and had fun with it. That took all the pressure off and we found another sound for this record that we were really excited about. After the songs started coming, the pressure was gone."

Along for that trip was bassplayer Stephen Bourke. The frontman for Step-Panther (which also features Hockey Dad's manager Daniel Radburn – and Stephenson) as well as solo work under the SM Jenkins monicker, Bourke had played on all the band's albums, but only recently made the step up to performing live with them – Stephenson and Fleming realising their sound had developed to the point where they couldn't do the songs justice by themselves any more. But at this stage, he wasn't officially inducted into the band. "I don't think Steve really wants to be in Hockey Dad," Stephenson said, suggesting he gets all the fun while being able to dodge the drudgery of photo shoots and interviews. "He's okay playing with us now and has done all the recordings, but it's super casual. I think we're happy to stick with that and see how it all goes."

To record the new album, the band toyed with a few options, even considering heading to Ibiza before deciding to return to Seattle. "We just decided it was best to go back to where we know," Stephenson said. "When you go into a new studio it takes you a few days to get used to the place, to where things are and how to go about it. Because we'd already been there, going back the second time eliminated all that worry and we could get straight into it."

The weeks spent at Sofala had paid off, with the band having 30 songs to choose from for the new album. They'd also decided to take their time working on them, to see where they could go. "We had a unanimous decision that we would get more creative," Fleming said. "We would write a song, then peel it back and think 'what else could we do?'. We would try and figure out different little ways that we could spice it up."

The new album was to be called *Brain Candy*, which was both a spin on "ear candy" and a reference to the diverse sounds on the album. "The concept is for it to be like a little bag of mixed lollies," Stephenson said. "Every song on the record triggers a little bit of a different emotion or just a little taste in your mouth. It's a lolly, it can be sweet or it can be sour, but ultimately it's just there for a treat."

The first treat from the album came in November with the release of *I Missed Out*. The song was a good choice first-up; it was catchy and didn't step too far from the Hockey Dad sound many were expecting. "I remember just listening to lots of riffs and I kind of just wanted to write a song where

I play a riff," Stephenson said. "I just wanted to shred a solo for four minutes, and it kind of works out."

The subject matter of the song dealt with the problem of being away touring and missing out on what family and friends were doing at home. There would soon be an unexpected irony in the song when COVID hit and the band had nothing to do but stay at home. "We were gearing up to send ourselves back into the world again," Stephenson would say after the release of the album. "But then we got stuck at home for a couple of months. It's been good because we've been able to hang out with friends and family, we've been able to surf, reconnect with our old lives. But now I miss my old, *old* life."

The first taste of something different from *Brain Candy* came in February, with the release of the song *Itch*. "The demo started off as a delicate, droned-out kind of song," Stephenson said. "As we started recording it in the studio and adding drums and guitars we realised the potential it had for an epic fuzzed ballad so we ran with it. It's definitely the most non-Hockey Dad song we have recorded."

The video for the song, featuring Fleming and Stephenson being chased and then bitten by the undead, would set in play the zombie theme the band used to promote the album release later in the year. Directed by Laban Pheideas, the band headed to Los Angeles to film it. "We did a video with him a few years ago and we left this one all up to him," Fleming explained. "It was the first time we've ever said 'here's our song, just make up a video for it' and we'll see what happens. So he was like 'let's go zombies'."

"The make-up and wardrobe was probably the funnest

but also the most uncomfortable part of the day," Stephenson said. "We were coated in thick body paint and face masks during the steamy LA day while skating. But it was worth it to creep people out who were walking by us."

Around this time the band was planning for a big year on the back of the release of *Brain Candy*. "We're going to put the record out and then start touring," Stephenson said. "We're going to be going all over the world once again, which I'm really looking forward to. And at the end of the year I suppose we'll just start working on the next record once all this touring is done. Should be good."

But it wasn't. By March NSW was in lockdown, which put paid to any plans the band had to tour. The release of the album – slated for May 29 – was pushed back to the end of July because the lockdown meant vinyl pressing plants were shut down.

The Yours and Owls team managed to run what was one of the last music festivals before the lockdown – a MacCabe Park double-header with the Farmer and the Owl Festival on February 29 and A Sunny Afternoon the day after. The second gig, with headliner Missy Higgins along with Kate Miller-Heidke, Something for Kate and Ash Grunwald was pitched to an older crowd than Farmer and the Owl. "I think it's nice to be able to do something for one group of people," Tillman said, "but then also be able to use that same site and do something totally different that appeals to a whole bunch of different people."

Hockey Dad wasn't on the bill for either of the shows, meaning they missed a chance to play live for months before the country was hit by a certain pandemic. Instead, they had to be happy with the release of a third *Brain Candy* single in April, *In This State*. It was the first song they finished during the recording sessions for the new album. The song gained its stripes when it impressed You Am I's Tim Rogers. "We came up with most of it the weekend of Splendour in the Grass" Stephenson said. "We had just played a You Am I song with Tim and whilst rehearsing for it, I was playing around with the opening guitar chords. Tim seemed to like them, which got us even more excited to finish it and start playing it live."

The band didn't exactly sit around twiddling their thumbs waiting for the *Brain Candy* release date. In May, they released an EP of their first demoes – *Early Days* – recorded months before the *Dreamin'* EP came out. "We had no idea what we were doing at the time," the band said on their Facebook page, "and we sure as shit didn't expect to still be doing all of this seven years later ... so we thought we'd share these with you to say thanks heaps for supporting us after all these years." But fans had to be quick, the EP – which included two previously unreleased songs in *Mr Sunshine* and *Sambuca at Six* – was only available on Bandcamp for one day.

"In lockdown we were trying to keep ourselves interested," Stephenson said, "and we dug up these first demoes that we'd ever done. It was strange listening back to them. They didn't sound anything like we do now. It was fun to see that starting point, to see what we were doing – it was pretty crap."

There was also the planning for their novel COVID-safe way of playing a few gigs to launch *Brain Candy* come July – a pair of drive-in shows at Bulli Showground (long the home of the Illawarra Folk Festival). "We've never been to a regular drive-in theatre before so we have no idea what's going on," Fleming said. "The tickets for the first show just went straight away, which is awesome. People are obviously super-excited for live music and it's a good way to do it – everyone's safe and in the comfort of their car."

Tagged Alive at the Drive-In, the promo material echoed the zombie theme of the *Itch* video, and there was talk the band would play the shows in zombie get-up. However, things changed at the last minute. Just three days out, the NSW Chief Health Officer told residents to avoid gatherings of more than 10 people, which prompted Balunn Jones from Yours and Owls to remind people the drive-in shows were legal under the public health order – at least for now. "The issue that we are facing is that that could change at any moment," he said. "If there is an outbreak tomorrow or across the weekend, the NSW government could change that … and then we would have to postpone the event."

That's exactly what they ended up doing – though not because of COVID. Days of heavy rain had made the Bulli Showground "unusable" and so the shows were postponed just two days before the release of *Brain Candy*. That left them scrambling to come up with other ways to plug an album in the world of COVID. One of those approaches was already in place – Fleming and Stephenson driving around delivering special *Brain Candy* packs that included branded Hockey Dad stuff in a "collectable" cereal box. "We basically chose a bunch of people who had pre-ordered the album," Fleming said. "So we're driving around delivering these pre-ordered albums. Some of the people weren't even home though, it was quite funny. So many times we were greeted by a family member who had no idea who we were."

The other way to plug the album came on the fly – less than a week after the drive-in shows were cancelled the band played an online "live-scream" of a concert at Wollongong's Regent Theatre, just up the road from the Music Farmers store. Everything was hush-hush before the show for fear of Hockey Dad fans milling around outside the theatre begging to be let in. Inside Stephenson, Fleming and Bourke played the album live front-to-back (plus a cover of Pavement's *Cut Your Hair*) while dressed in zombie make-up as other socially-distanced zombie friends sat in the audience.

The makeshift album launch worked a treat – *Brain Candy* debuted at No2 on the Australian charts, only held off from the top spot by a surprise album release by Taylor Swift. Along with the album's release came an eerily appropriate single for these COVID times – *Germaphobe*. Totty frontwoman Kelly Jansch played the germaphobe in question for the video.

"At one point we were having so much fun that we almost forgot about the storyline I had planned and just started to figure out different scenes as we went along," Fleming said. "The peak of fun was the final scene where we started throwing home-made slime at each other, which quickly turned into a 'how are we going to clean all this' moment."

But, aside from the gig in the theatre and those two rescheduled drive-in shows in October, Hockey Dad couldn't do much of anything gig wise. Thanks to COVID, they'd be stuck at home for the year, having not played a real gig since February.

Like Hockey Dad, Totally Unicorn went the livestream route during the pandemic. In August 2020, they launched the 18-minute animated live concert Totally Unicorn: Live from the Magical Mind of Bunkwaa. Animated by artist Craig Bunkwaa, its aim was to support those friends in the music industry affected by the pandemic, via the creation of a GoFundMe campaign.

"Many of our friends in the music industry have been hit hard by the global pandemic," the band said on Instagram. "People whose livelihood depends on live music. Roadcrew, sound engineers, artists – all of them have had their careers and income put on hold. Tough times indeed."

Labelmates Bad//Dreems were in the unfortunate position of being in the UK on tour when the whole COVID situation went crazy. They'd played some support slots for the DMA's, including a huge show at the Brixton Academy, and only managed to get through of a few of their own shows before the worsening situation of the virus forced them to axe the rest of the tour and head home while they still could.

"The shows in Europe, they were the first to go," Cameron told *Rolling Stone*. "They limited the number of people that could gather and then it continued day by day. With all the changes that were happening, it just seemed ridiculous to be going on and playing shows when they were just talking about closing schools.

"Then, we were worried about getting back. We knew that we were going to have to quarantine when we got back, so that was going to mess with everyone. Some people that had bought pre-sale tickets weren't even turning up, so you could see the writing on the wall. We made the decision then to pull the pin."

Cameron looked on the bright side and saw the forced self-isolation and then the lockdowns as a chance to grab a huge chunk of uninterrupted writing time (singer Ben Marwe even wrote an acoustic COVID tune, *I Wanna Self-Isolate With You*). He also realised the band was in the enviable position of being at the end of an album cycle, unlike Hockey Dad who had an album to plug and no shows to play.

Bad//Dreems also managed to put out a new song – *Desert Television* – recorded during some downtime in the UK before they had to scarper. They used the studio of Rory Attwell, from Test Icicles and Die!Die!Die!. "He just had a bit of time to kill," Cameron said, "so we went into a rehearsal room in Brighton and worked on a few songs and then we recorded those over a couple of days in his little shoebox studio in Hackney. *Desert Television* was one of those songs. They were really only planned to be demoes, but that one we were happy enough given the state of everything. We may as well chuck it out."

30

Having signed up one Adelaide band in Bad//Dreems, Farmer and the Owl decided to go back there and get their second out of town band. A fourpiece Dreamo band, Paradise Club started in 2017, releasing its first single *Saturday Night*.

More than three years later the album that single came from would be released. "Our debut album began in 2016 as 30-something demos that turned into 15 recordable songs," songwriter and singer Gere Fuss told The Music. "Those initial 15 songs were recorded in our producer/drummer Jack Newlyn's childhood bedroom at the start of 2017.

"Creating an album is easy, you just need a bunch of songs. But making an album that you're satisfied with is another story. That's why it took like almost four years – we just kept disliking our old stuff."

They finally found 11 songs they liked enough to release their debut on Farmer and the Owl in July 2020. Musically it was upbeat, sounding like it came from the soundtrack of an '80s movie but Fuss' lyrics often took a darker slant.

"When I do reflect, I realise I'm more comfortable writing about the bleaker times," he said. "It's not that I haven't tried to write with a positive meaning, and a couple songs on the album are maybe a bit happier, but I just find myself being less engaged and satisfied with what I'm doing.

"Maybe I feel like I owe these darker moments in my life some sort of justice."

An example of this is the very sweet sounding *All You Got*. The light tones of the music are instantly uplifting and create a happy mood, but the subject matter of the lyrics is going in a rather different direction.

"At the end of 2018 I learnt about some family stuff that was going on," Fuss explained. "At the start of 2019 a close friend passed away. A month later my dog died. It was one of the worst times of my life but I learnt a lot from what had happened.

"The song is about that period of my life, how I should never take the time I have with people for granted, and how thankful I am to have a supportive network of family and friends. It's fucked up how certain things can make you feel helpless and isolated, yet how resilient and understanding of the world you can become."

Fuss puts the split in moods between words and music down to his attempts to be more positive in his songwriting – something comes out more in the tune than the lyrics. And he has a lot of chances to practice upbeat songwriting; there are folders and folders of song ideas at home.

"Sometimes I might be halfway through making a

sandwich and then I go, 'Yeah there's a song' and I'm off back in my room making the song," he told The Beat. "It can be random moments that will bring it on. I might hear something outside and I'll go, 'Yeah, fuck that's a song'. I'm always doing it."

Having signed two out-of-Wollongong bands in a row, Farmer and the Owl took things a step further, doing a deal with an out-of-Australia band. Boston indie rock act Vundabar was started by Brandon Hagen and Drew McDonald in high school in 2013. Running their own Gawk label they released three albums before hooking up with Farmer and the Owl.

Taylor became a fan of the band in 2017 when they played with Hockey Dad on a US tour. "The first time I saw Vundabar, they totally owned a show at the Bowery in New York," he said. "They were fun and full of energy but beneath all of that were some really amazing songs.

"After seeing them a few more times across the US on tour with Hockey Dad and getting to know them, I really wanted to help introduce the band to Australia."

So they signed a deal to release the band's new album *Either Light* in Australia. Hagen told the Alston Pudding blog that distribution was the big hurdle they had to overcome while owning their own label. "It was kind of just the last piece that we couldn't really do on our own in a way that was effective," he said. "If you want a record you can get it at a show or online, but it's not really in record stores."

For *Either Light*, the band worked in the studio with a producer for two weeks, which was a big step up from the time spent on their last two albums (recorded in three days and a week respectively). A key influence on the album was the TV series *The Sopranos* – lead character Tony Soprano even gets a namecheck in the song *Codeine*.

"I'd literally just watched *The Sopranos* two times through while I was writing the record, and I feel like Tony Soprano is an archetype for a lot of the American experience in a way," Hagen told Spin.com. "He's the ugliness and the underbelly of capitalism and our culture. A lot of the record sort of deals with this looming sense that we might be doomed, and I see Tony as this character where from the first scene, you know he's fucked. He's a doomed hero, and in that sense, he's a great symbol for what life is like now."

Though they were released in lockdown, the Paradise Club and Vundabar albums were already in train before COVID changed everything. It wasn't the same story for the Farmer and the Owl's third long-player of the year, which would be hit by heavy delays in vinyl pressing. Early on in the lockdown the idea formed to put out a new compilation, along the lines of the *Beached Friends* series of a few years earlier.

"It's something we've wanted to do for ages, but I guess it's never been a big priority and always been pushed aside," Taylor said. "The first two weeks of lockdown, everyone was like 'what is everyone going to do'?"

But the lockdown saw record pressing plants close down and, by the time they reopened, there was such a backlog of work, that the Farmer and the Owl double album *Family Values* had its release date pushed back to late 2020. Oddly enough for a vinyl-centric label, the CD version of the 17-track *Family Values* was released first.

The core of the release was new, live or unreleased tracks from most of the label's acts – The Pinheads, Paradise Club, Totally Unicorn, Vundabar, Bad//Dreems, Tropical Strength and TEES. Former signing Bec Sandridge along with Tumbleweed and Mother and Son were also there. And of course Hockey Dad made an appearance, with a cover of You Am I's *Purple Sneakers*. "We played that live at Splendour in the Grass in 2018," Stephenson said. "Tim Rogers from You Am I came up and sang with us, which was cool. I [had a] fan moment, but I think my dad was having a bigger fan moment."

For Taylor, curating a Farmer and the Owl mixtape was one of his favourite things about running a record label. "It's like making a playlist that actually becomes a real-life tangible product," he said. "For *Family Values* it was exciting to not only come across some of the fresh new sounds from our local area but also dig into the archive of covers that our artists have delivered as well as highlight new music and lost tracks from most of the F&O family of artists."

The cover featured artwork by Christopher Zanko – a former member of The Pinheads. The painting of an orange-brick house – located on the Princes Highway in the northern Illawarra suburb of Bulli - had previously seen him named a finalist in landscape painting's Wynne Prize.

"He's had a long association with the label from the start, as far as being a musician goes," Taylor said. "In that time, he's developed as an emerging artist too ... one of the best local artists and Australian [contemporary] artists. His artwork is so iconically Wollongong as well ... and suburban Australia."

Late in 2020, to the joy of their fans who had been waiting since 2013, Tumbleweed put out some new music. For several years, Tumbleweed had been talking about doing something like Sub Pop's Singles Club, where they released a song every month for a year The words turned into action in October 2020 – a year before the band's 30th anniversary – with the digital release of *Shadowland* – the first piece of new music from the band since 2013's *Sounds From The Other Side* album. Singer Richie Lewis called it "the best thing we've ever done".

"*Shadowland* is about the uncertainty of the future," he said. "These are strange times, dangerous and divisive times. When the truth is not believed, there is little you can trust or count on."

In late November, the second song, *Rebellion* went up online – the two tunes were also released as a double A-side single. "*Rebellion* is about feeling helpless, watching a slow train wreck, yet kicking against the inevitable and having a glimmer of hope that maybe we can change its course," Lewis said.

Both songs were recorded by former Radio Birdman vocalist Rob Younger. While he and Lewis both sent their kids to Thirroul Public School and ran into each other during the afternoon pick-ups, they never got anything happening until now.

"We thought it was about time we did something together, so we gave him a call to see he was up for doing a string of singles that was a homage to the music that turned us onto cool music, the bands we aspired to be like," Lewis said. "He was keen to be involved."

To close out what was a pretty crappy year Farmer and the Owl put out an EP with an appropriately apocalyptic title. It was a limited vinyl release of Bad//Dreems' 2013 debut EP *Badlands*. "We never released it on vinyl and the only hard copies that exist are the CDs that we released when we released it," said singer Ben Marwe. "So, we've been wanting to do it for years because people always ask if they can get one, but then we never have them printed. So that's kind of why we're going with it and I'm pretty happy about it actually."

Afterwards

With a book like this, you have to find an ending somewhere, no matter how arbitrary it may seem – hence the 2020 cut-off. But of course, the Wollongong music scene didn't stop at the end of 2020, despite what it may have looked like thanks to COVID. So this section is to touch on a few things that happened post-2020 and pre-publication.

The big one was the fact that Yours and Owls ended up being the first music festival held in Australia – and, according to some, the world – since the COVID shitstorm started. While other festivals simply pulled the pin and decided to wait another 12 months, Yours and Owls took a more positive approach. Heading into the usual October festival dates they opted to play it safe and push it back to January. At the start of December 2020 they realised a lot of the regulations were still undecided, so they pushed it back another few months to April 2021.

All the while there were some massive hurdles; the

COVID safety plan, for instance. The plan had to be lodged as an exemption to the Public Health Order in place at the time. If the restrictions eased, then the plan had to be reapproved. "Five weeks out from the event, we got a tentative notice, 'if the COVID situation remains the same, we expect your plan will be approved'," Tillman told *NME*. "It normally takes six months to plan a festival. At that point, we were like, 'okay, it's a gamble, but we need to press go'. We got our final sign-off from all other local stakeholders maybe a week and a half out from the event."

On top of that was the need to move up the road to a different venue – Thomas Dalton Park – so as to better implement the COVID safety plan. That involved splitting the crowd up into four self-contained sectors with a revolving stage in the middle. Oh, and the punters all had to be seated, so Yours and Owls needed to hire 14,000 white plastic bistro chairs and then cable tie them together to stop people moving them around.

But, to the surprise of many, the festival actually happened – even though with the seats and social distancing it didn't look like any festival anyone had been to before. While pleased to have pulled it off, Yours and Owls were lucky if they broke even. "Every step of the way we've been told by everybody 'this isn't going to go ahead', it's been met with constant negativity," Tillman told the *Mercury*. "If we were thinking financially, or thinking in hindsight or coldly, it isn't the smartest decision but you know there's a moral and an emotional thing that goes along with it which is why we have decided to push ahead."

In May, news broke that Yours and Owls were involved

in a plan to turn the much-loved CBD movie theatre the Regent into an Enmore Theatre-style venue. The promoters were teaming up with Joe McGuinness, the man behind ventures like popular Thirroul restaurant/bar José Jones. Yours and Owls' Balunn Jones had lodged the liquor licence application, which included a description of the group's plans for the venue.

"The Regent Theatre has great potential to enhance the artistic and cultural activities of the Illawarra," Jones wrote. "It is a beautiful old building that is being restored for regular public use.

"The business mission and goals [are] to establish a nationally recognised entertainment venue that presents live music and other performance arts of the highest level.

"The diverse spaces in the venue are being utilised to provide as many attractions as possible. This includes presentation of live performances, art shows, meeting spaces and food and beverage service."

The Music Farmers label continued its respect of the city's musical history in March, releasing another piece of the past on vinyl. In a gatefold album with extensive liner notes, they released all the studio recording from Proton Energy Pills. Meant to be released on Record Store Day 2020, it missed that target, thanks to the COVID pandemic.

Unfairly, the band has served as little more than a footnote for Tumbleweed; the latter grew out of the former, albeit without guitarist Stuart Cunningham (singer Dave Curley survived briefly as a member of Tumbleweed too, before the band sacked him). Tumbleweed's success came on the trail already blazed by the Protons; that band had done the hard yards, breaking through into the Sydney market, signing with Waterfront Records and making the top 10 independent charts.

At the time what they achieved was a big deal, because in the 1980s and 1990s Wollongong bands just didn't make any headway in the Sydney scene. Even then they served as an example to other musicians in Wollongong of just what was possible.

Cunningham was instrumental in the vinyl re-release. Suffering from cancer, when the idea was first discussed in 2019 he was keen because he wasn't sure he'd still be around for the release – so having the music out there on vinyl gained a new imperative. Fortunately, Cunningham got better and was able to get his hands on a copy of the Protons on vinyl.

In preparation for the release, Cunningham had to go back and listen to the old tunes. That's something no musician looks forward to; almost none of them ever sit down and listen to their own albums.

"There was a bit of trepidation going in," he said. "I'm thinking 'am I going to cringe listening to this?' It's really heartening with the Protons recordings the cringe factor was not there at all. I was really proud of the recordings and songwriting – for such young guys it's really good stuff."

Taylor from Music Farmers said the Protons came from a different time, where you had to create your own places to play. "I was a bit too young when they were around," he said, "but from what Dave has always told me, there was nowhere. There was no set venues to play original music, so they'd hire out halls, put on their own shows. That started original bands putting on their own shows in Wollongong, and from that, places like the North Gong and the Oxford started doing regular live stuff again."

Limited to 300 copies, there was such a demand for the Protons album that it entered the ARIA vinyl album charts in the first week of release – at No11. It would also be the year's biggest seller at Music Farmers.

By the end of May, things had gone pear-shaped again. After the start of the Delta outbreak of COVID, the government tightened restrictions, just days before the Yours and Owls all-ages show at the University of Wollongong. Those restrictions saw the festival – to be headlined by Hockey Dad – postponed and then cancelled. "To say we are bummed would be a massive understatement," the promoters said on the Yours and Owls Instagram page, "but we have all been here before and we know the steps so please follow the guidelines being asked."

With different states having different rules, interstate shows were an option for some. Hockey Dad headed to Queensland in June to play afternoon and evening gigs at the Fortitude Music Hall in Brisbane on Saturday June 26 and a show in the same city the night after. All of those shows had already been rescheduled three times due to COVID.

And all but the afternoon show had to be rescheduled again. As the band headed out for the encore of the arvo show they got a tap on the shoulder from the tour manager. The Queensland government had changed the definition of a hotspot – and backdated it. Hockey Dad – who had tested negative for COVID – had made it to Queensland on June 23, a day before that state declared Greater Sydney a hotspot.

But the government backdated it to June 21, which meant the band had to leave immediately and enter 14 days of hotel quarantine.

"The hardest part for me was just being on such a high from the show," Fleming said, "and dropping to such a low in an instant. We did everything by the book. And it all just fell apart so quickly. It was really hard for us to comprehend. And it still is."

Things kept getting worse. Bands thought long and hard about whether they held off releasing their new album until after they could tour it, and gigs got cancelled left, right and centre. Yours and Owls had teamed up with Vivid to stage *Pacific Highway*, which was a celebration of Wollongong and Sydney music in August. On the bill were Totally Unicorn and Scab Baby but of course COVID wasn't going to let that happen – it got cancelled too (though it would be rescheduled for January 2022).

Wollongong City Council tried to help out with a range of measures, including hiring music photographers Anna Warr and Chris Frape for the *City of Sound* photography exhibition in the mall. Among the musos having their pictures taken were Stephenson and local bands Tropical Strength, Floodway and the awesomely named Hellcat Speedracer.

Farmer and the Owl didn't let the COVID lockdown stop them from signing artists or releasing vinyl. Though they'd learned from the long delay experienced with vinyl copies of the *Family Values* comp arriving months after the release date. So the plan was there would only be release dates announced when the label believed they could deliver on them.

In September they picked up Canberra-bred but

Melbourne-based fourpiece Moaning Lisa. "Wollongong has always been close to our hearts," the band said in a release. "We love that Farmer and the Owl have small-town roots and then these big worldwide aspirations."

The connection came after the band sent an email with new music to label manager Kate Marning on a Friday night. "We've all been fans of them for numerous years now, so it was super-flattering that they may be interested in working alongside us."

The label released four singles from the band ahead of the October 2021 release of the *Something Like This But Not This* album. "It's our first album and so we wanted to capture who we are and who we have been as a band throughout this first part of our existence," the band statement said.

"The original thought behind the tracklist was to capture the dynamics and flow of our live set. We wanted to replicate the energy we have when we play on stage together but also experiment and do things we can only achieve with the luxury of recording in a studio."

The video for *Inadequacy* saw them working with pro wrestlers – as you do. "We were really inspired by the intimacy and the communication that's inherent in wrestling," said singer-guitarist Charlie Versegi. "You have to be so in sync and have so much care for your craft and the people you're working with to make it happen. So many times throughout the shoot, [wrestlers] York and Ritchie would stop and check-in with each other, or take a pause to talk about safety.

"Wrestling serves as a perfect visual accompaniment for *Inadequacy* – the intensity and suspense you feel seeing it performed combined with the self-awareness and strength that goes into training."

The band's full-length debut hit the streets in October. The recording started in Sydney but, with COVID beginning to rear its ugly head again, the band decided to hotfoot it back to their Melbourne base to wait it out in the hope they could return. It soon became clear that wasn't an option and, as luck would have it, a friend who lived within the restrictive radius of the Melbourne lockdown had a recording studio at home. So not only could they finish the album, they could take their time without racking up a huge studio debt.

"We were able to experiment a little bit more," Versegi explained. "As much as we come into recording sessions super prepared – and make sure that we can play everything perfectly before we show anyone – it was cool to be able to sit back and try out some different things.

"We could be more experimental with some synth tracks that we've used and putting different harmony ideas and stuff on that we probably usually would have had to put aside for the sake of getting things done within a certain timeframe."

Totally Unicorn, the heaviest band on the label, released four singles in 2021 – two out of lockdown and two in it. The first was *Like*, an attack on social media released in January. The song came about due to boredom brought on by the 2020 lockdown. The second single, written and released during the 2021 lockdown, was *Trust Fund Glee* – a tale of the have-nots attacking the have-it-easys.

"*Trust Fund Glee* is an ode to anyone who has fought for every inch of ground on the road to achieving their dreams," explained guitarist Aaron Streatfeild, "only to be surpassed by someone fortunate enough to have financial backing. It bemoans those who buy their way through life."

Or as vocalist Drew Gardner succinctly put it, "This is a 'fuck you' to the people that never have to worry about tomorrow".

The concept for the eye-catching animated video came from bassplayer Dean Podmore, but COVID turned its completion into a race against the clock. "A few weeks before shooting, the COVID situation in Sydney began to worsen," Streatfeild said, "with another lockdown imminent, we scrambled to put together a contingency plan.

"With most of the concept remaining, I shot some green screen footage and sent it off to our friend Carl Whitbread [of the Sydney band Lo! and graphic artist extraordinaire] to turn our humble footage into the vision Dean had originally intended.

"As with any musician or band over the last two years, COVID has stomped over most of our plans, tours and releases. So, in some ways, this clip is a testament to overcoming the doom and gloom the pandemic has held over our lives."

The third single, *Yeah, Coach* came out in October and – like the earlier singles – continued the development of the band's sound from the *Sorry* album. "This song is about the social pressures that come with getting older," singer Gardner said.

"Financial security, starting a family, making sensible decisions but at the same time being content with where things are at present. Who knows, things may change tomorrow but right now I don't want to hear it." It came with a slightly disturbing video of Gardner pushing a wheelbarrow with a hooded, apparently dead, body around the streets.

Just before Christmas, the band released the single *Fri(ends)*, which Gardner said was about people you used to know. "People that were once staples in your everyday life, now strangers you pass in the street," he said. "It's something that most people experience in life and it's even more relatable now, with so many of us relying on screens to stay in touch – which, let's face it, isn't enough to sustain some relationships."

Announced at the same time was the February 2022 release of their new Famer and the Owl album *High Spirits/Low Life*, which included *Fri(ends)* and *Yeah, Coach*, but not the two singles released in 2021.

In March, The Pinheads released the *New Love Dawn* single, a funky number the band felt was the perfect remedy for the mess than was 2020. "Why not boogie your way out of a year that should be forgotten fast?" the band reckoned.

But, as history showed, COVID wasn't done with us yet. It came back not long after the release of that single, forcing the band to be one of many that had to postpone or cancel tour dates. Instead of touring, the band got San Francisco-based producer Al Lover to remix the single. "Al's remix takes the song to a whole new realm, with flavours reminiscent of '90s Manchester and a sprinkle of dub for good measure," the band said.

In December, The Pinheads released the single *Heart of Darkness* – inspired by the Joseph Conrad novel of the same name. "The tempo and groove are deliberately slimy and soggy, pushing and pulling," the band said. "Lyrically, it's the story of someone getting deeper and deeper into a realm of insanity or something very strange, which is mirrored by the way the song gives you a feeling of a weird night out where you can feel a flowing force that pulls you along."

Tumbleweed also got into the singles swing late in their 30th anniversary year. While the lockdown largely put paid to the "singles club" idea because they couldn't get together and record anything (and the idea was to record something timely and immediately relevant) the band did manage to contribute to one side of a split seven – the other coming from Sydney psych-rock outfit Grinding Eyes.

Released on the tiny Tym Records label, Tumbleweed's tune was a cover of The Factory's *A Path Through the Forest* – one of only two singles the UK psychedelic band ever released. The cover version was subtle and understated – it was hard to pick the band as Tumbleweed.

In November, the band formally kick-started their 30th birthday party. They reappropriated the idea of a special box to collect the 'singles club' releases and announced a collection of 12 of the band's seven-inchers in a box along with a booklet and T-shirt. The release, limited to 500 copies, omitted any of the singles from *Return to Earth* and *Mumbo Jumbo* due to issues with getting the rights to re-release them. That collection would be another vinyl release that would overshoot its street date – though not because of the pandemic. The release was delayed when the pressing plant's seven-inch machine broke down.

Gigs throughout most of 2021 were hard to come by so bands had to take whatever came their way. Tumbleweed got lucky with their 30th anniversary shows; their five-night residency in the week of Christmas squeaked in just before another COVID outbreak saw events cancelled yet again.

For Hockey Dad, the COVID mess of 2021 meant they opted to play a live streamed performance for the University of Wollongong's online graduation ceremony in mid-October. The graduates sat and watched at home while the band played in the UniBar. The booking was part of the university's approach to make amends for its widely panned first attempt at an online graduation in March 2020. That event wasn't even live; the ceremony was pre-recorded and the graduates' names just scrolled up the screen like the end credits of a movie.

The band also took a bit of a left turn, teaming up with Sydney wine store Built to Spill to release their own wine – self-deprecatingly called House Red. In doing so, they joined the likes of The Chats, Cosmic Psychos, Cub Sport, Paul Kelly and The Amity Affliction, all of whom had already paired up with Built to Spill. "It's a shiraz that is completely vegan, no gross stuff added," the band said on Facebook. "A little spicy, a little slurpy and altogether a nice drop."

There was also a surprise album release – a live recording compiled from the Drive-In shows of a year earlier. "The drive-in shows were such a strange and exciting experience for us," the band said.

"The idea was so foreign, and we had no idea how it was going to play out. We wanted to record and release the show as a little memento from a very weird time in the entertainment industry where conventional gigs were out the window.

"Hopefully it brings back fond memories if you attended any of the gigs. If it's your first listen we hope you enjoy the show and we are sure you'll love the horns."

He meant car horns, by the way, not a brass section. The label got stung again by vinyl pressing delays due to COVID, having to push back the release date a few weeks to early November. When it did finally hit the streets, it was very well-received. It entered the national charts in the third spot; only Radiohead's expanded re-release *Kid A Mnesia* and Abba's *Voyage* blocked their way. In the independent album charts it was better – they grabbed the No1 spot.

The Yours and Owls team found they quite liked the autumn feel of the 2021 festival and so in November, they announced it would back at the same time in 2022. Making things much easier was a $700,000 federal government grant, which cushioned the blow to the bottom line in the wake of the 2021 show.

Because they were ploughing ahead while nothing much was going on musically, they managed to snap up a lot of artists keen for some shows. "We were able to get in early and book acts when not much was going on," Tillman told the *Mercury*.

"Having gotten [a music festival] out of the way and was successful, that gave a lot of the artists confidence that we'd be able to pull it off again when most events and different operators were not even booking line-ups during that time."

Befitting a newly post-COVID world, there was only one overseas act in the November 10 announcement – New Zealand singer Benee. She had been booked for the 2021 show but had to pull out due to the border closure between

Australia and New Zealand. The 2022 bill also included Hilltop Hoods, Bliss n Eso, Flight Facilities, Jungle Giants and Peking Duk. The local talent wasn't forgotten either. Around 35 per cent of the bill included musicians from the Illawarra and South Coast. That included Hockey Dad bassist Stephen Bourke, longtime punkers Topnovil, Good Lekker, Chimers and Hellcat Speedracer.

The future of that 2022 festival was looking a bit shaky by the end of 2021. A resurgence of COVID saw Yours and Owls deciding to cancel the planned New Year's Eve party at the North Wollongong Hotel. The 2022 Yours and Owls festival was in April and, if COVID had taught us anything, it's that plans can change quickly, but the team must have been casting a wary eye to their already-booked festival.

A few days after the November 2021 festival announcement Farmer and the Owl unveiled their new label signing. They returned to their hometown focus, signing up Illawarra rapper Kid Pharoah. While a step away from the sound the label was known for, it wasn't its first rap connection – local rap artist Angelo the Poet appeared on the *Family Values* compilation. In a statement, the Farmer and the Owl team tagged Kid as "one of the most interesting acts to come out of Wollongong in a while".

"Stylistically, in the last couple of years some interesting new artists totally different to what the local scene has typically produced have begun to emerge," the statement continued. "As we've dug into each of them, Kid Pharoah's fingerprints have been in there somewhere as a producer, collaborator or feature artist."

His first song for the label – *Burn the House Down* – had

echoes of The Prodigy but with a rapid-fire vocal delivery. In announcing his signing, Kid Pharaoh said he was looking to shake things up.

"I'm eagerly seizing the opportunity to break down barriers and present a fusion of genres divergent to the local norm - all while challenging perceptions of what a rap artist can do," he said.

The year 2021 closed out with a surprising blast from the past. Thirty years after they broke up, there was a new Proton Energy Pills single out. It had an unusual birth; three fans of the Protons had decided to pull the band's unreleased tunes from live bootlegs and other sources and then re-record them. They got in touch with singer Dave Curley and guitarist Stewart Cunningham to see if they wanted to take part – and the new vinyl was released on New Year's Eve.

Looking back at that late 1980s period that spawned the Protons, Curley remembered Wollongong was a bit of punchline everywhere else – and hometown bands were thought of as inferior.

"You were automatically a second class citizen if you're from Wollongong," Curley said. "Wollongong was made fun of, its only appearance in the media was to be made fun of – at least that's how I remember it from my childhood and I think that cultural cringe did go with that.

"Funnily enough, that was the way that we were treated by people running local venues. If we ever did get a gig at a pub here it was almost a locally enforced thing that 'local bands aren't in the same league as touring bands'."

That's certainly not something anyone could say about the Wollongong music scene these days. But it was the efforts of those who went before that allowed this fourth golden age to be as great as it is.

Bonus content: I didn't know they played here

For Wollongong music geeks of a certain age, it can be a bit of a parlour game to throw out the name of a well-known band, adding the kicker 'did you know they actually played a show in Wollongong?'.

It's less of a thing these days, with the Yours and Owls festival regularly bringing in the big names. That also seems to have led to a diminishing of the city's inferiority complex to the extent that it no longer seems surprising that the big names would chose to take the stage in Wollongong. But I can tell you, many of us remember a time when it was unbelievable that an international performer (or even a big national act) would come to our town.

While I have touched on a few of these visits in the text of *Lull City*, it just wasn't possible to shoehorn them all in. So here's a heap more, which perhaps shows us that other people thought Wollongong was worth turning up for a gig.

In December 1977, almost a year before releasing their iconic *Parallel Lines* album, Blondie played a show at the Wollongong Town Hall as part of the band's first Australian tour. Crowded House would play at the same venue in 1986.

Plenty of people remember punk legends The Ramones turning up for a show at Waves in January 1991. But that wasn't their first visit to the city – the Bruddas also played at the Wollongong Leagues Club on their first Australian tour in July 1980 – with Matt Finish the odd choice for a support act. On that tour, Wollongong and the Gold Coast were the only non-capital city shows.

A month later, on August 10, The Cure turned up on their *Get a Dose of The Cure* tour. Weeks later on August 24. The Vapors played the same venue on the back of their No1 single *Turning Japanese*.

In 1979 UK punk act The Stranglers performed at the Cabbage Tree Hotel in Fairy Meadow, the same place where the infamous Johnny Thunders played in 1986. Up the road is the Charles Hotel (named after Charles Waterhouse, of the Waterhouse racing dynasty that owned the pub). There's a rumour that Iggy Pop was slated to play a show there on his 1983 tour but pulled the pin due to a poor turnout.

In 1990, the biggest music venue at the time opened up. Waves at Towradgi filled a gaping hole in the market in the days before the Wollongong Entertainment Centre was built. Prior to Waves, the top venues in terms of size were the city's leagues clubs, meaning the city likely missed some big names due to the lack of a large place to play. Among Waves' list of famous international acts are Ice-T (1992), Faith No More and Alice in Chains (1993), Duff McKagan, Helmet and Beastie Boys (1994), The Offspring and L7 (1995), Mr Bungle (1996), Public Enemy (1998) and Sepultura (1999).

After it was opened in 1998 with a performance by Bob Dylan, the Wollongong Entertainment Centre played host to the biggest bands to visit town. These included Garbage and Alanis Morissette (1999), Tool (2002), Jack Johnson (2003) Meat Loaf (2004), Bryan Adams (2005), 'Weird Al' Yankovic and Pink (2007) and Brian Wilson (2010)

Around the same capacity as a decent-sized leagues club, the University of Wollongong hall tended to stick with Australian artists. However, they did book The Presidents of the United States of America in 1997, more than a year after their breakthrough *Lump* single. British acts XTC (1979) and The Fall (1982) also played on campus, as did indie darlings Pavement in 1993. The university also booked a few bands to play in the city's Master Builders Club, including Sex Pistol John Lydon's band PiL in 1989 and Mudhoney a year later.

PiL had played a few years earlier at Shellharbour Workers, which managed to land a few big names in the 1980s including a two-night stand for Motorhead in 1984, and Iron Maiden in 1985

Throughout the 1970s and 1980s, Australian acts on their way up would stop off in Wollongong. INXS played at Corrimal Leagues as early as 1979, which was before they had released their first single *Simple Simon*. They were regular visitors in the following few years playing shows at Dapto

Leagues, Woonona-Bulli Football Club, Wollongong Leagues, Port Kembla Leagues and the Charles Hotel.

From 1979, Midnight Oil became a common sight in the city's leagues clubs before moving to the likes of Waves and the university in the 1990s. Cold Chisel were down here since the mid-1970s playing shows two or three times a year with the Northern Suburbs Leagues Club and Mt Pleasant Sports Club being regular venues.

BIBLIOGRAPHY

BOOKS
Davis, Joseph, *DH Lawrence at Thirroul*, Collins, 1989
Engleheart, Murray, *Blood, Sweat and Beers*, HarperCollins, 2016
Eklund, Erik, *Steel Town: The Making and Breaking of Port Kembla*, Melbourne University Press, 2002
Hagan, Jim, and Wells, Andrew (eds), *A History of Wollongong*, University of Wollongong Press, 1997
Humphries, Glen, *Friday Night at the Oxford*, Last Day of School, 2018
Humphries, Glen, *Healer: The Rise, Fall and Return of Tumbleweed*, Last Day of School, 2020
Jones, Jaeson, *The Executives: Their Aim Was To Please You*, self-published, 2015
Linton, John Suter, *Bound by Blood*, Allen & Unwin, 2004
Nichols, David, *Dig: Australian Rock and Pop Music 1960-85*, Verse Chorus Press, 2017
Stacey, Terence J, *The Battles of the Sounds*, Moonlight Publishing, 1995
Stafford, Andrew, *Pig City*, University of Queensland Press, 2014
Vereker, Richard (with Abernathy, Mark), *The Fast Life and Sudden Death of Michael McGurk*, Allen and Unwin, 2010
Walker, Clinton, *Suburban Songbook: Writing Hits in Post-War/Pre-Countdown Australia*, Goldentone, 2021
Walker, Clinton, *Inner City Sound*, Verse Chorus Press, 2005
Wheeler, Warren, *Steel City Sound* exhibition catalogue, Wollongong Art Gallery, 2014
Wood, Anne, *More Tales From Our Streets*, A Wood, 2000
Wood, Anne, *Tales From Our Streets*, A Wood, 1999

NEWSPAPERS AND MAGAZINE
Barlass Tim, and, Smith, Alexandra, 'Father who lost son to overdose at Defqon.1 says don't stop festival', *Sydney Morning Herald*, September 18, 2018

Begley, Patrick, and Evans, Michael, 'Absolutely tragic: Premier vows to shut festival down after two overdose deaths', *Sydney Morning Herald*, September 17, 2018.
Bishop, Karin, 'Songs of youth win award', *Sydney Morning Herald*, December 29, 1990
Brandson, Barry, 'The Del-Fi's are waiting until Ossie thinks they are ready', *Illawarra Mercury*, December 6, 1961
Butler, Joshua, 'Bands get chance to break out', *Illawarra Mercury*, May 22, 2014
Butler, Joshua, 'Bar strikes fresh note', *Illawarra Mercury*, September 6, 2013
Butler, Joshua, 'Beautiful noise to sound out at MacCabe Park, *Illawarra Mercury*, April 11, 2014
Butler, Joshua, 'Creating a band brand', *Illawarra Mercury*, September 10, 2014
Butler, Joshua, 'Fresh hope for bars and music venues', *Illawarra Mercury*, January 10 2014
Butler, Joshua, 'Fun-filled festival returns bigger and better', *Illawarra Mercury*, October 4, 2014
Butler, Josh, 'Group aims to hit chord', *Illawarra Mercury*, August 24, 2013
Butler, Joshua, 'Hallelujah chorus for gig strategy', *Illawarra Mercury*, February 20, 2014
Butler, Josh, 'Hockey Dad's top run of musical form continues', *Illawarra Mercury*, August 13, 2014
Butler, Joshua, 'Illawarra's Live Music Taskforce gets to work', *Illawarra Mercury*, August 23, 2013
Butler, Joshua, 'Music festival with a difference', *Illawarra Mercury*, September 30, 2013
Butler, Joshua, 'Noise rule changes music to their ears', *Illawarra Mercury*, March 7, 2014
Butler, Joshua, 'Parkside: DJs Making a Big Noise', *Illawarra Mercury*, May 13, 2004
Butler, Joshua, 'Yours and Owls going out with bumper party', *Illawarra Mercury*, July 17, 2013

Carty, Lisa, 'Concert security outrage', *Illawarra Mercury*, February 3, 1986

Carty, Lisa, 'Storm Aid adds $40,000 to fund', *Illawarra Mercury*, December 17, 1998

Carty, Lisa, 'Storm Aid concert funds stalled', *Illawarra Mercury*, June 5, 1999

Carty, Lisa, 'Storming back: Festival celebrates Wollongong's spirit', *Illawarra Mercury*, November 20, 1998

Casey, Bill, 'The forgotten idol', *Illawarra Mercury*, December 11, 2003

Clarke, Peter, 'Concert-goers plan to rock Bob Millward', *Illawarra Mercury*, February 4, 1986

Clarke, Peter, 'Steelers may lose liquor licence', *Illawarra Mercury*, February 4, 1986

Cornford, Philip, 'Flood victim take on insurers', *Sydney Morning Herald*, October 8, 1998

Cornford, Philip, 'The big flood insurance castaways fight for justice', *Sydney Morning Herald*, October 19, 1998

Cosgrove, Shady, 'Light goes out at the Bulb', *Illawarra Mercury*, July 24, 1999

Crabb, Brendan, 'Look who was at Wollongong's Last Frost festival', Illawarra Mercury, August 20, 2017

Crabb, Brendan, 'Rock duo in isolation', *Illawarra Mercury*, June 29, 2021

Crabb, Brendan, 'The Greens 'Sniff Off' campaign to be present at the Yours and Owls music festival this weekend', *Illawarra Mercury*, September 28, 2018

Delfino, Frank, '200 ban: unionists threaten Laws boycott', *Illawarra Mercury*, September 7, 1979

Delfino, Frank, 'Casino key to $50m resort bid', *Illawarra Mercury*, December 20, 1974

Delfino, Frank, 'Millions promised by casino', *Illawarra Mercury*, December 21, 1974

Delfino, Frank, 'The king meets his opponents', *Illawarra Mercury*, September 8, 1979

Duffy, Jodie, 'School of rock', *Illawarra Mercury*, November 4, 2006

Duncan, Moragh, '2 Vox FM: The Sounds of Silence', *Illawarra Mercury*, July 19, 1989

Duncan, Moragh, 'Community radio gasps for air time', *Illawarra Mercury*, July 20, 1989

Duncan, Moragh, 'Making waves', *Illawarra Mercury*, July 24, 1993

Failes, Geoff, 'Band backing floods in', *Illawarra Mercury*, November 5, 1998

Failes, Geoff, 'Chronology of a disaster: after the flood – two years on', *Illawarra Mercury*, August 17, 2000

Failes, Geoff, 'Stuart Park hoons to face tougher council', *Illawarra Mercury*, October 19, 1993

Halliday, Anne, '2 Vox venture is set to make waves by June', *Illawarra Mercury*, February 12, 1988

Han, Esther, 'New laws to hold drug dealers responsible for NSW music festival deaths', *Sydney Morning Herald*, October 23, 2018

Hannan, Liz, 'Ousley car plan wins enthusiast', *Illawarra Mercury*, March 15, 1994

Heininger, Peter, 'Leagues club bans pop concert', *Illawarra Mercury*, May 10, 1979

Humphries, Glen, 'Brothers don't band together for October's Yours and Owls festival', *Illawarra Mercury*, May 31, 2019

Humphries, Glen, 'Legendary Wollongong band Proton Energy Pills on vinyl again', *Illawarra Mercury*, March 19, 2021

Humphries, Glen, 'The tragedy and triumph of the 1998 floods', *Illawarra Mercury*, August 13, 2018

Humphries, Glen, 'Thirst' column, *Illawarra Mercury*, November 19, 2011

Humphries, Glen, 'Tumbleweed come out of the shadows with some new music', *Illawarra Mercury*, October 14, 2020

Humphries, Glen, 'Wollongong's devastating flood of August 1998', *Illawarra Mercury*, June 6, 2016

Kennedy, Sharyn, 'Gong Beat', *Illawarra Mercury*, March 14, 1969

Kennedy, Sharyn, 'Gong Beat', *Illawarra Mercury*, August 1, 1969

Kennedy, Sharyn, 'Gong Beat', *Illawarra Mercury*, August 8, 1969
Kennedy, Sharyn, 'Gong Beat', *Illawarra Mercury*, September 5, 1969
Kennedy, Sharyn, 'Gong Beat', *Illawarra Mercury*, October 25, 1969

Langford, Ben, 'Regent Theatre revival set to rock with Yours and Owls, McGuinness', *Illawarra Mercury*, May 21, 2021
Langford, Ben, 'Savvy operators introduce funky to city nightlife', *Illawarra Mercury*, November 22, 2013
Love, Tony, 'Radio 2OO, club in a rock first', *Illawarra Mercury*, September 21, 1979

Mardon, Cydonee, 'Nurses running to show the love', *Illawarra Mercury*, March 19, 2013
McCabe, Kathy, 'Aussie music festivals are being urged to address gender imbalance in line-ups', *Daily Telegraph*, June 15, 2016
McCabe, Kathy, 'Banging a 'Gong', *Daily Telegraph*, September 29, 2018
McIlwain, Kate, 'CBD liquor view sought', *Illawarra Mercury*, January 9, 2015
McIlwain, Kate, 'Drinking culture at clubs draws scorn', *Illawarra Mercury*, January 15, 2015
McIlwain, Kate, 'Humber decision on ice', *Illawarra Mercury*, December 3, 2014
McIlwain, Kate, 'Long road for Humber', *Illawarra Mercury*, March 12, 2015
McIlwain, Kate, 'Small bars, big benefits', *Illawarra Mercury*, April 13, 2011
McIlwain, Kate, 'What you won't see at this year's Yours and Owls festival', *Illawarra Mercury*, July 31, 2018
Minus, Jodie, 'Red tape silences shop's music shows', *Illawarra Mercury*, October 28, 2008
Mitchell, Peter, 'Four arrested in police crackdown', *Illawarra Mercury*, February 20, 1995
Morrissey, Daniel, 'New station puts strain on old rivals', *Illawarra Mercury*, October 3, 1991

Mouhtouris, Alethea, 'So what's the solution?', *Illawarra Mercury*, March 3, 1994

Myler, Janine, 'Gong Beat', *Illawarra Mercury*, March 20, 1970

Nelson, Peter, 'N-Lets: Good time avant-garde', *Roadrunner*, June 1979

Palathingal, George, 'Hockey Dad review: Ratbag rockers winning over fans with waves of fun', *Sydney Morning Herald*, September 9, 2018

Parkins, Brianna, 'Farmer and the Owl festival-goers choose what to pay', *Illawarra Mercury*, January 13, 2015

Parkins, Brianna, 'Small venues set bar high', *Illawarra Mercury*, February 7, 2015

Patterson, Glynnis, 'Eatery 'under siege',' *Illawarra Mercury*, June 1, 1993

Patterson, Glynnis, 'Screaming crowd forces police retreat', *Illawarra Mercury*, March 1, 1994

Patterson Glynnis, 'Stuart Park hoons pelt officers', *Illawarra Mercury*, October 26, 1993

Patterson, Glynnis, 'Stuart Park hoons will die – police', *Illawarra Mercury*, June 2, 1993

Paver, Chris, 'Explosion rocks Wollongong CBD', *Illawarra Mercury*, August 29, 2012

Randall, Sheridan, 'Hidden gems – better business', *Illawarra Mercury*, August 2, 2011

Ritchie, Emily, and Calvert, Alana, Defqon.1 deaths backlash: 'Close this down forever', The Australian, September 17, 2018

Savage, Desiree, 'Eco-friendly camping at Wollongong music festival', *Wollongong Advertiser*, May 31, 2017

Savage, Desiree, 'Fans fuming after hour-long queues at Jimmy Barnes' Wollongong concert', *Illawarra Mercury*, February 13, 2018

Savage, Desiree, 'Festival rule 'overreaction'', Illawarra Mercury, February 19, 2019

Savage, Desiree, 'Gong's accidental festival', *Illawarra Mercury*, October 2, 2015

Savage, Desiree, 'Here's what The Saints, Ali Barter and YouTube have to do with Wollongong', *Illawarra Mercury*, November 1, 2018

Savage, Desiree, 'Solar-powered bars, compost at Wollongong's Yours and Owls festival', *Illawarra Mercury*, July 25, 2019

Savage, Desiree, 'Wollongong Mayor labels new NSW Government festival rules an 'over reaction'', *Illawarra Mercury*, February 19, 2019

Savage, Desiree, 'Wollongong Mayor's rock star speech at Sydney protest to keep music festivals alive', *Illawarra Mercury*, February 22, 2019

Savage, Desiree, 'Wollongong's Yours and Owls festival announce lineup for 2022', Illawarra Mercury, November 10, 2021

Savage, Desiree, 'Yours and Owls 2017 the best festival yet', *Illawarra Mercury*, October 1, 2017

Savage, Desiree, 'Yours and Owls claim new NSW music festival regulations could wipe them out and hurt national economy', *Illawarra Mercury*, February 13, 2019

Savage, Desiree, 'Yours and Owls used to lure volunteers to Puckeys Estate reserve', *Illawarra Mercury*, August 17, 2018

Schekowski, Margaret, 'The alternative advertising agency', *Illawarra Mercury*, November 6, 1982

Simpson, Bill, 'Radio 2 Double 0 moving up to Fort Drummond', *Illawarra Mercury*, May 7, 1979

Simpson, Bill, 'Wave FM no longer rules airwaves', *Illawarra Mercury*, September 28, 1995

Simpson, Nathan, 'Radio revolution sweeps Illawarra', *Wollongong Advertiser*, January 25, 1995

Sjostedt, Arne, 'Two piece gathers momentum', *Canberra Times*, December 16, 2010

Sorenson, Tina, 'Last few insurers play Scrooge at Xmas', *Illawarra Mercury*, December 22, 1998

Stewart, Alison, 'Sherbet rocks Wollongong', *Illawarra Mercury*, August 21, 1978

Taylor, Vicki, 'FM station moves out of the bathroom', *Illawarra Mercury*, March, 26, 1982

Thompson, Angela, 'Complaints shut down live music at The Patch', *Illawarra Mercury*, February 13, 2013
Thompson, Angela, 'Illawarra bands rally round to support paralysed mate', *Illawarra Mercury*, January 12, 2013
Thompson, Angela, 'Café owners charged over graffiti', *Illawarra Mercury*, May 26, 2012
Thompson, Angela, 'Café owners graffiti charges dismissed', *Illawarra Mercury*, November 28, 2012
Thompson, Angela, 'Drug dogs sniff out 43 revellers at Yours and Owls festival', *Illawarra Mercury*, October 1, 2018
Thompson, Angela, 'Vandals leave ugly 'bomb' on bar wall *Illawarra Mercury*, March 17, 2012
Tonkin, Shannon, 'GPT tour reveals transformation of CBD site', *Illawarra Mercury*, December 2, 2012
Tonkin, Shannon, 'Owls of protest as wall art goes', *Illawarra Mercury*, February 7, 2012
Tonkin, Shannon, 'Paralysed bar owner fined for drink driving', *Illawarra Mercury*, September 5, 2013

Unknown, '$10,000 concert loss rocks hapless Wolves', *Illawarra Mercury*, October 2, 1984
Unknown, '200 hotel criticised by SM', *Illawarra Mercury*, October 13, 1979
Unknown, '2WL celebrates 25th birthday', *Illawarra Mercury*, October 9, 1956
Unknown, '2WL waves hello to FM', *Illawarra Mercury*, July 4, 1992
Unknown, 'A midsummer night's Oils', *Illawarra Mercury*, February 1, 1986
Unknown, 'A wild night', *Illawarra Mercury*, February 3, 1960
Unknown, 'American pop stars' holiday eve concert', *Illawarra Mercury*, April 23, 1970
Unknown, 'Appalling catastrophe', *South Coast Times*, August 2, 1902
Unknown, 'Ball boycott as Minutes ticked off', *Illawarra Mercury*, August 29, 1968
Unknown, 'Ball was quiet, after all', *Illawarra Mercury*, August 31, 1968

Unknown, 'Ban on at midnight: top pops lose out', *Illawarra Mercury*, May 15, 1970

Unknown, 'Bare bodies pass censor', Illawarra Mercury, April 1970

Unknown, 'Battle stations! Another voice hits the airwaves', *Illawarra Mercury*, January 10, 1978

Unknown, 'Big Stuart Park plan passed', *Illawarra Mercury*, October 23, 1958

Unknown, 'Casino finances heroin trade', *Illawarra Mercury*, July 6, 1977

Unknown, 'Billy Thorpe concert flops', *Illawarra Mercury*, April 5, 1976

Unknown, 'Casino assessment released', *Illawarra Mercury*, February 4, 1975

Unknown, 'City dance erupts into brawl', *Illawarra Mercury*, May 9, 1969

Unknown, 'City hears casino case', *Illawarra Mercury*, March 4, 1975

Unknown, 'City says big hello to 2 Double 0', *Illawarra Mercury*, January 1, 1979

Unknown, 'City vetoes casino plan', *Illawarra Mercury*, April 15, 1975

Unknown, 'Coast pop show to cost $7000', *Illawarra Mercury*, April 28, 1970

Unknown, 'Conservatives oppose casino', *Illawarra Mercury*, February 11, 1975

Unknown, 'Council defers casino decision', *Illawarra Mercury*, April 22, 1975

Unknown, 'Council lifts ban on caravans in Stuart Park', *Illawarra Mercury*, February 23, 1966

Unknown, 'Delay won't stop pop promotion', *Illawarra Mercury*, December 10, 1975

Unknown, 'Disappearance of Stuart Park lessee', *Illawarra Mercury*, July 19, 1963

Unknown, 'Discotheque owner defeated by problems', *Illawarra Mercury*, July 9, 1970

Unknown, 'Dreadful explosion at Mt Kembla', *Illawarra Mercury*, August 2, 1902

Unknown, 'Firm to open skating rink', *Illawarra Mercury*, September 23, 1967

Unknown, 'Fire inquiry: the destruction of the rink', *Illawarra Mercury*, September 3, 1889

Unknown, 'Firebug runs riot in radio station', *South Coast Times*, August 8, 1966

Unknown, 'Floodwaters did cover casino site', *Illawarra Mercury*, March 13, 1975

Unknown, 'Hold-up held up star', *Illawarra Mercury*, May 17, 1969

Unknown, 'Hot group meets cold reception', *Illawarra Mercury*, May 22, 1972

Unknown, 'I want my name cleared', *Illawarra Mercury*, July 7, 1977

Unknown, ' "I want to hold your hand" in Keira Street' South Coast Times, March 5, 1964

Unknown, 'Ice rink bills too hot to go on', *Illawarra Mercury*, January 14, 1970

Unknown, 'It's off! Council says no to pop festival site', *Illawarra Mercury*, December 23, 1975

Unknown, 'It's porn power!', *Illawarra Mercury*, December 18, 1975

Unknown, 'Johnny hits rock bottom', *Illawarra Mercury*, July 7, 1978

Unknown, 'Last tenant leaves Stuart Park', *Illawarra Mercury*, October 3, 1964

Unknown, 'Laws signs with 200', *Illawarra Mercury*, September 7, 1979

Unknown, 'Little Richard 'sent' teenagers', *Illawarra Mercury*, October 2, 1957

Unknown, 'Malicious gossip', *Roadrunner*, July 1979

Unknown, 'McCabe [sic] Park to become garden', Illawarra Mercury, August 12, 1948

Unknown, 'Meeting to air radio needs', *Illawarra Mercury*, June 18, 1986

Unknown, 'Music group set own standard', *Illawarra Mercury*, April 30, 1970

Unknown, 'New-look disco planned', *Illawarra Mercury*, July 8, 1971

Unknown, 'No 2JJJ relays to region', *Illawarra Mercury*, July 27, 1983

Unknown, 'No to Rowe show in town hall, *Illawarra Mercury*, July 11, 1967

Unknown, 'Our big rock-in Sunday', *Illawarra Mercury*, March 26, 1970

Unknown, 'Our Cook Day today', *Illawarra Mercury*, April 28, 1970

Unknown, 'Park scheme experiment', *Illawarra Mercury*, December 22, 1958

Unknown, 'Police alerted on pop concert', *South Coast Times*, July 13, 1967

Unknown, 'Pop festival doomed', *Illawarra Mercury*, December 30, 1975

Unknown, 'Pops v Pink Pussy Cat', *Illawarra Mercury*, August 30, 1968

Unknown, 'Radio 200 fined for breaches', *Illawarra Mercury*, May 19, 1979

Unknown, 'Radio 2WL stays right in tune', *Illawarra Mercury*, March 12, 1983

Unknown, 'Radio station's appeal succeeds', *Illawarra Mercury*, April 10, 1979

Unknown, 'Rejuvenation of eastern Crown Street, Illawarra Mercury, April 18, 1968

Unknown, 'Rockers thrill 5000 crowd', *Illawarra Mercury*, April 17, 1979

Unknown, 'Rowe show shifted to Corrimal', *Illawarra Mercury*, July 12, 1967

Unknown, 'Sherbet lays 2200 in aisles', *Illawarra Mercury*, June 29, 1976

Unknown, 'She's only sixteen! Starting a teenagers' night spot', South Coast Times, December 19, 1963

Unknown, 'Spotlight on Yours and Owls', *Coal Coast Magazine*, Issue Two, Winter 2018

Unknown, 'Station emphasis on music: radio aims at younger market', *Illawarra Mercury*, January 11, 1978

Unknown, 'Stuart Park closed to campers', *Illawarra Mercury*, June 17, 1964

Unknown, '30 New Year's 'revellers' arrested', *Illawarra Mercury*, January 2, 1982

Unknown, 'This rocked a large cordon of police', *Illawarra Mercury*, October 11, 1968

Unknown, 'The Beach Boys hit high note', *Illawarra Mercury*, April 24 1970

Unknown, 'The Disaster at Mt Kembla', *Sydney Morning Herald*, August 1, 1902

Unknown, 'The Elite Skating Rink', *Illawarra Mercury*, April 6, 1889

Unknown, 'They waited … 15 hours', *South Coast Times*, July 17, 1967

Unknown, 'Tin Panners plan happening', *Illawarra Mercury*, December 27, 1969

Unknown, 'Teenagers mob pop singer', *Illawarra Mercury*, December 29, 1969

Unknown, 'Tornadoes are young, but …', *Illawarra Mercury*, September 29, 1961

Unknown, 'Tuned in: our incredible cover star, musician Bec Sandridge's debut album is hitting high notes', *Coal Coast* magazine, issue 10, September-November 2020

Unknown, 'Wagga council may ban play', *Illawarra Mercury*, March 30, 1970

Unknown, 'Warning – leave the grog home', *Illawarra Mercury*, February 1, 1986

Unknown, 'Wee Liz gets big break on pop show', Illawarra Mercury, December 4, 1968

Verity, William, 'Take two: Louise Keyte and Katie McKenzie', *Illawarra Mercury*, April 28, 2012

Visentin, Lisa, NSW festival licensing scheme on the chopping block, Sydney Morning Herald, May 13, 2019

Walker, Donna, 'Car enthusiasts in high revs over 'hoon' insult', *Illawarra Mercury*, June 7, 1993

Walker, Donna, 'Park signs aim to put hoons in a spin', *Illawarra Mercury*, February 25, 1995

Walsh, Kate 'Scanning right space', *Illawarra Mercury*, November 9, 2012

Zalunardo, Paul, 'Cool change on its way to the city', *Illawarra Mercury*, November 12, 1998

REPORTS AND JOURNALS

Baker, Sarah, Cantillon, Zelmarie, and Nowak, Raphael, *Sounds of Our Town – The Wollongong Edition*, Sounds of Our Town, 2020

Cantillon, Zelmarie, Baker, Sarah, and, Nowak, Raphael, 'A cultural justice approach to popular heritage in deindustrialising cities', International Journal of Heritage Studies, May 27, 2020

Donaldson, Mike, 'Redback Graphix', *Australian Left Review*, No 77, 1981

Ehrlich, Brenna, 'Hockey Dad: Five albums that changed my life', Tidal, February 9, 2018

Gallan, Ben, 'Mild-mannered bistro by day, eclectic freak-land at night' – the Oxford Tavern as heterotopia and cultural asset', UOW honours thesis, 2010

Graham, Harriet, 'Inquest into the death of six patrons of NSW music festivals', State Coroner's Court of NSW, November 8, 2019

'Review of the operation of the Music Festivals Act 2019, NSW Government, June 2020

Southall, Nick, 'The WOW factor: Wollongong's unemployed and the dispossession of class and history', *Illawarra Unity* journal, Volume 8, Issue 1, December 2008

Southall, Nick, 'WOW: The Wollongong Out of Workers Union', *Illawarra Unity* journal, Volume 6, Issue 1, January 2006

State Coro

'The music and arts economy in NSW', NSW Parliament Planning and Environment committee hearing transcript, July 4, 2018

'Wollongong City Council Cultural Plan', Wollongong City Council, January 2014

WEBSITES

Apter, Liam, 'Some thoughts, feelings and images from Last Frost festival', Pilerats, 2017

Bonadies, Ben, 'Vundabar's *Either Light* at the end of the tunnel, Alston Pudding Music Blog

Boutros Tommy, 'Hockey Dad: On Haunted Houses, Bending in and Weet -Bix, lunchboxtv, January 30, 2018

Butler, Joshua, Radar Illawarra

Butler, Joshua, Bleached

Chapman, Cassidy, '2018 Yours and Owls Festival review', Scenestr. October 6, 2018

Chesler, Josh, 'Vundabar were inspired by *The Sopranos* on *Either Light*', Spin.com, March 13, 2020

Colburn, Randall, 'Hockey Dad announce new album, *Blend Inn*, share *Homely Feeling*', Consequence.net, October 20, 2017

Condon, Dan, 'Farmer and the Owl was like no other festival in the country', Double J website, March 5, 2019

Condon, Dan, 'Why Farmer and the Owl is bringing boundary-pushing music to regional Australia', Double J website, February 26, 2019

Davies, Hayden, 'Exclusive: Stream Tropical Strength's debut album *Zutti* with a track-by-track walk-through', Pilerats

Davies, Hayden, 'The chaos of Cry Club, the band that will never be boring', Pilerats, 2020

Dias, Avani, Laneway organiser warns 'high-risk' classification could end its Sydney leg', Hack, February 25, 2019

Earp, Joseph, 'Ben Tillman on the evolution of Yours and Owls festival', The Industry Observer, June 16, 2017

Fuss, Gere, 'More Comfortable Writing About Bleaker Times': A Deep Dive Into Paradise Club's Debut LP', The Music, July 21, 2020

Gregoire, Paul, 'Don't kill live music: an interview with festival promoter Ben Tillman', Sydney Criminal Lawyers blog, February 20, 2019

'How I started a boutique Aussie music festival and how you can do', Tone Deaf, September 24, 2015

Jenke, Tyler, 'What happens to a band when COVID-19 cancels their tour?', Rolling Stone, April 2, 2020

Jenke, Tyler, 'Track by track: The Pinheads take us through New Album *Is This Real*', Tone Deaf, July 4 2019

Jolly, Nathan, 'Hang on did the NSW festival laws actually just get worse?', The Music Network, October 21, 2019

Katzif, Mike, 'Review: Hockey Dad *Boronia*', NPR, August 4, 2016

Lowrey, Tom, 'Second pill-testing trial at Groovin' the Moo hailed a success as partygoers dump dangerous drugs', abc.net.au, April 29, 2019

McCarthy, Dylan. 'Mother and Son', Tone Deaf, October 10, 2013
Martin, Lisa, 'Pill testing at Groovin the Moo festival potentially saves seven lives, organisers say', *The Guardian*, April 29, 2019
Mixdown, 'Totally Unicorn say their sorrys' (sic)

Neville, Brendan, 'Bad//Dreems: a band that aren't afraid of anything or anyone', Happy Mag

Radas, Zoe, 'Bad//Dreems; Alex Cameron gives the skinny on *Doomsday Ballet*, Stack, October 18, 2019

Scott, Tim, 'Stream early recordings from '80s Australian punks the Sunday Painters', VICE, January 25, 2015
Shemesh, Yasmine, 'Hockey Dad's vibes are the result of a lifelong friendship', On the A.Side, August 16, 2016

The Music, 'Premiere: The Pinheads – The Pinheads, May 11, 2017
'Tropical Strength to release album *Zutti* on May 11, 2018', Grande Rock, May 4, 2018
Tunbridge, Brooke, 'Bad//Dreems explain their new sound on *Doomsday Ballet*', Volume Media, September 11, 2019

Underwood, Alex, 'Hockey Dad lets us in on the road trip playlist that's kept them alive during their US tour', Pilerats

Welby, Augustus, 'Crafted over three-and-a-half years, Paradise Club's debut album is finally here', The Beat, July 14, 2020

Wheeler, Warren, Steel City Sound, various pages

Young, David James, 'Hockey Dad and the Village That Raised Them', LNWY, May 2018

'Yours and Owls is one of the best bloody festivals in Australia', Savage Thrills, 2018

INDEX

2 Double O (See i98fm)
2-Tapes 31
2WL (See Wave FM)
30 Days of Yes 156-157
5x5x5 121
5 Crown Lane 77-78, 218

A.B. Original 164
ABBA 275
A Comedy of Errors 57
A Hard Day's Night 13
A Ruffian 178
A Sunny Afternoon 250
Abstract Classic 7, 101-102
AC/DC 29
Adam Buckland Ensemble 60
Adams, Bryan 281
Aints, The 209
Albion Park 20, 240
Alice in Chains 171, 281
Alison Wonderland 191
ALL 64
Alloy Forces 64
Amigos Restaurant 53
Amity Affliction, The 274
Amyl and the Sniffers 209
Angelo The Poet 276
Angels, The 163
Angus and Julia Stone 191
Anomie 74
Antony and the Johnsons 177
Apple Candy dance 22
Arcade Fire 170
Archy Punker 227
Arkell, Frank 42
Armstrong, Luke 116
Asteroid B-612 70

At The Drive-In 164
Austinmer 4
Australian Music Prize 175
Avanu, Tanya 228

Babymachine 68-69, 114, 121, 122, 124, 191
Bad//Dreems 111, 126, 234-236, 254-255, 256, 260, 262
Baker Boy 236
Baker, Sarah 201
Balgownie 162
Bandstand 16
Bara, Brad 236
Barcode 79-80
Barkley, Glenn 64
Barnes, Jimmy 168-169, 208, 229
Barnett, Courtney 141, 156, 175, 236
Bass Drum of Death 126
Batrays 109
Beach Boys, The 27-28
Beached Friends 107, 109, 137, 150-51, 259
Beaches 156
Beachhouse 209
Beastie Boys 281
Beatles, The 12-13, 123
Bee Gees 15, 18
Bellambi 154, 160, 240
Belmorgan Property Group 65-66
Benee 275
Beniuk, David 59-60, 163
Bennett, Michael 139, 140
Bennie James and the Hesitant Few 122
Berejiklian, Gladys 211-213, 216
Berkeley 14, 112

Berkeley High School 14
Besgrove, Jacqui 68
Beverley, Ben 136
Big Top festival 155
Blakey, Cath 192
Blink-182 59, 149
Bliss n Eso 70, 275
Blondie 71, 280
Blue, Vera 148, 236
Bluejuice 70
Bluesfest 213
BMG 238
Bonnie 'Prince' Billy 177
Bootleg Rascal 117
BotBots, The 178
Bourke, Stephen 247, 276
Brown, David 39
Bracode 67-68, 115, 124
Bradbery, Gordon 96, 201, 214
Braithwaite, Daryl 168
Brandon Park 48-49
Brother Brick 70
Buckland, Adam 60
Bugaloo 24
BugGirl 78
Built to Spill 274
Bulb 59
Bulldoze All Bowlos 121, 122
Bulli 114, 240, 260
Bulli Pass 161, 241
Bungalows, The 90, 136
Burdon, Eric 163
Burling, Nathan 122-123
Burrows, Lucy 52
Bushfires 239-245
Butterfly 32
Byrnes, Ossie 14, 16

Callaghan, Michael 44
Cameron, Alex 235, 254
Campbell, David 164
Camp Cope 175

Cantillon, Zelmarie 201
Capitol Hall 23, 27
Carmel E-Klastic 32
Casey, Bill 17
Casinos (both legal and illegal) 53-54, 112-113
Castro's 85
Cerezo, Lio 130-131
Challenger 7 70
Charles Hotel 11, 30, 280, 281
Chastity Belt 148
Chats, The 274
Chimers 184-185, 276
City of Sound 268
Checkmates, The 15
Clapton, Richard 163
Clark, Nate 125
Cleves, The 23
Cloher, Jen 156
Clouds, The 4
Cloud Control 155
Coffin Cheaters 14
Cochrane, Eddie 10
Coke Ovens 46
Collegians 26-27
Collins, Trina 121, 122
Computer Town 99
Coniston 47, 241
Coniston Hotel 47
Conran, Peter 56-57, 115-116
Cold Chisel 168, 282
Coledale 240, 241
CondoFest 207
Cook, James 1, 27
Cornford, Maryanne 61
Corrimal 9, 12, 18, 31
Corrimal Community Hall 9, 19, 21, 29, 30-31
Corrimal Leagues Club 279
Cosmic Psychos 274
Cosmic Z 64
Crash Craddock 12
Crowded House 280
Crown Theatre 10, 12

Cry Club 182-183, 203
Cub Sport 155, 191, 274
Culprits, The 59-60
Culture Bank 107
Cunningham, Stewart 70, 265-266
Cure, The 69, 280
Curley, David 63, 64, 265
Curley, Lenny 121, 125
Curnow, Aaron 176-177

Dalla Pozza, Simon 74-76
Dappled Cities 97
Dapto 29, 240
Dapto Leagues Club 281
Dapto Showground 29
Darling Downs 114
Davis, Wayne
Dawn Collective, The 72
Deafhaven 209
Deane, Belinda 115-116
Dear Seattle 227
Death Cab for Cutie 171, 172
Del-Fi's, The 16-17
Derek's Accent 18
Defqon.1 210, 212-213
Dettol 59
Devlin, Johnny 12-13
Diamond, Neil 113
Dicey Rileys 116
Diesel 168
Dinky Crash 64
Dliver 72
DMA's, The 175
Doing It Locally 40
Dodgy World 60
Donnelly, Stella 209
Don't Kill Live Music rally 214
Downtown Motel 52
Downunder Records 18
Doyle, Marty 114-115
Dragon 27
Drop-Offs, The 184
Dropping Honey 69-70, 122
Dune Rats 154, 164, 182

Dylan, Bob 281
DZ Deathrays 126

Earl's Court 120
Easybeats, The 29
Eat My Chainsaw 63
Eilish, Billie 246
El Sanchez 75, 233
Enfant Terrible 191
English, Jon 34, 207
English, Luc 237
English, Noah 237
Erika's Jive 61, 163
Erwin, Kerrie 115
Escarpment, The 137
Evans, Peter 32
Evol 38, 125, 184
Executives, The 17-18, 124

Fairgrounds 155
Fairy Meadow 48, 79, 103, 116, 241, 280
Faith No More 281
Fall, The 281
Falls Festival 110
Family Values 157, 259-261, 268, 276
Fangin' Felines, The 184
Farmborough Heights 240, 241
Farmer and the Owl (festival) 21, 97, 98, 105, 125-126, 154, 208-210, 214-216, 250
Farmer and the Owl (label) 7, 106-107, 109, 131, 137, 137, 140, 149-150, 157, 167, 170, 176, 187-188, 189, 218, 236, 256, 258, 259, 262, 268, 276
Farnham, John 22, 24, 180, 234-235, 237
Farrier, Will 180
Fast Times at Ridgemont High 151, 152
Feik's Device 122
Festival crackdown 201-215

Festival of Wollongong 207
Figtree 28, 241
Fire Fund 244-245
Fireworks Café 61
Fists, The 72
Fleming, Billy 98, 100, 101, 109, 111, 158, 171, 172, 173, 190, 218, 244, 248, 251, 252, 253, 268
Flight Facilities 275
Floodway 268
Flume 170
Flying Circus 24
Flying Fish Café 57
Foo Fighters 171, 172
Frape, Chris 268
Fraternity 25
Freshwater 23
Fugazi 64
FUgG 60-61, 75, 114, 115
Fumes, The 70
Fuss, Gere 256-258

Gallan, Ben 56-57
Gang of Youths 136
Garbage 281
Gardner, Drew 140, 141, 209, 220-221, 222, 270, 272
Garrett, Peter 236
Geoff & The Spicolis 151-152
Gilbert, Warwick 30-31
Girls Get Loud 68
Gimme Head 146
Gluyas, Greg 64
Golden Plains 216
Gong Beat 20, 22
Good Lekker 191, 276
Gooseberry Island 4
Gordon Bruce 37
Grand Hotel 35, 79
Grant, Simon 88
Gravity 65-66
Greetings from Wollongong (movie) 44-45
Grinding Eyes 273

Grinspoon 155, 158
Groovin' the Moo 211-212
Grunwald, Ash 250
Gurrumal 175
Gym Instructors 122

Hagan, Brandon 258
Happy Accident 49
Hard-Ons, The 78
Harp Hotel 79
Hawke, Bob 42
Hee Haw 60, 75
Helensburgh 17, 70
Helmet 281
Hellcat Speedracer 268, 276
Helter Smelter 116, 121-122, 198-199
Higgins, Missy 149, 250
High Beam Music 60, 75, 106, 232
Hiltop Hoods 275
Hoadley's Battle of the Sounds 25-26
Hockey Dad 7, 100, 102, 103, 104, 105, 106-107, 117, 118, 124, 126, 129-131, 136, 137, 142-146, 151, 153-154, 155, 156, 170-175, 176, 186, 190-191, 198, 203, 209, 218, 227, 236, 238, 244-245, 246-253, 254, 267-268, 273-275, 277
  Albums/EPs
  Blend Inn 157, 170-174, 246
  Boronia 142-146, 152, 157, 171, 172, 173
  Brain Candy 246-253
  Dreamin' 7, 107, 109-110, 111. 142, 172, 174, 251
  Early Days 251
  Live at the Drive-In 274-275
  Songs
  A Night Out With 144
  Can't Have Them 130, 143
  Germaphobe 253
  Get Free (cover) 174
  Girl With Two Hearts 143
  Homely Feeling 157-158, 170, 171, 173

I Missed Out 248-249
I Wanna Be Everybody 171, 173, 190, 246
I Need a Woman 110, 124, 143
In This State 250-251
Itch 249
Join The Club 157, 246
Jump The Gun 143
Lull City 108, 109, 110
Mr Sunshine 251
Purple Sneakers (cover) 156, 260
Sambuca at Six 251
Seaweed 109
So Tired 144
Sweet Release 173, 175, 246
Two Forever 144-145
Homewrecker 191
Horror My Friend 224, 226
Hospital the Musical 139
How Machines Work 76-77
HOPE festival 115-116
Humber 95-97
Hunt Brothers 64
Hunting Grounds 98, 103
Husband Wants a Wife 237
HyFest 116-117
HyTest 78, 116, 122, 125, 126

I98fm/2 Double 0 34-37, 207
Iacurto, Raf 233
Ice-T 281
ICAC 80-83
Illawarra Folk Festival 114, 214, 251
Illawarra Hotel 59
Imagination, The 16
Immolate 78
Impedance Records 70, 78, 106, 218
Independent Music Monthly 59
INXS 229, 281
Infusion 71
Ireland, Tim 72
Ironworkers Club 44, 59
Iron Maiden 281

Irwin, Nick 78, 106, 198

Jacob 227
Jamberoo 114
Jane, Maddy 244
Jansch, Kelly 182
Jarman, Bodie 219
Jeb Taylor Hotel 191
Jebediah 126
Jeff St John and Copperwine 20, 24
Jenkins, John 59
Jenny Broke the Window 109
Jezebels, The 156
Jimmy and the Boys 27
Johnny Johnson and the Rebels 11, 124
Johnson, Jack 281
Johnson, Vivien 30
Jones, Balunn 86, 137, 193, 252, 265
Jose Jones 265
Jungle Giants, The 191, 275

Kangaroo 4
Kanine Records 130-131
Kelly, Paul 274
Kemblastock 114-115
Kennedy, Dennis 45, 47
Kennedy, Sharyn 20, 22-23
Kenning, Shane 121, 122
Kerr, Bob, 15
Kuepper, Ed 209
Kevin Borich Express 29
Kid Pharaoh 276
King Gizzard and the Lizard Wizard 98
King, Zondrae 21-22
Knipe, Toni 21

L7 281
La La La's 184, 228
Ladyhawke 148
Lahey, Alex 164
Lake Illawarra 4-5, 99, 112
Lake Illawarra High School 101, 110
Lake Illawarra Hotel 101
Lane, Damien 69-70
Laneway Sydney 215-216
Lang, Robert 171-173
Last Frost festival 155
Lawrence, DH 3-4
Laws, John 36-37
Leadfinger 70, 78, 121
Lewis Erica 67
Lewis, Richie 188-189, 244, 261-262
Lee, Derek 17
Leo de Castor and Friends 23
Leftards, The 177
Liberteen Ranch 85, 93, 136
Like a Version 236
Ling Yeow, Poh 139
Little Prince, The 86
Little Richard 10-11, 124
Little River Band 28
Live at the Wireless 174
Living End, The 101, 110
Lorde 170 Los Tones 97
Los Pintar 227
Loud Whisper 102
Lydon, Johnny

MacCabe, Henry 205-206
MacCabe Park 21, 34, 38, 98, 168-169, 206-208, 209
McCann, Barry 54
McCartney, Paul 13
McKagan, Duff 281
McKinnon, Peter 45-46
Machine, Kristy 68-69
Machine Translations 97
Macklemore 171
Mad Polly 149
Maidza, Tkay 148

Mambali 236
Man Bites Dog 48
Manfred Mann's Earth Band 28
Manzini, Michael 180
Marksmen, The 14-16, 25
Marning, Kate 269
Martin, Ann 93-94, 185
Marwe, Ben 254, 262
Mascis, J 209
MasterChef 139
Master's Apprentices 23
Master Builders Club 281
Matt Finish 280
Matthews, Wendy 163
Matt Finish
Mayhew, Rebecca 67, 68, 125
Meat Loaf 281
Mental as Anything 163, 168, 169
Mercury BlueScope Band Competition 102-103
Meredith 216
Merinda 5
Merry Widows 60
Mess Hall, The 126
Methyl Ethyl 191
Middle Kids 175
Midnight Oil 4, 48-49, 203, 236, 279-282
Mighty Morphin Power Rangers 143
Miller-Heidke, Kate 250
Millward, Bob 49-50
Minutes, The 15
Mirage 35
Mistaken Identity 49
Moaning Lisa 268-270
Mocambo 21
Moginie, Jim 4, 203
Mojo Hands 125
Monstrous Blues 60, 72, 75, 114
Morgan, Beth 81-82, 225
Morris, Jenny 163
Morris, Russell 20-21
Morrisette, Alanis 281
Morrissey, Daniel 39

Moss, Ian 168
Mother and Son 7, 78, 90, 97, 218-220, 260
Mother Goose 27
Motorhead 281
Mountain Sounds 213
Mr Bungle 281
Mt Keira 241
Mt Kembla 114, 204-205, 240
Mt Kembla mining disaster 204-205
Mt Ousley 162
Mt Pleasant Sports Club 282
Mt St Thomas 37
Mudhoney 279
Mudlungs 59, 64
Music Farmers (store) 76-79, 97, 120, 184, 220, 224
Music Farmers (label) 106, 108, 218, 233, 265-267
Musicoz 8, 70-71
Mutated Noddies 48
My Bloody Valentine 69

N-Lets 32
Nabilone 120, 122
Neville, Brian 22-24
New Christs 78
Newcastle 195, 200-201, 215
Newton-John, Olivia 17
Nguyen, Diana 210, 212
Nice Folk, The 121
Nirvana 171, 186
Nixon, Merv 36-37
No Dress Regulations 64
NOFX 64
Noble, Peter 213
North Beach Kebabs 80, 83
North Gong Hotel 6, 67, 244, 266, 276
North Wollongong 80
Northern Bowl 22
Northern Suburbs Leagues Club 282
Nowak, Raphael 201-202
Nunggarrgalu, Don 236

O'Brien, Steve 121
Ocean Alley 191
Offspring, The 281
Ohana 72, 139, 179
O'Keefe, Johnny 10, 17, 28
Olbrich, Arnie 14
Oliveri, Nick 78
Oliver's 22-23
Osbourne, Ozzy 179
Otis Bar 86, 149
Outset festival 20-21
Oxford Tavern 6, 7, 50-53, 54-60, 65-67, 72-73, 79, 88, 115, 122, 202, 225, 227, 266
Oxley, Rod 82-83

Pancake Day 115
Pantera 179
Paradise Club 256-258, 259, 259
Parkside DJs 136
Parkinson, Doug 22, 34, 207
Patch, The 11, 79, 103, 116, 198-199, 280
Pauljevic, Nigel 212
Pavement 253, 281
Peking Duk 191, 275
Performing baboon 3
Pham, Joseph 210, 212
PHFAT 126
Phillis, Jodi 4
PiL 281
Pill testing 210-213
Pinheads, The 7, 107, 126, 131, 136, 137, 151, 154, 164, 203, 209, 228-229, 236, 259, 260, 273-274
   The Pinheads 154
   Is This Real 228-229
Pink 281
Pink Fits, The
Pink Pussycat Ball 15-16
Pioneer Hall 21
Plant Room 47, 61
Player, Jez 229
Plum, Thelma 148

Podmore Dean 271
Pop, Iggy 280
Porcelain 67, 70-71
Port Kembla 123, 128-129, 185
Port Kembla Leagues Club 281
Port Kembla steelworks 2, 41-42, 47, 127-129, 229
Porter, Neil 15
Post Malone 246
Pounderhound 72
Preatures, The 136, 137, 164
Presets, The 164, 170
Presidents of the United States of America 281
Project Contemporary Artspace 121
Proton Energy Pills 45, 47-48, 61, 70, 124, 265-267, 276-77
Psyfari 213
Pulse 59
Public Enemy 281
Pyjama Tops 26

Queens of the Stone Age 78
Quilty, Ben 178

Rad Bar 92, 94, 105, 106, 108, 111, 176, 209, 224, 225-228
Radburn, Daniel 92, 103, 107, 111, 130, 226-227, 247
Radiators, The 146
Radio ban 34
Radio Birdman 4, 29-31, 77, 203, 261
Radiohead 275
Raengal, Peter 45
Raised as Wolves 227
Ramones, The 280
Rand, Chris 179
Ratatat 85
Redback Graphix 44-45
Redback Music 59
Redback Records 6, 77
Reddy, Helen 18
Reeves, Charles 'Chicka' 54
Regent Theatre 253, 265

Rex Hotel 11
Reyne, James 163
Richie and the Creeps 114
Rick and the Bad Boys 18
Riley, Heather 183
ROADS 233
Robinson, Steven 57
Rolling Stones, The 112-113, 123
Rollins, Henry 185
Rose Tattoo 29
Rowe, Normie 18-19
Ruby Tuesdays 180-181
Russell Vale 240
Russell W 178
Ryan, Paul 178

Safia 117, 164
Sam Allen 236
Samonella Dub 136
Sampa The Great 148
Sandon Point 84, 85
Sandridge, Bec 7, 136, 137, 148-150, 151, 164, 203, 260
Saints, The 203
Scab Baby 268
SCABZ 230
Scamm 35
Scarborough 240
Scooter Rock Chix 68
Schultz, Julianne 41-42
Scobie, Annabelle 181
Segression 72, 124, 179
Sepultura 281
Servo, The 185
Sex Pistols
Shadowski, Chuck 104
Shark, Amy 175, 236
Sherbet 25, 28
Shifter 60, 64, 75
Shihad 75
Shining Bird 97, 109, 126, 136, 137, 156, 178, 203, 244
Short Fuse 177-178
Side Effect X 72, 179

Sing, Sing, Sing 17
Six O'Clock Rock 16
Skating rinks 51-52, 53
Skyhooks 28
Slipknot 179
Slugfuckers, The 32
SM Jenkins 247
Smith, Adam 86, 89, 197-198
Smith Street Band, The 136
Smith's Hill 33
Snider, Shaun 181
Social Outcasts 63
Socketwood 63-64
Solid Effort 151
Solomon Wright Crusade 20
Something for Kate 250
Soul Agents 18
Southall, Nick 43
Spilt Milk 146-147
Spit Chewy 181-182, 191
Splendour in the Grass 155, 251
Sports, The 27
Spunk Records 176-177, 178
Spy Vs Spy 49
Stanwell Park 131, 148, 240
Stanwell Tops 240
Starr, Ringo, 13
Steel City Blues 41-42
Steel City Sound (exhibition) 73, 123-124, 218
Steel City Sound (website) 120-121
Steel City Pictures 44
Steel Town Sounds 48
Stefanovic, Alex 16
Stefanovic Karl 16
Step-Panther 92, 109, 126, 227
Stephenson, Zach 98, 100, 101, 130, 158, 172, 173, 190-191, 227, 244, 247, 248, 249-250, 260
Sticky Fingers 117
Stiffys, The 104
Storm Aid 163-164
Storms of 1998 160-163

Storm Water Action Group (SWAG) 162-163
Strange Tenants 49
Stranglers, The 280
Stratton, Nathan 184, 228
Streatfeild, Aaron 141, 222
Stuart Park 44, 133-135, 163-165, 191
Stumbling Jesus Mosquito 74
Sultana, Tash 175
Sunami 6, 8, 59
Sunday Painters 45-47, 115, 125
Sunray Farm festival 112-114
SURF³ 109
Svegie's Vegies 48
Sweet Sweet Bulbs 60
Swift, Taylor 253

Tabak, Glen 81-82
Table of Knowledge 2, 80, 83
Tamad Shud 20, 23
Tame Impala 85
Tarrawanna 14, 47, 186
Tarquin 32
Taylor, Dane 178
Taylor, Jeb 7, 58, 70, 74-79, 97, 105, 108, 125, 130, 167, 187, 197-199, 202-203, 218, 233-234, 245, 258, 260, 266
Teen Queen 207
TEES 107, 137, 167-168, 209, 260
Tek, Deniz, 29-31, 77, 203
Terminal Records 45-46
Tertangala 61
Teudt, Matt 219-210
The Australian Independent Music Show 40
The Good Trash 63
The Occy 122-123
The Sopranos 259
The Young Doctors 17
Third Eye Stimuli 177
Thirroul 3, 4, 11, 176, 241
Thirroul Pleasure Grounds 3
Thomas Dalton Park 264
Thomas, Denise 61
Thorpe, Billy 28, 163

Thumlock 60, 75, 120, 125, 231-233
Thundamentals 236
Thunders, Johnny 280
Tiki Coffee Lounge 53
Tillman, Ben 7, 84-86, 87, 88, 89-91, 94, 96, 106, 107, 108, 117-118, 136, 147, 155, 165-166, 169-170, 192-193, 208-209, 228, 234, 250, 264, 275
Tillman, Lizzie 167-168
Tin Pan Alley 20, 25
Tired Lion 148
Tommy M and the Mastersounds 87, 102
Tooke, Jonathon 183
Tool 281
Topnovil 276
Tornadoes, The 14
Totally Unicorn 7, 92, 139-141, 164, 203, 209, 220-222, 236, 253-254, 260, 268, 270-272
   Horse Hugger 140, 141
   Dream Life 220, 141
   Sorry 220-222, 271
Totty 182, 244
Towradgi 85, 163
Trans Electric Records 76
Tremors, The 14
Triple J/Double J 37-38, 110, 157, 170, 174-175, 215-216, 246
Tropical Strength 107, 189-190, 209, 260, 268
Tumbleweed 7, 47, 61-62, 72, 74, 75, 92. 103, 121, 123, 143, 170, 171, 186-188, 191, 207, 231, 232, 244, 260, 261-262, 265, 273-274
   Tumbleweed re-release 187-188, 218
   Shadowland/Rebellion single 261-262
Turkish Green Electric, The 23
TV Jones 30
Twilights, The 25

Unanderra 160, 240
Unearthed 38
Unearthed High 110
Unheard, The 47, 48, 115, 125
Unscene 122
University of Wollongong 6, 39, 56, 61, 79, 84, 97, 104, 109, 111, 153, 281, 282
Unsworth, Barrie 36
Up Down Festival 215
Urge Records 177
Urquhart, Felicity 70
Utterbox 68

Van Dyk, Ronny 60, 177-178
Vandenberg, Tim 31
Vanns, The 191
Vapors, The 280
Vellar, Frank 81-82, 225
Velvet Elevator 224, 226
Vennsquidink 122
Ventolin 74-75
Vereker, Richard 54
Versagi, Charlie 269, 270
Violent Soho 155
Vines, The 85, 174
Voight/465 32
Violet Crumble 25
Vox FM 8, 38-40, 59
Vulpes Vulpes 109
Vundabar 258-259, 260

Waifs, The 149
Walking Who, The 90, 92, 97, 109, 137
Wanderers, The 25, 124
Warumpi Band, The 236
Warner, Dave 26-27
Warr, Anna 268
Warrawong 22
Warren, Ray 179
Waterfront Records 47, 187, 266
Waterhouse, Bill 112
Waters, Kim 59
Wave FM/2WL 25, 33-37
Waves 85, 280, 282
Webster, Alastair 189
Webster, Russell 189, 178

Wedgetails from Windang 109
Wee Liz 18
Wesley Snipers, The 122
West Dapto 113, 114
Wheeler, ,Warren 7, 11, 61, 96, 116-117, 120-124, 185
Westfield Figtree 28
White Blanks 151
Whiteley, Brett 4
Whitlams, The 163
Williams, Brent 64
Willoughby, Kyle 101, 102
Wilson, Brian 281
Wilson, Marie 163
Wiilson, Miles 234-235
WIN Television 37, 48
Windang 7, 99, 100, 244
Wollongong (band) 180
Wollongong Art Gallery 73
Wollongong Central 78, 93
Wollongong City Council
   Corruption investigation 2, 80-83, 225
   Live Music Taskforce 93-95, 97, 98, 201
Wollongong City Skillshare 63
Wollongong Entertainment Centre 280, 281
Wollongong Leagues Club 280, 281
Wollongong Music Round Table 71-72
WollongongMusicScene.com 71-72
Wollongong Out of Workers (WOW) union 42-43
Wollongong Showground 20, 28
Wollongong Town Hall 15, 18, 21, 26, 28
Wollongong Youth Centre 63, 64, 68, 74
Wollongong Workers Club 35
Wombarra 75
Women's Music Collective 67
Wonderland Ballroom 22, 23, 155
Woolly Mammoth 174

Woonona 1, 27, 240
Woonona-Bulli Football Club 281
Wreckless Enterprises 177-178
Wright, Stevie 29
Wurramara, Emily 236

XTC 281

Yankovic, 'Weird Al' 281
Yeah, Yeah, Yeahs 177
Ye Luddites 121
Yes-Men, The 70
You Beauty 179-180
You Am I 157, 251, 260
Young, John Paul 163
Young and Pissed Off 43-44
Younger, Rob 4, 31, 261
Yours and Owls (café) 79, 86-90, 92, 94, 98, 120, 122, 225
Yours and Owls (festival) 44, 117-119, 120, 125, 132, 136-137, 146-48, 164-166, 168-170, 191-192, 195-197. 236-237, 263-265, 267, 275, 279

Zambian Goat Herders 58, 59 64
Zanko, Christopher 260
Zondrae's 21

If you liked this book why not check out my others, all which are available through my micropublishing company Last Day of School? (www.lastdayofschool.net)

Friday Night at the Oxford

The story that led to reunion of legendary band Tumbleweed. An in-depth look at Sunday Painters, a band decades ahead of their time. Iconic shows like HOPE, HyFest and the Steel City Sound exhibition. These are just of the more than 100 stories about Wollongong bands and events written by journalist Glen Humphries for the *Illawarra Mercury*, from 1997 through to 2018, and his own short-lived website Dragster.

The 200-plus pages of *Friday Night at the Oxford* provide a snapshot of what happened in the Wollongong music scene over the last 20-odd years – the bands, the venues, the events. It's a celebration of the music of a city.

So dig it.

Healer
The Rise, Fall and Return of Tumbleweed

With their long hair and fuzzed-up guitars, Tumbleweed rose out of the ashes of late-80s Indie band The Proton Energy Pills. Just over a year after their 1990 birth, they'd recorded with Mudhoney's Mark Arm, scored a support slot on Nirvana's only Australian tour (just as the grunge wave hit) and signed a US record deal.

The Wollongong band hit their peak of popularity in the wake of the 1995 album *Galactaphonic*. And then proceeded to shoot themselves in the foot. Guitarist Paul Hausmeister got the sack, and then drummer Steve O'Brien left in protest.

From there the band went downhill, releasing albums that met an increasingly uninterested public and playing shows in front of a half-dozen people. So it was no surprise when they called it quits in 2001.

With the acrimony that swirled around the members for years afterwards, it was hard to ever see the band getting back together. But in 2009 they managed to heal their wounds and reunite, releasing their fifth studio album a few years later and survive the sudden death of bassplayer Jay Curley.

Journalist and music writer Glen Humphries has interviewed the members of Tumbleweed numerous times and, in Healer, takes the first complete look at the band's career.

Sounds Like an Ending

Midnight Oil, 10-1 and Red Sails in the Sunset

In 1982, Midnight Oil was a band in trouble. Their last album, *Place Without a Postcard*, was supposed to be their big breakthrough but it hadn't worked out that way. So they found themselves in London, feeling the pressure of recording what was a "make or break" album. If this album went the same way as the last one, it could be the end of Midnight Oil. Out of the crisis came *10,9,8,7,6,5,4,3,2,1*, an album that changed everything for the band. It entered the charts and stayed there for more than three years. They started playing bigger venues - and they were able to pay back the bank manager.

Two years later, they headed to Japan to record the polarising *Red Sails in the Sunset*. It managed to do what *10-1* couldn't - give the band their first No1 album. But again the band found themselves facing the possibility it could all be over, courtesy of lead singer Peter Garrett's tilt at federal politics. If he wins, the band loses.

In *Sounds Like an Ending*, journalist and author Glen Humphries takes a track-by-track look at these two albums and the times and turmoil that fuelled them.

Alright! Queen at Live Aid

On July 13, 1985, the world tuned in to watch Live Aid beamed in from Wembley in London and John F Kennedy Stadium in Philadelphia. The massive event was spawned from Bob Geldof's idea six months earlier to raise money for Ethiopian famine victims through the release of the charity single, Do They Know It's Christmas?.

The iconic performance on that day came from Queen, a band that had been considering calling it quits just months earlier. Performing in front of an estimated audience of 1.9 billion people, the fourpiece stole the show and revitalised their career.

Alright takes a look back at Queen's performance on that day as well as revisiting the origins of the Band Aid single and the logistics behind getting Live Aid off the ground.

The Slab
24 Stories of Beer in Australia

Beer. You know it and, chances are, you love it. But you might not know the part beer has played in Australian history. Right from the start beer was there. It was on board The Endeavour when Captain Cook set sail for Australia. It was drunk not long after the First Fleet landed in Botany Bay.

It was there when World War I soldiers got a skinful and ran riot in the streets of Sydney. It was there during the era of six o'clock closing where people were still drinking it long after the little hand had passed the six. It was even there when it really shouldn't have been - when Canberra declared itself an alcohol-free zone.

What? You didn't know the nation's capital used to be dry? Well, then you need this book. You'll also find out just what the hell Voltron has to do with Victoria Bitter.

"History as it should be written. With beer. About beer. Crisp. Refreshing. Won't cause bloat."
John Birmingham, author of Leviathan

James Squire: The Biography

After getting caught swiping a few chickens from a neighbour, James Squire was sentenced to seven years in Sydney Cove. You could say it was the best thing he ever did – it led to him become a brewer, policeman, property tycoon, respected citizen and a bloody rich guy. But if all you know about James Squire is what you've read on labels on beer bottles, then you really don't know that much at all. This book – the first biography of Squire – separates the facts from the well-known myths. He never stowed away on the First Fleet ship carrying female convicts and didn't get lashed for stealing the ingredients to make beer.

He was also a man who may have used a false name on his daughter's birth certificate, loathed people who cut down trees on his property and got along far better with the natives than most of the other white newcomers.

Along the way you'll also discover a few other things about Sydney Cove, including Captain Arthur Phillip's efforts to get his hands on some Aboriginal heads for a friend, the early Australian fondness for cider rather than beer, the fight rival brewer John Boston had over a dead pig and the marine who tried to trade his hat for an Aboriginal child.

Night Terrors: The True Story of the Kingsgrove Slasher

Between 1956 and 1959, suburban Sydney was terrorised by a phantom known as the Kingsgrove Slasher. A peeping Tom, he graduated to breaking into houses to watch people sleep before later slashing women and girls with a razor while they lay in their beds.

He punched a 21-year-old woman into unconsciousness, breaking her teeth and cutting her mouth, hit a teenage girl in the face with a piece of wood and slashed a deep wound across the stomach of a 64-year-old woman. The Slasher also groped teens in their beds, and one of his 18 victims was just seven years old.

Night Terrors is the first detailed account of the Kingsgrove Slasher case. It draws on hundreds of newspaper articles written at the time - which show the level of fear in the community - as well as the transcripts from the court hearings, which had been sealed since 1959. The result is a true-crime book that might make it hard for you to go to sleep at night.

EBOOKS

The Six-Pack Stories from the World of Beer

From stories of monks making beer, to rumours of an unpleasant secret "ingredient" in a world-famous drink, there are plenty of great stories about beer. And six of them are captured in this ebook.

Beer is Fun!

Oh look, it's the best moments from Beer is Your Friend, the blog that won a national beer writing award and also inspired Dale to leave a comment "give ur self an uppercut u oxygen thief".

Why should you buy this book? Because it's 300-plus and it'll cost you just $2. What else in life will give you loads of entertainment for just $2? Go on, buy it. If you don't like it, I'll give you your money back. Well, that's a lie, I won't give you a cent, because I plan on holidaying in The Bahamas with the $2 you give me.

www.ingramcontent.com/pod-product-compliance
Lightning Source LLC
Chambersburg PA
CBHW020315010526
44107CB00054B/1852